WE SHALL OUTLAST THEM

PUTIN'S GLOBAL CAMPAIGN TO DEFEAT THE WEST

HANNA NOTTE

W. W. NORTON & COMPANY
Independent Publishers Since 1923

Printed in the United States of America
First Edition

Manufacturing by Lake Book Manufacturing
Book design by Chrissy Kurpeski
Production manager: Julia Druskin

ISBN 978-1-324-11701-8

W. W. Norton & Company, Inc., 500 Fifth Avenue, New York, NY 10110
www.wwnorton.com

W. W. Norton & Company Ltd., 15 Carlisle Street, London W1D 3BS

Authorized EU representative: EAS, Mustamäe tee 50, 10621 Tallinn, Estonia

1 2 3 4 5 6 7 8 9 0

The strongest of all warriors are
these two—Time and Patience.

—LEO TOLSTOY, *WAR AND PEACE*

Midway upon the journey of our life
I found myself within a forest dark,
For the straight-forward pathway had been lost.

—DANTE ALIGHIERI, *INFERNO*: CANTO I
FROM *THE DIVINE COMEDY*

CONTENTS

Introduction: I Think War Is Coming 1

PART I:
SECURING ECONOMIC LIFELINES

CHAPTER 1 The Shadow Fleet 17

CHAPTER 2 Tales of Laleli and Alabuga 32

PART II:
WAGING THE WAR OF NARRATIVES

CHAPTER 3 Our Friend, the Soviet Union 51

CHAPTER 4 Russia Cannot Be Canceled 67

PART III:
PLAYING CLOSE TO HOME

CHAPTER 5 The Art of Survival 89

CHAPTER 6 The Oligarch's Plan 103

CHAPTER 7 Geography Is Everything 117

PART IV:
PLAYING FARTHER AFIELD

CHAPTER 8 Too Much Upheaval 135

CHAPTER 9 Phoenix from the Ashes 155

Part V:
FRAGMENTING INTERNATIONAL ORDER

CHAPTER 10 When the Elephants Fight . . . 171
CHAPTER 11 Hostess with the Mostest 188

Part VI:
DEFEATING THE WEST

CHAPTER 12 There Must Be Fear 205
CHAPTER 13 Of Saboteurs and Spies 223
CHAPTER 14 Disruptor in Chief 244

CONCLUSION We Shall Outlast Them 261

Acknowledgments 275
Notes 279
Index 293

WE SHALL OUTLAST THEM

Introduction: I Think War Is Coming

He made them wait, as usual. Ministers and parliamentarians, priests and soldiers, governors and oligarchs—they had all assembled in Gostiny Dvor, the Old Merchant Court in Moscow's bustling Kitay-gorod district, to listen to Vladimir Putin take stock of one year of war against Ukraine. It was February 21, 2023.

Igor Sechin, the head of Russian oil giant Rosneft, sank into a chair next to Gazprom chief Alexey Miller and whispered something in his ear. Sergey Shoigu, the Russian defense minister, and Kremlin spokesman Dmitry Peskov cracked smiles as they mingled with the crowd. Elsewhere in the massive hall, Elvira Nabiullina, the head of Russia's central bank, sat by herself, seemingly immersed in gloomy thoughts.

Finally, a male voice announced via loudspeaker: "The President of the Russian Federation, Vladimir Vladimirovich Putin." It was the prompt for the audience to stand and watch Putin walk resolutely toward the rostrum, accompanied by a festive burst of trumpet fanfare. When the president began speaking, it was not just to the elites assembled at Gostiny Dvor but to the entire Russian nation. The spectacle was aired on countless outdoor video screens, looming over passersby at Moscow's Varshavka Sky shopping center and in the port city of Sevastopol in annexed Crimea.

Having laid out why his decision to invade Ukraine had been justified—in fact, necessary—Putin detailed how Russia was adapting to the new circumstances brought about by the war. The West's gamble to make the Russian people suffer through sanctions had failed. Russian companies were expanding business ties with non-Western partners. Efforts were underway to ditch the dollar in Russia's trade. As Putin's philippic against the West dragged on, Dmitry Medvedev, the former president turned nuclear scaremonger, briefly dozed off. "We will develop cooperation with friends," Putin assured his audience. Centuries of Western hegemony, in his telling, were finally coming to a close.

Putin concluded his address with a bombshell: Russia would suspend its participation in the New START—the last remaining nuclear arms control treaty with the United States and a vestige of a bygone era of cooperation. The conditions of confrontation with the West permitted no other choice. The audience broke out into rapturous applause. But as Russia's national anthem played, a sense of foreboding dampened the mood. Some sang along dutifully, others stared into space. Despite the rosy picture painted by Putin, those assembled knew Russia was not out of the woods. Outlasting the West would not be easy. And everyone would have a part to play in meeting the challenges still to come.

TEN YEARS PRIOR TO PUTIN'S ADDRESS, IN 2013, I FIRST VISITED Russia as a graduate student and spent a summer in a small, Soviet-style apartment on the outskirts of the city of Yaroslavl owned by a widow named Irina. Irina and her family offered my introduction to everyday life in Putin's Russia. My host rose at the crack of dawn each day to prepare copious amounts of *kasha* (porridge) and *syrniki* (small, thick pancakes) for breakfast. When I left the plate half-full, she grumbled that I would never find a husband unless I gained a few pounds. Sometimes, Irina's grandson Alexey and his friends would drive me around aimlessly in an old Lada and show off their stash of moonshine in the trunk. I remember that summer as a time of tough battles with Russian grammar, intense listlessness at night, and endless curiosity in the Russia that surrounded me: harsh and a bit madcap.

To work on my grammar, I had daily lessons in a rundown middle school, building on the language classes I had taken at Cambridge University and, before that, in Trier, a small, predominantly Catholic town in West Germany where both Karl Marx and I were born. Growing up post-reunification, near the border with France, Russia seemed like a remote place that was politically far less relevant than Germany's Western partners. My paternal grandfather talked often about the Allied forces who had deployed to our region at the end of World War II. He spoke fondly of the Americans, to whom he said we owed a great deal of gratitude for reintegrating Germany into the international community after the horrors of the Holocaust. He never spoke to me about the Soviet Union. It was music, rather than an awareness of the deep entanglement of Germany's history with Russia's, that drew me to study the language and country to which I would end up devoting my professional life. Born into a family of musicians and hoping to become a professional violinist, I spent my formative years in a house filled with the sounds of Rachmaninoff's Preludes and Tchaikovsky's Symphony No. 5—works steeped in melancholy and echoes of nostalgia. Russian music struck a chord deep within the dreamy kid that I was.

But politics and history soon became my primary focus, as I studied political science at Cambridge University and then international relations at Oxford. When I traveled to Yaroslavl for my sojourn with Irina in 2013, I knew that tensions between Moscow and Western powers were ratcheting up. I arrived in Russia as US whistleblower Edward Snowden was finding refuge in the country, prompting the Obama White House to postpone a planned US–Russia presidential summit. Putin had been back in the Kremlin for a little over a year, and the spirit of the Obama Medvedev–era "reset"—an attempt to improve relations in 2009 and 2010—had dissipated. The Kremlin had already requested that Washington wrap up its US Agency for International Development (USAID) programs in Russia, while the US Congress had passed the Magnitsky Act, imposing sanctions on Russian officials suspected of human rights violations, prompting the Russian Duma to ban US adoptions of Russian children in response. It was a time of growing unease, but Russia and the US were still occasionally cooperating, for instance in destroying Syria's chemical weapons in 2013.

Living in Moscow for nearly a year from early summer 2015—by that time a PhD student and temporarily affiliated with the Carnegie Moscow Center and the Institute of Oriental Studies of the Russian Academy of Sciences—I watched as elite suspicion of Westerners grew. Putin had annexed Crimea the year before, causing Europe and the US to level harsh sanctions against Russia. 2015 was also the year Russian forces intervened in the Syrian civil war to save the Assad regime from collapsing, the Russian military's first large-scale operation outside the post-Soviet space since the end of the Cold War. Buoyed by rising oil prices, Russia's growing military prowess, and his consolidation of authoritarian stability at home, Putin became more and more emboldened in his conduct abroad.

In the years that followed, I visited Russia frequently for conferences and meetings as I concluded my PhD and started working for a small private mediation outfit. Russia–West relations continued on a downward trajectory, while the Kremlin also tapped ever more brazenly into the state's dictatorial potential. With time, I felt that I was under closer scrutiny during my visits and that my Russian interlocutors spoke less freely.

By October 2021, relations between Russia and the West had reached a new low, snowballing after accusations of Russian interference in the 2016 US presidential election and the US withdrawal from the 1987 Intermediate-Range Nuclear Forces (INF) Treaty. At that time, I flew to Sochi for the annual meeting of the Valdai Discussion Club, a conference some dub the "Russian Davos," following a two-year hiatus caused by the pandemic. Russian and international guests mingled in the hallways of the Polyana 1389, a hotel named for its elevation of 1,389 meters above sea level in the mountains surrounding the Black Sea resort. I had recently joined the James Martin Center for Nonproliferation Studies, a US think tank, and was in Sochi to understand where Russian foreign policy was headed in general, and how the Russians thought about the prospects of practicing nuclear arms control with the US in particular. Times were tense, and arms control was one of the few remaining areas the two sides were still willing to discuss.

Having undergone multiple COVID tests over several days, attendees were awaiting Putin's appearance. The Russian leader's paranoia during the pandemic was well known. His meetings with foreign heads of state, during which attendees would sit at opposite ends of a comically long table, had become the source of widespread ridicule. For security reasons, Putin would not be joining us up in the mountains at the Polyana, so on the last day of the conference, the other guests and I huddled into luxury vans and made our way down the winding roads to Sochi's Olympic Park.

Over the years, Putin's Valdai speeches had become an occasion for him to attack the West and expound his vision for Russia. What had started as an intimate gathering in which Putin joined foreign guests onstage was now a one-man show before an audience of a few hundred. As we—academics, journalists, Russia watchers—began the typically long wait for Putin in the foyer, we talked over canapés and coffee. Well over an hour later, we were called into the big hall, where bodyguards lined the walls. After we sat tight for yet another hour under the scorching heat of the stage lights, Putin finally walked up to the podium.

He took a seat next to Fyodor Lukyanov, editor in chief of the journal *Russia in Global Affairs*, who has been moderating the event since 2017. ("I cannot quit as long as the president likes it," Lukyanov later told me.) Seated some fifty feet from the audience, Putin clearly had not shed his fear of germs.

Having followed Putin's estrangement from the West over the years, I was familiar with his anti-American diatribes. But for this speech—his last major settling of accounts with the West before the invasion of Ukraine four months later—Putin managed to outdo himself. He delivered a fiery attack on Western liberalism, inveighing against "monstrous things" like cancel culture and a society he declared was forcing transgenderism onto children. "Let's call a spade a spade," he said. "This simply verges on crimes against humanity under the banner of progress." Seated some ten rows in front of me, Margarita Simonyan, the country's propagandist-in-chief, rose from her seat to thank Putin. "As a mother of three young children," she exclaimed, she was grateful to the president for the protection of Russians from "the tentacles of liberal fascism."

The speech felt different from his previous appearances at Valdai. Putin railed against what he considered the West's disrespect for Russia's security interests, even touched briefly upon nuclear weapons—but much less than I had expected. This speech was about ideology. His attacks on Western liberalism reflected an effort to rally hard-core conservatives and supporters of traditional values around Putin—inside Russia, but also outside of it.

I was back in Moscow four months later, in February 2022, to attend another event, this one dedicated to Russia's role in the Middle East. Faisal Mekdad, the Syrian foreign minister, had come to speak and wax lyrical on his country's ties with Russia. But I found it hard to focus, unsettled by the rapidly evolving news updates on what seemed like a looming catastrophe.

On February 21, after delivering a belligerent, contemptuous, and nostalgia-laden speech, Putin had signed decrees confirming the Kremlin's official recognition of two breakaway territories in the Donbas, the predominantly Russian-speaking region of eastern Ukraine which the Kremlin depicts as historically Russian. The move could be seen as a prelude to further escalation, since it allowed Putin to move more troops and weapons to eastern Ukraine. Russian forces had already amassed at the Ukrainian border.

On February 22, the day before Russians celebrate Defender of the

Fatherland Day, I took a stroll around Moscow. It was unexpectedly mild for the time of year, with none of the snow that usually blankets the Russian capital in the gloom of winter. The city, it seemed to me, exuded an atmosphere of normality, but also some undefinable sense of foreboding.

I think war is coming, I texted a friend from Moscow's Sheremetyevo Airport as I waited to board my flight the next day. A few hours after I landed in Vienna, Russia launched its full-scale invasion of Ukraine.

THE MOST ASTUTE OBSERVERS OF RUSSIA HAVE LONG DEBATED the precise moment Putin turned away from the West. When did the Russian leader have a change of heart, and why? After all, when he first rose to power in 2000, he seemed set on constructive relations with Washington—offering Russian cooperation on counterterrorism and Afghanistan after the 9/11 attacks. Some situate Putin's moment of reckoning around 2004 or 2005, when democracy protests dubbed the Rose and Orange Revolutions swept across Georgia and Ukraine, which the Kremlin blamed on Western meddling. Others point to Putin's infamous "Munich speech" criticizing American hegemony in 2007 as clear proof of the Russian leader's chilling feelings toward the West. Still others believe Putin's point of no return came much later, after the short-lived "reset" in US–Russia relations collapsed in the early 2010s.

The riddle of Russia–West relations is wrapped in the even bigger enigma of what generally animates Russia to act the way it does. Those understanding Russian foreign policy as rooted in insecurity view the country's long and porous borders as the source of a perennial sense of vulnerability that impels Russian leaders to seek to control buffer zones. Counterviews posit that Russian foreign policy is primarily driven by ideology, that its impetus to control neighbors is a means to entrench autocratic rule at home. Or they foreground a distinctly Russian quest for international status and respect in seeking to explain the country's conduct abroad.

This book does not aspire to conclusively settle that fundamental debate—though to me, Putin's decision to launch a full-scale, high-risk invasion of Ukraine in February 2022 appeared to spring from a long-nurtured cultural/ideological obsession with the victim rather than any proximate Western actions that threatened Russian security. Still, the story of Putin's growing estrangement from the West over the years, a story that reached its erstwhile apex in 2022, is one of contingency and complexity. Over time, Putin nurtured an intuition of US decline, watching what he considered an increasingly rotten American culture, the country's growing polarization, the US debacles in Afghanistan and Iraq, and its (and Europe's) feeble response to the Russian annexation of Crimea in 2014. At the same time, Putin felt increasingly confident in Russia's own regional and global throw weight. He claimed some 20 percent of Georgia's territory in 2008, took Crimea, meddled in the 2016 US presidential election, and proved capable of projecting power into the Middle East and Africa. While Putin's resistance to American primacy in Europe grew stronger over the years, he also believed Russia finally had the power to push back.

Invading Ukraine, Putin sought to demonstrate that the United States did not write the rules internationally. If Russia could prove this point in Europe, at the heart of the liberal international order, it would midwife a post-Western order globally. His land grab in Ukraine, Putin surely surmised, would give Russia enormous leverage to shape Europe's future security landscape. Putting Western states—chiefly the United States—in their place, Russia would emerge as a privileged pole in an international power system not unlike the nineteenth century's Concert of Europe. Russia's war against Ukraine would prove an accelerator of this struggle over global order, since it hastened Russia's decoupling from the West. But it would mark just one round of a larger contest. Like the judo player Putin was in his youth, he thought in terms of bouts and tournaments.

Putin's claims about the West transforming Ukraine into its lackey, posing a threat to Russia, may have struck a chord across Russia's population, among elites and average people alike. Still, it was Putin's whim to wage war. He may have counted on a short invasion, on Russia's ability to quickly create a fait accompli in Ukraine that the West would have to swallow. Instead, his invasion dragged ordinary Russians to a place where most would not have gone freely: a long war, and a deep and lasting rupture with the West of the kind not seen since the heights of the Cold War.

And so, confrontation with the West became the central organizing principle of the country's foreign policy. After February 2022, Russia adapted its entire global statecraft—that is, the art of wielding power abroad through economic, military, political, and propagandistic means—to prosecute the war and pursue its global campaign against the West.

In 1956, Soviet leader Nikita Khrushchev expressed supreme confidence in communism's ability to conquer the world. "Your grandchildren will live under socialism," he declared in a television broadcast. "We will bury you," he told Western diplomats at a Moscow reception. Apparently, he did not mean the adversary's physical elimination, but rather that the USSR would outlive the West in a systemic struggle. Some seven decades later, Putin followed in Khrushchev's footsteps, adamant that Russia stand firm against its enemies in a new battle of wills.

Outlasting the West, the Kremlin understood, would require *stoykost*. *Stoykost* is an old Russian virtue, derived from the verb *to stand*, which captures the ability to endure hardship without giving in, and which I had first encountered back in 2013 in Irina—a woman who lost her husband decades ago to the bottle, her hands coarsened by the work in the dacha's garden, her household chores her everyday companion. But outlasting the West also required that Russia reinvent itself on the global stage. Many expected the country to turn into an international pariah following its invasion of Ukraine. But in fact, the war marked the arrival of a newly outward-facing Russia—the subject of this book.

Most essential to outlasting the West was Russia's economic

adaptation. Before 2022, the West had counted on its own centrality to the worlds of finance, technological innovation, and commerce, hoping the threat of massive sanctions would deter Putin. Once the war began, the West wagered that punishments and restrictions would sufficiently impair Russia's economy and war machine. But Russia found an oil lifeline in China and India, assembling a "shadow fleet" of tankers to ship its crude in defiance of an oil price cap. Central Asia, the South Caucasus, and Turkey emerged as conduits for trade, and Iran, North Korea, and China as reliable sources of weaponry or dual-use goods. Technocrats worked overtime to ensure Russia could settle payments for its imports and exports, notwithstanding its exclusion from the dollar-dominated financial architecture.

Russia also took its confrontation with the West into the global information space. In the years leading up to the invasion, Russia had already presented itself as a bastion of traditional values, fostering an alternative to a Western-led order. Putin's Valdai speech centered on culture war issues was a prime example of this strategy. After February 2022, the apostles and amplifiers of Russia's propaganda went into a veritable frenzy. They told receptive audiences that the war in Ukraine was part of a larger struggle against Western "neocolonialism," curating media ecosystems supportive of Russia.

With its resources sunk into Ukraine, the Russian military was forced to adapt its presence in other regions—retreating in the Middle East and the South Caucasus, while exploiting opportunities to go on the advance in the Sahel. Russia pursued its global agenda in the hallways and plenaries of international diplomacy. It boycotted traditional venues for negotiation and threw wrenches into established institutions, including the United Nations, while trying to rally support from the Global South. At the same time, Russian diplomats hustled to elevate and expand clubs that excluded Western states, like the BRICS alliance comprising Brazil, Russia, India, China, and South Africa. Moscow froze cooperation with Western capitals on issues of global concern, such as nuclear arms control. Russian politicians and propagandists rattled the nuclear saber, and Moscow stepped up its attempts to sabotage critical infrastructure in Europe.

One important reason why Russia has held its own internationally, and in some cases even gained ground, has had less to do with its own efforts and more with the agendas of others. In a May 2023 speech, Fiona Hill, a former Russia adviser to Donald Trump, characterized the Global South's position on the Ukraine war as a "proxy rebellion" against the US. "This is a mutiny against what they see as the collective West dominating the international discourse and foisting its problems on everyone else," she said. Hill was right, but she told only part of the story.

Confronted with the Ukraine invasion, many non-Western countries refused to be forced into a stark either-or choice between Russia and the West. Some sympathized with Russia's story about the war and its origins, because the Soviet Union once was a friend, because the West is hypocritical, or because of a genuine affinity for Putin's strongman politics. Others loathed the invasion but still had their reasons to stay on good terms with Russia. Their motives were more diverse than could be accounted for by the concept of "proxy rebellion." But collectively, these countries created a relatively permissive international environment for Russia to prosecute its war.

Not everything that Russia did was new. In some areas, the Kremlin merely doubled down on preexisting efforts, for instance in hustling to elevate the importance of BRICS, diversifying its economic ties away from the West, or engaging in a hybrid campaign in Europe. But the war also forced Russia's foreign policy into genuine adaptation, which encompassed several universes and was sometimes riven by contradictions: There was innovation, with Russia producing drones of Iranian origin and turning them into even deadlier weapons. There was improvisation, with Russia's curation of a shadow fleet of oil tankers. There was radicalization, with Russia's threats of nuclear apocalypse. And sometimes, there was restraint, such as when the Kremlin realized it could not afford to save Syria's Assad regime a second time. Putin's massive strategic gamble—thrusting Russia into a war against

Ukraine—generated a host of smaller cul de sacs for Russia's foreign policy, forcing it into contortions and, sometimes, even retreats. On more than one occasion, however, Russia also managed to turn adversity into opportunity.

THERE IS NO ONE FOR WHOM RUSSIA'S WAR HAS BEEN OF GREATER consequence than Ukraine. No one has suffered greater pain from Russia's onslaught than average Ukrainian men, women, and children. No one has resisted Russia more courageously than they have. Authors and journalists have told their stories from the ground, and many more stories remain yet to be told, heroes to be honored, and victims to be mourned. I recognize the Ukrainians' spirit in the face of great adversity, yet this book is not about the war in Ukraine. Neither is it an account of the drastic domestic changes that have swept across Russia, with the Kremlin cracking down on perceived enemies of the state and mobilizing human and material resources for the war—though I touch on some of these aspects by necessity.

Rather, this book tells the story of a more combative Russian statecraft and how it has manifested in the world. It is a book about Russia's many battlegrounds and the frontiersmen waging its struggle. It is a book about Russia's foreign policy adaptation, with its successes and its failures. And it is a book about the consequences of that adaptation for global order.

Those looking to understand Russia and the way it acts in the world usually zoom in on the metropole, but I was just as much drawn to the periphery. In my research for this book, I gravitated most of all to men and women in far-flung theaters, some of whom were swept up in Russia's confrontation with the West, while others became facilitators of Russia's agenda—sometimes gladly, sometimes unwittingly, sometimes opportunistically. Russia's effort to outlast the West, I believed, is a kaleidoscopic effort splintered into countless stories, the work of enablers at home and abroad. It is an effort that changes the lives of everymen whose footsteps may well have been ours—including in the most unexpected of places. And so, I set off on a journey around the globe: to the Arab Gulf states, Armenia, Finland, Georgia, India, Israel, Kazakhstan, South Africa, Turkey, the United Kingdom, and the United States. I spent time in the capitals of international diplomacy: Geneva, Vienna, and New York. I visited civilian shelters and military bases, party headquarters and presidential palaces, occupied territories and tense borderlands. I collected the stories of blatant propagandists and whistleblowers in hiding; refugees and refuseniks; activists and ambassadors; former prime ministers and former resistance fighters. I interviewed Russians in exile and Russians who drive their country's combative statecraft from Moscow.

They all helped me understand how it is that Russia manages to outlast the West. To make sense of Russia's place in the world, we need to inspect the sources of energy that propel it forward, energy that appears deliciously attractive to some while casting a dark shadow on others.

[illegible] of whose [illegible] now [illegible] of the [illegible] in [illegible] most unexpected [illegible] around [illegible] the [illegible] Kazakhstan, South Korea, [illegible] United Kingdom, and the United States [illegible] in the capitals [illegible] international [illegible] centers [illegible] New York. I visited [illegible] military bases, [illegible] I [illegible] the [illegible] Baltic [illegible] and watch [illegible] in [illegible] and [illegible]

This [illegible] the [illegible] of Russia's place in the world [illegible]

Part I

SECURING ECONOMIC LIFELINES

CHAPTER 1

The Shadow Fleet

THE *EAGLE S* IDLED IN THE WARMING FALL SUNSHINE. THE tanker had just delivered its precious cargo—tens of thousands of tons of Russian oil—to the port of Kandla in India's northwestern state of Gujarat. India's monsoon season was over, and Gujarat's famous festival period was in full swing. The port was bustling with activity. From space, the cranes towering above the vast container terminals resembled an ant colony at work.

The *Eagle S* had passed through many hands involved in its making, its management, and its exploitation for profit. Built at a Chinese shipyard in 2006, it was sailing under the flag of the Cook Islands, with a multinational crew of twenty-four members. Technically operated by a Mumbai-based entity called Peninsular Maritime India Private Limited, the *Eagle S* held an Indian safety management certificate that had been issued just recently. The ship's registered owner, however, was a murky Dubai-based company called Caravella LLCFZ.

As the *Eagle S* sailed westward from Kandla after delivering its load, a strong breeze whipped across the deck. Two hundred and twenty-eight meters long and thirty-two meters wide, the tanker slowly wound its way through the Gulf of Kutch, which was teeming with freighters transporting goods to and from the Indian coast. At last, it pushed ahead at full steam into the seemingly endless waters of the Arabian Sea.

Had it been up to Western nations, the *Eagle S* would not have been traversing the world's oceans. They suspected the tanker to be part of an infamous shadow fleet that ferried millions of gallons of Russian oil in defiance of Western sanctions, allowing Russia to earn the revenues it needed to continue waging its war against Ukraine.

When Putin annexed Crimea in March 2014, Senator John McCain called Russia "a gas station masquerading as a country." It was meant as an insult. But the Kremlin continued to earn handsomely on its hydrocarbon exports. Over the subsequent decade, oil and gas revenues accounted for between 30 and 50 percent of Russia's total federal budget income, making them the most important single source of cash for the Kremlin. By the time Russia invaded Ukraine in February 2022, it remained the world's largest exporter of oil and natural gas to global markets. On the eve of the war, the EU was buying around 50 percent of Russia's oil exports and over 60 percent of its gas exports. The United States was less reliant on Russian crude but still received 8 percent of its petroleum products from Russia. Russia's oil and gas revenues were so high that they sufficed to pay for its annual military budget almost twice over.

Once Russian tanks rolled into Ukraine, Western capitals were determined to nip that revenue stream in the bud. On March 8, President Joe Biden announced a full US ban on imports of Russian oil, liquefied natural gas (LNG), and coal. Europe considered a similarly comprehensive prohibition impossible. It needed Russia to secure sufficient energy supplies for heat, mobility, power supply, and industry. Still, the EU promised to cut its gas dependency on Russia by two-thirds over the course of 2022 and to end it entirely by 2030. It also banned Russian coal. As for oil, European nations rushed to buy more from other countries all around the world. But Europe was slow in shaking its dependence on Russia. During March and April 2022, Russia earned a whopping $44 billion for its exports of fossil fuels to the EU, benefiting from soaring commodity prices after the invasion.

By the summer, Western nations resolved to up the ante. As Putin addressed a virtual BRICS summit in late June, vowing to reroute Russia's trade to "reliable international partners," the G7—Canada, France, Germany, Italy, Japan, the UK, and the US, joined by the EU—were busy preparing for their own summit. At the top of their agenda: how to implement a price cap for Russian oil, in order to starve the Kremlin's coffers of attractive revenue.

The idea was that G7 countries would ban their companies from providing ships, insurance, or financing for Russian oil exports, unless the oil was purchased at or below a fixed price. As a rule, trade contracts require that oil transportation be insured. If Russian oil exporters wanted to have insurance from a Western provider and transport their oil on Western tankers, they would have to agree not to sell at prices above the cap. The West hesitated to push Russian oil out of the market entirely; it still accounted for too large a share of supply in an already tight global market. Excluding it from that market would drive up energy prices, and inflation, for the average consumer, including in America and Europe.

As the US Treasury took the lead in working out how a price cap might work, analysts raised doubts over its viability early on. Sergey Vakulenko, a fellow at the Carnegie Russia Eurasia Center who, until February 2022, held a senior position at Russian oil giant Gazprom Neft, was one of them. Western insurance providers could deny their services to Russian cargoes violating the cap, but they weren't the only game in town. The plan also did not consider how China and India—the former an existing, the latter a prospective buyer of large volumes of Russian oil—would respond to the price cap.

Notwithstanding such loose ends, Western governments had reason to be cautiously optimistic when the price cap of sixty dollars per barrel went into effect in December 2022. At the time, countries making up the price cap coalition wielded significant influence over global oil transportation. Their companies moved 55 percent of Russian oil and controlled 90 percent of the insurance market for such shipping.

But Russia was not going to concede defeat without putting up a fight. Its exporters adapted, shifting to rely on aging, off-the-books tankers such as the *Eagle S* to transport Russian oil. In doing so, they copied well-established Iranian practices. Russia assembled the fleet through a variety of measures, including by transferring tankers previously owned by Russian entities (such as the tanker group Sovcomflot) to new management companies (for instance, in the United Arab Emirates, or UAE), or by acquiring very old vessels that were slated for decommissioning. Operators of shadow vessels turned to bogus insurance outfits for maritime accident insurance certificates, outmaneuvering Western insurance providers. The Russian parliament also passed a law introducing a new formula for calculating tax revenues from oil, to ensure that the price cap would not significantly impact the Russian budget.

By summer 2023, it dawned on the price cap coalition that Russia was selling significant amounts of oil above the cap. The shadow fleet—tankers not owned, managed, or insured by an entity in the price cap coalition—had grown to around 153, and they were transporting over 50 percent of Russian oil exports. By spring 2024, the fleet comprised 435 vessels. It was a formidable feat in Russia's effort to fight back the West in the global sanctions war.

One man who profited handsomely from the emergence of the shadow fleet was Igor Sechin, the chief of Russian oil giant Rosneft and close ally of Putin. In early 2024, Rosneft reported an almost 50 percent surge in net profit for 2023. According to an investigation by *The Wall Street Journal*, Rosneft relied on a subset of the shadow fleet—some one hundred vessels directed by Azerbaijani traders—to transport its crude. By some accounts, Rosneft was responsible for about 40 percent of Russia's crude exports, and the "Rosneft shadow fleet" transported about half of that total.

Sometimes described as Russia's "Darth Vader," Sechin is a sturdy man, with a broad face, stern demeanor, and close-cropped hair. He represents, unlike anyone else, the mixing of political and financial power that has characterized Russia since the collapse of the Soviet Union. Born in Leningrad, now St. Petersburg, on September 7, 1960, Sechin studied French and Portuguese at Leningrad University. He then served in the army as a translator before being posted to Angola and Mozambique as part of a little-known Soviet trade body called Tekhnoexport, which is said to have supplied arms to Africa.

Sechin met Putin in the early 1990s on a trip to Brazil. It would be a fortuitous meeting. Sechin was the only official to move with Putin from St. Petersburg to Moscow for what would mark Putin's emergence on the national political scene in 1996. Putin named Sechin deputy head of his first prime ministerial administration in 1999 and soon afterward promoted him to deputy chief of staff during his first presidency. In those years, according to a US diplomatic cable published by WikiLeaks, Sechin's role was "so shadowy that it was joked he may not actually exist." In his biography of Putin, the British journalist and author Philip Short writes that Sechin served the Russian president with a "limpetlike devotion" and that the two men bonded over the fact they had both grown up in a poor suburb of Leningrad. That bond elevated Sechin to become a key player among Russia's *siloviki*—members of the Russian security services who would wield significant power in the country.

Sechin has served as the chief executive of Rosneft since 2012. Under his eye, the company struck deals with Italy's Eni, Norway's Statoil (now Equinor), and America's ExxonMobil. In 2013, Rosneft signed a $270 billion deal with China National Petroleum Corporation, through which the company committed itself to provide China with 365 million tons of oil over twenty-five years, tripling Russian supplies to its giant eastern neighbor. After the annexation of Crimea, Putin used Sechin to build closer business ties with Cuba and Venezuela.

In keeping with his shadowy reputation, Sechin usually shies away from the media. In March 2023, however, when the price cap coalition was just finding its footing, the Russian journalist Pavel Zarubin managed to catch Sechin on camera for a short moment during a state visit to Moscow by Chinese President Xi Jinping. Asking Sechin to reflect on Xi's visit, Zarubin reminded him: "Several years ago, you told me you know a Chinese word—*yuan*. Is there any new word you have learned since?" Sechin took a short pause and then replied, chuckling, "*Many* yuans."

Sechin had every reason to be in a good mood. In the first quarter of 2023, as Russia was assembling its shadow fleet, Russian oil exports to China rose by over 30 percent compared to the previous year. With such impressive growth, Russia soon overtook Saudi Arabia as China's top oil supplier. Other countries outside the price cap coalition turned to Russia, too. Turkey became an important buyer of Russian crude, while Brazil and Saudi Arabia gobbled up record volumes of Russian diesel. Most important, Russia started to sell unprecedented amounts of crude to India. Attending the India Energy Week in Bangalore in February 2023, Sechin laid into the price cap coalition. "Under conditions of unprecedented sanctions, pressure and confrontation with virtually the entire Western world," he roared onstage, "Russia was able to achieve results exceeding those of the world's leading economies." It amounted to a "major psychological victory," he said.

By summer 2024, Russia was transporting close to 70 percent of its seaborne oil exports on shadow tankers. Sergey Vakulenko's admonition had proved prescient. The implementation of the price cap suffered from widespread loopholes. And attestation fraud—shippers falsely claiming their Russian oil cargo was compliant with the price cap—was difficult to prove.

Faced with these predicaments, the price cap coalition had few good alternatives. In trying to regulate the oil price, it could have attempted to use political pressure on OPEC+, a club that consists of members of the Organization of the Petroleum Exporting Countries (OPEC) as well as other oil-producing countries, including Russia, that make collective decisions about oil output. The Biden administration had tried to convince Saudi Arabia, a leading member, to refrain from cutting back production and thereby push up prices in late fall 2022, just ahead of the price cap taking hold. But it had failed. The oil-rich countries of the Persian Gulf region, including Saudi Arabia and the UAE, showed little appetite in supporting measures that would hurt Russian oil income since they required high prices to support their own budgets.

Western nations learned early that in facing the Herculean task of reducing Russia's income from oil sales, they would not be able to count much on the Saudis or the Emiratis. And this, it turned out, was true in more than just one way.

FOR A RUSSIAN PALATE, THE MENU AT CHALET BEREZKA IN Dubai leaves little to be desired. Dark Russian bread, salad Olivier, Beluga vodka, and numerous types of pirozhki promise a culinary experience just like back home. Sprawled across the western rooftop of Dubai's luxury Nakheel Mall, the restaurant's terrace is dotted with cozy sofas that overlook Palm Jumeirah, the tree-shaped archipelago of artificial islands known for its glamour. Sechin is said to have celebrated New Year's Eve onboard a yacht anchored just off Palm Jumeirah's coast in 2022.

Dubai has drawn wealthy Russians for more than a decade. After Russia's annexation of Crimea led to a first wave of Western sanctions, real estate purchases by Russians in the UAE skyrocketed. Once the UAE introduced a value added tax in early 2018, some Russians left due to the increased cost of living, but another batch came during the COVID pandemic, taking advantage of its early reopening relative to other parts of the world. Some super-wealthy Russians, like the entrepreneur Andrey Melnichenko, legally obtained Emirati passports.

Yet another wave of Russian elites looked to Dubai as a safe haven after the invasion of Ukraine. As Western states sanctioned Russia and cut transport links, the UAE staked out a neutral position on the war and maintained direct flights to Russia. In 2022, Russians became the leading nonresident buyers of Dubai real estate. Foreign direct investment by Russian companies into the UAE increased by 34 percent in the same year. The number of Russian individuals and companies looking to set up businesses in the Emirates surged. Russian entrepreneurs felt they faced less discrimination—and fewer bureaucratic hurdles—than in Europe.

Dima Tutkov was one Russian to benefit from Dubai's accommodating business environment. He launched Angel Cakes, a brunch and coffee chain specializing in sugar- and gluten-free desserts, in his hometown of Volgograd in 2019. The business soon expanded into other Russian cities and in August 2022, Tutkov opened his first café in Dubai. "The decision was unrelated to the war in Ukraine," the forty-year-old entrepreneur told me when we met at one of his Dubai cafés in early 2025. Having decided to take Angel Cakes abroad, Tutkov and his team considered alternative cities like London. They had run the numbers: costs per unit, the expected tax burden, the bureaucratic expenses. Dubai had made the most sense, Tutkov told me, licking the remnants of a matcha-flavored dessert from his spoon.

In addition to building a new franchise in the UAE, Tutkov was able to run his Russian business, an advertising agency, out of Dubai. The war in Ukraine both hindered and helped, he told me. It initially complicated things like banking and logistics, because of the sanctions. But because many Russian service providers—for instance, those offering IT or payment services—flocked to Dubai, an emergent web of Russian infrastructure eventually made operations there easier.

After the invasion of Ukraine, Dubai did not just emerge as an attractive haven for hungry Russian entrepreneurs like Tutkov. It also became a prime location for the reregistration of sanctioned shadow fleet vessels. According to the Centre for Research on Energy and Clean Air (CREA), over two hundred oil tankers transporting Russian crude oil and oil products between December 2022 and December 2024 had owners listed in the UAE, many of them newly registered companies. Out of these, 164 were shadow tankers. The leading Emirati manager transporting Russian oil in 2023 and 2024 was a company called Sun Ship Management, with 230 million barrels accounting for 34 percent of all Russian crude oil transported by a coalition of Emirati companies.

Countering the reregistration of shadow tankers in Dubai proved as hard as beheading the Hydra: Each time a head was cut off, two more would grow in its place. Once Russia's Sovcomflot had transferred dozens of tankers to Sun Ship Management, the Emirati company was sanctioned by the US government. Most of the tankers were then simply transferred to another Emirati company, soon to be sanctioned as well. And so the game continued. By the time the *Eagle S* made its voyage from Kandla in Gujarat, its ownership, too, had been registered with a new Dubai-based company. That company, Caravella LLCFZ, appeared to operate just a single vessel—the *Eagle S*—and listed a business center at a luxury hotel as its address. Caravella LLCFZ seemed to live up to its name, derived from *caravel*—a small sailing ship developed by the Portuguese in the fifteenth century that was known for its light weight and its maneuverability.

The price cap coalition was irked by the ease with which shadow fleet tankers like the *Eagle S* could change ownership in Dubai, just like a chameleon changing color. In November and December 2023, the US Treasury's Office of Foreign Assets Control sanctioned several UAE-based companies and their associated vessels, including Sun Ship Management. The Emiratis tried to send conciliatory signals in response. In August 2024, they introduced a ban on ships bearing the flag of Eswatini, a nation known to transport Russian oil. But legal and financial loopholes and lax sanctions enforcement impeded a proper beheading of the Hydra.

The price cap and sanctions against vessels, the two principal levers used on Russian oil income, never fully worked. And regulating the volume of Russian oil sales more forcefully, by outright sanctioning that oil, always remained off the table for political reasons. Instead, Russian oil money kept flowing, Western states were always one step behind, and the UAE could reap the benefits.

Mohammed Baharoon, who heads the Dubai Public Policy

Research Center, told me the UAE was interested in what he called "unimpeded connectivity" with the rest of the world, because that benefited the country's economy. "If you want true connectivity, you cannot be on Team A, B, or C," he argued. The UAE viewed war and sanctions as clots in the arteries of trade, Baharoon said. Sticking with the medical analogy, he suggested that the US had come to overuse sanctions as a tool of statecraft, "just like a patient turning to antibiotics as if it were an aspirin."

Emirati officials echoed his view. Hamad Buamim, chair of the Dubai Multi Commodities Centre, a leading UAE free trade zone, said in an interview with the *Financial Times* that, "unfortunately, politics is driving decisions that are not commercially viable for the global economy." It was a not-so-subtle jab at the Western price cap coalition and its campaign against Russian oil. "The fact that the economy is not purely controlled by one side of the world makes these sanctions against Russia less effective," he went on to argue. "They are effective when you look west, but they are not really effective beyond that."

WHEN YOU LOOK EAST FROM DUBAI, RATHER THAN WEST, A different reality takes shape. A five-hour drive from India's Kandla port, on the other side of the Gulf of Kutch, Jamnagar emerges as if from nowhere. The Jamnagar district hosts one of the world's largest and most complex oil refineries, with manufacturing facilities, a petroleum refinery complex, a petrochemical complex, power generation facilities, and its own port infrastructure, all sprawling over 7,500 acres. The steel tonnage required for its construction would have been enough to build nineteen Eiffel Towers, the cement sufficient for ten Empire State Buildings. When it opened in December 2008, the *Financial Times* called Jamnagar "the big new kid on the refining block."

Reliance Industries, which operates the Jamnagar refinery, is India's largest private company. It is also one of the big winners in the Russian–Indian oil trade that exploded after the invasion of Ukraine.

Before February 2022, India sourced its oil primarily from the Middle East, especially Iraq and Saudi Arabia. Russian oil was less attractive to Indian refiners, in part because of high freight costs compared with those from Middle Eastern producers. With the drop in Russian prices, that changed. Russia's share of India's total import volumes rose from just under 3 percent in 2021 to 38 percent in 2023. By that point, India accounted for over one-third of Russia's crude oil exports.

India's rapidly growing population has driven an increasing demand for fossil fuels, making it the third-biggest consumer of electricity and oil in the world. But India imported growing amounts of Russian oil not just to meet its rapidly expanding domestic needs. It also had a substantial refining and reexport business to satisfy. India's refineries have profited handsomely since the Ukraine invasion, importing massive volumes of heavily discounted Russian crude that bolstered their profit margins. In 2023, India became the world's fourth-largest exporter of middle distillates (gas oil, diesel, and kerosene) and the sixth-largest for overall refined products. And the trend line continued to point upward.

It is easy to get a sense of India's insatiable hunger for energy while driving through rush-hour traffic in New Delhi, a megacity projected to become the world's most populous by 2035. During my visit in spring 2025, my taxi driver battled cars, buses, trucks, motorcycles, rickshaws, and tuktuks, to deposit me at Chanakyapuri, a posh part of New Delhi sprawling with embassies, mansions, and ministries. I was there to meet Ajay Bisaria, who understands India's energy trade with Russia better than most.

Until recently India's high commissioner to Canada, Bisaria is a trained economist, served as a diplomat for thirty-five years, and represented India at the World Bank. A Soviet specialist, he witnessed the end of perestroika on the ground while posted at the Indian embassy in Moscow, and was then at India's department of commerce when the Soviet-era trade in rupees was abandoned in favor of Indian–Russian trade in US dollars in the early 1990s.

It was a pleasant and unusually clear day when we met, after days of light rainfall had boosted New Delhi's usually dismal air quality index. Bisaria wore a well-tailored blue suit and appraised me with piercing, smart eyes. He saw India's decision to ramp up its purchase of Russian oil as pure economics. "Cheaper oil was available to us, so why not take advantage? This was the logic. It also helped reduce India's import bill," he said. Sechin would likely agree. Speaking at Indian Energy Week in the spring of 2023, just months after signing an agreement between Rosneft and the Indian Oil Corporation to significantly increase oil supplies to India, Sechin was fulsome in his praise for India as a country guided by "enlightened national interest" in pursuit of a foreign policy "free from pressure," by which he meant the Western price cap coalition.

India's oil partnership with Russia caught the attention of that coalition quickly. As early as April 2022, when India had barely begun to increase imports from Russia, Biden urged Prime Minister Narendra Modi to avoid going that route. By that summer, however, Indian imports were rapidly growing. Tensions only spiraled after the price cap was introduced. Ahead of an EU–India summit in May 2023, the EU's foreign policy chief, Josep Borrell, argued that Brussels should move to crack down on third countries refining Russian oil and then selling the products to Europe. "If diesel or gasoline is entering Europe . . . from India and being produced with Russian oil, that is certainly a circumvention of sanctions," he said. Indian officials were not pleased. External affairs minister Subrahmanyam Jaishankar urged Borrell to study the EU's own regulations more carefully. "If Russian crude is substantially transformed, it's not treated as Russian anymore," he said.

When I asked Bisaria about such Western criticism, he recalled that "there was some pressure from the US at the beginning, but India did not yield." There was a feeling in India, he said, that China was benefiting from cheaper Russian energy, "so why shouldn't we?" Western states had no right to criticize India—a sovereign nation, the world's largest democracy, and a country that has its own history with Russia—over its trade decisions, especially since Europe itself continued to benefit from cheap Russian energy.

Hardeep Singh Puri, India's minister of petroleum and natural gas, went even further during an interview with the BBC's *HARDTalk*, arguing that India was doing the world a service by taking Russian oil off the market. "Let me enlighten you," he said as he laid into the journalist. "What the US told us is that they *wanted* us to buy as much oil from Russia as we liked, as long as we bought it at a reasonable price. And that was music to my ears. . . . If we hadn't bought Russian oil, the price would have gone up and you would have had even more inflation in Europe than you currently have."

Puri may have had a point, yet India was still enabling Russia to skirt the oil price cap. According to data assembled by CREA, 331 shipments of oil arriving in India's port of Sikka between February and September 2024 cost an average $90.80 per barrel. In that period, 65 percent of those tankers were subject to the cap. Had the price cap been applied properly, it would have cut Russia's revenues by 34 percent. Embracing an unexpected opportunity to buy cheap oil, India had thrown Russia the most critical of economic lifelines.

IT WAS EARLY DECEMBER 2024 WHEN IGOR SECHIN ARRIVED IN the Emirates for another visit. This time, he would stay in Ras Al Khaimah, a city smaller and more laid-back than Dubai. Delivering a keynote speech at an economic forum, he was bullish on the oil sector. The world was still far from reaching peak demand for fossil fuels, he argued, and it was foolish for the West to try to squeeze Russia out of the energy market. With a wealth of natural resources estimated at $100 trillion, Russia could—and, in fact, had the responsibility to—ensure reliable energy supplies to its foreign partners over the long term.

Sechin had reasons to be confident. First, Rosneft was about to clinch another massive deal with Reliance Industries. Second, as it approached the three-year anniversary of its invasion of Ukraine, Russia had continued to fill its state coffers through exports of key commodities: LNG, fertilizers, and nuclear fuel. But no exports were more important than oil. In 2024 alone, Russia had earned almost $200 billion on oil exports, with a large share evading the price cap. The Europeans had played a rather inglorious part in the story. While shunning Russian crude oil, they had bought record quantities of refined products based on Russian crude—especially from India. According to CREA, the EU paid more for these imports in 2024 than it sent in financial aid to Ukraine.

Finding ways to sell its oil, Russia had managed to generate the income it needed to prosecute the war in Ukraine. But the effects of Russia's adaptation went further. Russia and the consumers of its oil, eager to avoid the reach of sanctions, created shipping fleets composed of the likes of the *Eagle S*, surrounded by a whole industry of agents providing insurance and maintenance. In doing so, they fueled the fragmentation of global oil shipping and heightened the risks of environmental disaster. And finally, by reorienting its oil exports to India, China, and other non-Western countries, Russia had put in place a solid foundation for deeper ties in the east and south.

Such was the state of affairs as 2024 ended, and the West had exhausted its tools of economic coercion vis-à-vis Russia—or had it?

In mid-January 2025, with just days left in office, the Biden administration hit the shadow fleet with its biggest blow to date. It sanctioned 183 vessels, from both Russian and international owners, and several UAE-based ship managers and oil traders. The decision sent shock waves through global oil markets. While India tried to appear blasé about it, its oil imports from Russia declined in February, falling to their lowest level since January 2023. But India's oil trade with Russia would prove more resilient than Western states had hoped—and this wasn't to be the last blow it would withstand.

Unperturbed by the commotion, the *Eagle S* had settled into tranquil waters after enduring an ordeal of its own. On Christmas Day 2024, the ship was temporarily detained by Finnish police, suspected of having damaged an underwater cable while heading through the Baltic Sea en route from the Russian port of Ust-Luga to Egypt. The incident raised alarm bells in Western capitals, forcing officials back to their office desks over the holiday. Was the *Eagle S* not just a shadow tanker, they wondered, but also involved in Russia's campaign of sabotage against critical undersea infrastructure in Europe? While investigating the damage, police arrested some of the crew and escorted the vessel into Finnish waters. There, it remained anchored off the old town of Porvoo.

The people behind Caravella LLCFZ warned through a lawyer that, given all the fuss, they might abandon the vessel. If the *Eagle S* should need to find a new owner, so be it.

Eventually, it would traverse the world's seas again, ferrying oil to hungry consumers on faraway shores. The price cap coalition wouldn't tire in trying to get the better of Russia, eventually turning the screws on India, escalating its crackdown on the shadow fleet, and even taking aim at Sechin's Rosneft directly. But Russia would find new ways to export its most precious resource—just as it would manage to import the merchandise it needed to keep its people content, and bring in the men, munitions, and materiel it required to prosecute its war.

CHAPTER 2

Tales of Laleli and Alabuga

FOOD SHORTAGES, RATION CARDS, RAMPANT CRIME. THIS IS HOW most Russians remember the chaotic days after the fall of the USSR. Almost overnight, the optimism and sense of opportunity that had characterized the late-1980s era of glasnost and perestroika gave way to gloom and deprivation. The strict Soviet-era regulations that had kept supply chains and prices under control for decades suddenly ceased to exist. Hyperinflation ravaged average people's savings. Supermarket shelves were empty. Between 1990 and 1993, alcohol consumption increased dramatically, as did the number of alcohol-related deaths, especially among working-class men. Those who did not live through the events will have difficulty grasping just how bad things got in Russia. Rising to power at the end of the 1990s, Putin would always remember this period as Russia's decade of humiliation—and the collapse of the USSR that precipitated it as "the biggest geopolitical catastrophe of the century."

Putin, who worked in the office of St. Petersburg Mayor Anatoly Sobchak at the time, was forced to supplement his income by moonlighting as a taxi driver. Others turned to what became known as the "suitcase trade" to earn some extra rubles. Men and women from Russia (they were called *chelnoki*, which translates as shuttles) traveled to Turkey—especially to the Laleli market in Istanbul's Fatih district—filling their luggage to the brim with textiles and light consumer goods and then taking them back home to sell. While the Laleli market became especially famous, this type of unregulated trade enveloped the entire Caspian and Black Sea region. At its peak in 1993–94, an estimated ten million Russians were involved in the shuttle trade, whose volume came close to ten billion US dollars per year. Even civil servants participated to top up their meager salaries. Putin's future spokesman Peskov, then working for the Russian foreign ministry, ferried cars between Russia and Turkey.

The 1990s were a harsh decade for Russia, with real per capita GDP falling by 42 percent from 1990 to 1998. Still, Russia's trade regime became more open and liberal, and the country began seeking partners in the West. In 1997, Russia signed a bilateral partnership and cooperation agreement with the EU, regulating trade with the bloc. Coming to power on the heels of the devastating 1998 financial crisis, Putin took further steps toward economic reform, and Russia started benefiting from rising oil prices over the coming decade. In 2012, Russia joined the World Trade Organization, taking its integration into the global economic system to yet another level.

That integration was first challenged in 2014. After Russia annexed Crimea, the EU restricted Russian access to finance, arms, and specific technologies, prompting Russia to retaliate by banning imports of some EU agricultural and food products. Living in Moscow at the time, I remember my disappointment at the disappearance of French cheese from Russian grocery stores. The US, meanwhile, issued sanctions related to the annexation of Crimea and, eventually, Russian cyber-activities and alleged electoral interference. But Russia's connectivity to Western markets was far from severed. On the eve of the Ukraine invasion in February 2022, Russia remained the EU's fifth-largest trading partner, and it imported one-third of its goods from the EU.

When the full-scale invasion came, that would change dramatically—and Russia would embark on furious and varied efforts to ensure it could maintain access to the goods and services it both wanted and needed to see it through the war and avert economic collapse.

In the six months after the invasion, as Western states were coming up with the oil price cap, they were also rolling out sanctions package after sanctions package, targeting everything from Russia's access to the EU's capital markets to Russia's transport and technology sectors. They introduced measures that prohibited the export to Russia of a broad variety of goods—electronics, luxury items, and any dual-use products, meaning those that had both civilian and military applications. Over the course of 2022, EU exports to Russia plunged by 40 percent.

Putin responded with a law on parallel imports, which allowed importers to bring goods into the country without obtaining permission from the original manufacturer. The Russian government published lists of goods that individuals and companies could move into Russia duty-free and from third countries.

Russian traders flocked back to the Laleli market—as did I, to get a glimpse of what this "Laleli 2.0" trade looked like in practice. It was midmorning in May 2023 when I set off for the market on foot from Istanbul's Taksim Square. In the early hours, bursts of heavy showers had provided some relief after what had been unusually warm days, even for Turkey. As I approached the Laleli district, located close to the Istanbul University campus, I noticed more Cyrillic signs. *Optovaya i roznichnaya*, which means "wholesale and retail," was written on many of the shop windows. The area felt far from the beauty of other Istanbul neighborhoods, like historic Sultanahmet or colorful Beyoğlu. It struck me as a conglomeration of forgettable buildings, crammed with similarly forgettable stores. Some sellers had unpacked their wares on stalls outside their storefronts with flashy signage, half-blocking the pavements. By 10 a.m., many people were already out and about, hunting for a good bargain. "Look, this is the color you wanted, a soft red," I overheard a saleswoman say in heavily accented Russian, unwrapping a blouse from plastic foil.

During the months before my visit, sales from Laleli to Russia had risen sharply, yet unlike in the early 1990s, goods were shuttled no longer in suitcases or buses but in cargo planes. Retailers from Russia purchased wholesale packages of clothing and other consumer goods. An individual shuttle trader usually bought goods for a minimum of $500 and would earn a markup of 30 percent upon selling the wares wholesale back in Russia. "Because the US and EU countries closed their doors to Russia, Russia turned to Turkey," the head of the Laleli Industrialists and Businessmen's Association told *The Wall Street Journal.*

Russia's harsh economic decoupling from the West did not just revive the hustle and bustle in Istanbul's Fatih district. It also gave rise to much broader economic activity that saw trade flows of unprecedented proportions, routed via third countries, into Russia. As EU exports to Russia dropped precipitously, there was an unusual surge in European exports to countries in Central Asia and the Caucasus. At the same time, Russian imports from these trading partners took off. This phenomenon came to be known as the "Eurasian roundabout," a term coined by the European Bank for Reconstruction and Development.

Turkey was a key node in this roundabout. In 2021, the country had not even been among Russia's top ten foreign trade partners. After the Ukraine invasion, the trade turnover between the two countries more than doubled. The roundabout trade also engulfed Russia's neighbors in the South Caucasus and Central Asia. Exports into Russia from Armenia, Azerbaijan, Georgia, Kazakhstan, Kyrgyzstan, Tajikistan, Uzbekistan, and Turkey collectively increased by 33 percent in 2022, compared to the previous year.

Most ominously for Ukraine and its Western supporters, the roundabout trade fed the Russian war machine by allowing Russia to import a variety of dual-use goods that could be repurposed for weapons. Turkish companies functioned as intermediaries involved in smuggling Western-origin microchips and machine tools into Russia. In the first nine months of 2023, Turkey reported exports worth $158 million of forty-five goods that the US had listed as "high-priority" (to *not* export) to Russia and Eurasian countries suspected of acting as intermediaries for Moscow. This was a threefold increase compared to 2022. The former Soviet republics in Central Asia and the South Caucasus became major transshipment hubs for US and European chips, lasers, measuring instruments, electronics, and other dual-use products headed for Russia. Seemingly harmless electronics like these came in handy for the manufacturing of aircraft, cruise missiles, armored vehicles, and tanks. The same applied to chips stripped from the most common household appliances. After the Ukraine invasion, European exports of washing machines, refrigerators, and even electric breast pumps to Russia's neighbors exploded. Shipments of these appliances to Russia from the same countries grew commensurately. End consumers in Russia faced significantly higher prices for many of the imported goods, forced to absorb the additional costs for logistics and services in third countries. Still, thanks to an elaborate infrastructure of intermediaries specialized in facilitating Russia's trade and payments, Russia could import almost any product, produced in any part of the world, if it so wanted. It was always one step ahead of the West.

Western governments tried to rein in the Eurasian roundabout, a beast that seemed to keep growing in size and sophistication. Just as they had targeted the oil-ferrying shadow fleet, they tried to restrict Russia's ability to import goods that were key to its prosecution of the war. The EU's consecutive sanctions packages added ever more items to the lists of merchandise that Russia could not buy. The EU also stepped up its sanction enforcement efforts, with member states launching investigations into suspected violations by their companies. In addition, Western states ramped up their export licensing controls, measures meant to control the possible end use of items. In an effort to make sure nothing and no one slipped through the cracks, senior American and European officials visited Turkey and countries in Central Asia and the South Caucasus to press governments to choke off trade patterns they believed were helping Russia evade restrictions. The US also took aim at individual entities from these countries, which carefully tried to balance their relations with Russia and the West. But if sanctioning shadow fleet vessels amounted to playing a game of Whac-a-Mole, so did taking on the roundabout trade. Governments needed a vast bureaucratic machinery to parse the data, given the fragmented landscape of small businesses, consultancies, and intermediaries involved. And targeting, say, companies in Kazakhstan or Turkey with a broad brush risked punishing those that did not export sanctioned goods to Russia—and antagonizing their governments in the process.

Over time, the US turned to a more politically sensitive, yet effective tool: secondary sanctions. Secondary sanctions target third parties, like banks and financial institutions, that do not directly violate sanctions but engage with individuals or entities that do. An executive order signed by Biden in December 2023 allowed US authorities to disconnect foreign banks from the US financial system for violating sanctions against Russia. EU countries were more hesitant to apply such measures, struggling to agree among themselves and pointing to past instances in which secondary sanctions failed to achieve the desired result. Still, because the world economy relies so heavily on the US dollar and the financial institutions through which it flows, US secondary sanctions were powerful.

By spring 2024, two years into the Ukraine invasion and thirteen rounds into the EU's sanctions packages, Putin's Russia had achieved the dubious distinction of becoming the most sanctioned country in the world. More than 2,100 individuals and entities and 58 percent of prewar EU exports to Russia had been subjected to restrictions. Yet, even as this kaleidoscope of restrictions became ever more elaborate and expansive, it proved insufficient to choke off Russian imports. As *The Economist* coolly noted, over 80 percent of the world, if measured by population, and 40 percent, if measured by GDP, were not enforcing any sanctions on Russia whatsoever. And those countries that did were struggling with Russian adaptation.

Why did the Eurasian roundabout survive? To begin with, new trade routes and transport arrangements facilitated it. For instance,

Russia used obscure shipping and logistics companies to import goods, just as it used them to export its oil. Bracing itself for an indefinite future under Western sanctions, Russia also increased investment into the construction of non-Western transport routes linking it to trade partners in Asia and the Middle East. One such route was the International North-South Transport Corridor, designed to link Russia and the Indian Ocean via Iran.

Russia also benefited from long-standing institutional ties to partners in the Eurasian roundabout. Armenia, Belarus, Kazakhstan, and Kyrgyzstan, together with Russia, form part of the Eurasian Economic Union (EEU), founded in 2015 to spur economic integration among its members. The group offered several advantages, including that trade between EEU members was not subject to routine customs checks and that entrepreneurs could register businesses in partner states with relative ease. One case uncovered by researchers at the Organized Crime and Corruption Reporting Project showed how Russians were quickly able to register intermediary companies on Kazakh soil in order to purchase drones abroad and then export them to Russia.

Finally, even though US secondary sanctions posed serious challenges to the roundabout trade, and to the Russian economy more generally, Russia found ways to soften that blow, too. Taking inspiration from the barter exchanges of the old Laleli trade, Russia's technocrats would make sure to deprive the US dollar of some of its potency.

If there is one technocrat who helped Russia weather the storm of the West's economic onslaught, it is Elvira Nabiullina. A former economic adviser to Putin, Nabiullina became the first woman to run Russia's central bank—or the central bank of any G8 country, for that matter—in 2013. For several consecutive years, Forbes named her among the world's one hundred most powerful women, until Putin invaded Ukraine and she was removed from the list.

Born in October 1963 in Ufa, a city in western Russia known for its oil refineries, Nabiullina grew up in modest conditions. Her father was a chauffeur, and her mother worked in a local factory. Nabiullina graduated from the department of economics at Lomonosov Moscow State University in 1986 and soon after the collapse of the Soviet Union started her career as an economic technocrat, working her way up to minister of economic development. When Putin was reelected as president in 2012, she became his special economic adviser, before being appointed to head the central bank the following year. She won plaudits at home for steering Russia's economy through the first barrage of Western sanctions following the annexation of Crimea in 2014 and then through the COVID pandemic.

Those who know her have described Nabiullina as focused, always well prepared, and an advocate of market forces—despite her Soviet-era economics education. She is also notoriously hard to read. Kremlin watchers have resorted to deciphering clues about policy decisions from the brooches Nabiullina chooses to wear on the occasion of major announcements. In March 2020, she wore a brooch in the form of a *nevalyashka* doll, a traditional Russian toy that pops back up when pushed over, as policymakers sought to shore up the economy against the COVID pandemic.

Nabiullina decided to wear no brooch at all during a widely anticipated press conference on February 28, 2022, just four days into the invasion of Ukraine. She appeared exhausted, dressed all in black, as if she had entered a period of mourning. Rumors soon ricocheted that Nabiullina had tried to resign because of her opposition to the war. Whatever her personal feelings might have been, in late April 2022 the Duma, Russia's parliament, confirmed Nabiullina for five more years as chairwoman of the central bank. Fifty-eight years old at the time, Nabiullina would be one of the key technocrats steering Russia's foreign economic adaptations, especially in monetary matters, which were so crucial to its ability to persevere against the West in this new era.

In addition to targeting the shadow fleet and the Eurasian roundabout, Western states imposed unprecedented financial sanctions on

Russia. Within days of the invasion, the EU froze the Russian central bank's assets. Western governments also moved swiftly to expel Russia from the SWIFT banking communications system. SWIFT, the Society for Worldwide Interbank Financial Telecommunication, is key to most global banking transactions because it authenticates the identities of banks sending and receiving money. Disconnected from SWIFT, Russian banks found it a lot harder to conduct international transactions.

Forced to react to such drastic Western measures, Nabiullina had a solid base upon which to build. Under her watch, long before 2022, the central bank had both grown its reserves and shifted them away from the US dollar toward gold, the euro, and the Chinese renminbi. Russia had also experimented for years with settling trade in nondollar currencies. In 2014, Russia launched the System for Transfer of Financial Messages, a homemade equivalent to SWIFT whose aim was to create a closed communication system for Russian banks that the US Treasury would not be able to monitor. Several Russian banks had also joined a Chinese messaging platform, the Cross-Border Interbank Payment System, making Beijing an important partner in Moscow's de-dollarization efforts. Even though both Russia and China continued to rely heavily on SWIFT, they laid a foundation for de-dollarizing transactions between themselves, years before the invasion of Ukraine.

After February 2022, Russia needed to take such de-dollarization efforts to an entirely new level. Russia's technocrats came up with innovative solutions, further boosting trade in nondollar currencies and putting in place the infrastructure to use cryptocurrencies. Businesses even turned to the clandestine, barter-like exchanges that had been typical for the Laleli "suitcase trade," altogether eliminating the need for any bank transactions. Speaking in St. Petersburg in June 2023, Putin proudly announced that the share of the dollar and euro in Russia's exports would be halved by the end of the year. What he failed to mention was that Russia's much-vaunted de-dollarization was slowly but surely turning into yuanization. Russia's economic dependence on China was growing, and not just in monetary matters. Soon, China would account for more than 30 percent of Russia's export revenues and provide over 40 percent of its imports, including dual-use goods. That reliance gave Beijing growing leverage over Moscow when it came to trade negotiations. And with Russia's economic ties with the West severed, there was no escaping that growing dependence and asymmetry. Some in Moscow must have worried about it—and the political implications going forward—but a deepening vassalage to China was the price Putin was willing to pay for chasing his dream of dominating Ukraine.

Nabiullina's monetary policy did not please everyone, either. Russian oligarchs were angry at her move to curb inflation by hiking interest rates, which squeezed their profit margins. Sechin complained that Nabiullina's monetary policy was inhibiting the modernization of his oil refineries. But as Russia marked the three-year anniversary of the war, she remained firmly in the saddle.

Reviewing successes and challenges in the face of Western sanctions during an address to the Duma in early April 2025, Nabiullina struck an overall upbeat tone. Yes, cross-border payments had become more difficult, but the central bank was working with businesses to solve difficulties as and when they arose. Referring to the West, she told lawmakers: "They were counting on a serious disorganization of our financial system, but that did not happen. Trading partially shifted to a different format." She concluded her remarks by suggesting that "tectonic changes in global trade are unfolding before our eyes, and it is still very difficult to judge where they will lead the global economy—and how they will affect Russia."

But as Nabiullina knew full well, in the most sensitive areas, Russia's wartime trade remained largely insulated from the long arm of the US Treasury. A sinister alliance of Iranian drone technology, North Korean munitions, and Chinese electronics had emerged to ensure that Russia's battlefield needs would not go unmet.

On one of her first outings as minister for economic development in November 2007, just two months after Putin had appointed her to the role, Nabiullina traveled some five hundred miles east of Moscow to Russia's majority-Muslim Republic of Tatarstan. She was there to attend the festive opening ceremony of the Alabuga Special Economic Zone. Photographs show a youthful Nabiullina, wearing a dark coat and a large pink scarf, standing in what looks like a massive warehouse, surrounded by a crowd of male officials in dreary suits and ties. During the 2010s, Nabiullina, herself from an ethnically Tatar family, would frequently visit the special zone as it continued to develop, benefiting from attractive investment conditions such as low taxes. Long home to significant oil and gas production and heavy industry, Tatarstan would turn into a tech hub as well, thanks to Alabuga.

By 2021, the Alabuga Special Economic Zone hosted, among other things, the Alabuga Polytech college, conceived as an educational center to produce brilliant specialists in areas like chemistry, engineering, and industrial robotics—an "Elon Musk funnel" of sorts. It has recruited Russian high school students to participate in dual work-study programs, allowing them to focus on subjects like drone technology. Slickly edited videos with upbeat music show young students donning protective suits and building components of the Albatross M5, a Russian reconnaissance drone. What the videos do not show is that since spring 2023, the school has also been involved in manufacturing the Iranian-designed Shahed 136 armed drones, according to several groundbreaking investigations. To that end, the school even sent hundreds of students to Iran for specialized training.

Emerging as the primary hub for the assembly of the Shahed 136 (rechristened by Russia as "Geran-2," named after the geranium flower), the Alabuga Special Economic Zone came to occupy a special place in Russia's effort to import the parts, people, and knowhow it needed to prosecute the war in Ukraine. The Shahed 136—a loitering munition, also called a suicide or kamikaze drone—became the backbone of Russia's deep-strike campaign into Ukraine. Russia made several upgrades to the drone, increasing its speed and altitude and making it more resistant to jamming. Russian payments for Iranian drone technology went through obscure UAE entities, and Russia also delivered gold bars as part of the transaction.

In addition to Alabuga Polytech, another entity became critical to Russia's ability to churn out a steadily growing number of Shaheds. In 2022, Alabuga launched an educational program called Alabuga Start, offering two- or four-year work programs in areas like hospitality, catering, and front desk services. The program was tailored exclusively to foreign women between the ages of eighteen and twenty-two, especially from Africa and former constituent republics of the Soviet Union that are now part of the Commonwealth of Independent States. Alabuga Start sought recruitment help from African government representatives and leveraged Russia's growing activity within BRICS to spread the word.

To attract students, Alabuga Start promised plane tickets to Russia, competitive starting salaries, a certificate upon conclusion of the program, and career advancement opportunities. The flashy promises, however, obscured more sinister realities. The majority of participants ended up working in Shahed production. In Alabuga Start's flagship educational program, "Composite Materials Production," for instance, participants were trained in gluing, cutting, painting, and assembling "items"—skills required for the labor-intensive production of drone airframes. Program administrators used dating apps like Tinder and Badoo to reach out to young women and lure them to Russia with promotional material that painted a future filled with love, marriage, and children. Leaked documents in 2023 reviewed by the Institute for Science and International Security (ISIS) revealed that internally, Alabuga Start participants were derogatorily called "mulattoes." In interviews with the Associated Press, some of the African women employed at Alabuga Start complained of long hours under constant surveillance, of broken promises about wages and areas of study, and of working with caustic chemicals that left their skin itching. In spring

2025, Interpol in Botswana began investigating Alabuga Start for alleged human trafficking after reviewing its social media posts.

As of summer 2024, more than 90 percent of those employed at Alabuga Start, as well as around one-third of students at Alabuga Polytech, were working in drone production, including of the Shahed 136, according to the ISIS. Using data from January through August 2024, the institute calculated that Alabuga had achieved an annual production rate estimated at about 4,700 drones per year. Ukraine has claimed an even higher number, estimating in spring 2025 that Alabuga had produced over six thousand Shaheds in 2024 and was aiming for eight to ten thousand in 2025.

These drones wrought constant destruction across Ukraine's cities, infrastructure, and the electricity grid. Sent in swarms, they were meant to saturate Ukrainian air defenses and erode civilian morale, usually descending upon cities during the night and leaving people running for the shelters. Thousands of Ukrainian homes were regularly left without power due to the strikes. By spring 2025, the facilities at Alabuga used to produce the Shahed had doubled in size, and it seemed that Russia had established a second production line in the city of Izhevsk, west of the Ural Mountains. Thanks to that expansion, Russia was able to further up the ante, sending record-breaking numbers of drones into Ukraine.

The production of Shahed drones at Alabuga became the most visible and vilified manifestation of the expanding weapons trade between Russia and Iran after the invasion of Ukraine. But it was not the only one.

Since the 1990s, Russia has provided important military and nuclear assistance to Iran, from tanks and surface-to-air missiles to help in constructing its nuclear power plant at Bushehr. But there was little in terms of military technology that Tehran could offer Moscow in return. The dynamic was one in which, by and large, Russia was the patron and Iran the client.

That changed after the invasion of Ukraine. In the summer of 2022, Iran started to transfer—by aircraft or via shadow vessels crossing the

Caspian Sea—not just the Shahed 136, but also artillery shells, small-arms ammunition, antitank rockets, mortar bombs, and glide bombs to Russia. In September 2024, after many months of rumors and speculation, US officials confirmed that Iran had begun delivering several hundred close-range ballistic missiles to Russia as well.

Iran was not the only partner Russia could count on to feed its military campaign. China emerged as by far the most important provider of dual-use goods. Days before the Ukraine invasion, China and Russia had declared a "no limits" strategic partnership. Delivering dual-use components rather than finished weapons allowed China to keep Russia in the fight while claiming plausible deniability. Chinese exports to Russia of items like microelectronics, machine tools, telecommunications gear, radars, optical devices, and sensors rose by over 60 percent during the first two years of the war. By 2024, US officials raised concerns that China was no longer just exporting dual-use goods to Russia, but also giving at least some direct military support.

The last partner to enter the fray was North Korea. The isolated and secretive East Asian nation had maintained close ties with the Soviet Union and then with Russia for decades. In September 2023, eighteen months into the Ukraine war, North Korean leader Kim Jong Un visited Russia's Far East to meet with Putin. It was his first known trip outside the country in over four years. Kim traveled for over twenty hours in an armored train with an entourage that included his defense minister, top generals, and the director of the munitions industry department. As his train rolled into the city of Komsomolsk-on-Amur, a red carpet was rolled out at the railway station for officials to greet him. During the six-day visit, Putin and Kim exchanged rifles as gifts. Once he returned home, Kim ordered the provision of large-scale military assistance to Russia.

From fall 2023, North Korea emerged as the most consequential supporter of Russia's war, if measured by the sheer volume of weapons. It sent huge quantities of artillery shells, short-range missiles, and antitank missiles. By fall 2024, the Ukrainian general staff estimated that over half of the shells used by Russia came from North Korea.

Around that time, Kim made a decision that Western officials had long deemed unthinkable: He sent thousands of North Korean troops to fight alongside Russian soldiers. Once they were deployed to Russia's Kursk region and encountered Ukrainian soldiers, bizarre reports emerged about these North Koreans who were setting foot into a foreign country for the first time in their lives. Never having enjoyed unfettered access to the internet before, they were said to be watching a lot of pornography. Russian commanders ordered them to commit suicide, if need be, by blowing themselves up with grenades, to evade imminent capture by Ukraine. And they came with exceptional morale and loyalty to the homeland they served. "Even in times when the sky collapsed, it was the arms [of the motherland] that protected our lives; I always feel reassured because I am held in those benevolent arms," read a notebook left by a dead North Korean soldier and retrieved by Ukrainians. Russia also lured other foreign nationals—Africans, Bangladeshis, Nepalis—to fight in Ukraine, often under the false premise of civilian work. But North Koreans represented by far the biggest contingent.

Russia's turn to North Korea for soldiers shocked the world—but not Pavlo Klimkin. The trained physicist studied in Moscow and dealt with Russia extensively after joining Ukraine's foreign service in 1993. Three months after Russia annexed Crimea, Klimkin became Ukraine's foreign minister, a role in which he served until 2019. "The problem is that many people in the West don't understand the Russian mentality," Klimkin told me. "How you achieve results and how you do foreign policy is understood differently from the classic politician in the West." Intrigued, I asked Klimkin to elaborate. "If you started as a young officer in the KGB," Klimkin explained, "and after that you did your career in the FSB [Russia's Federal Security Service], you see the world in a different way. You have some tenacity. You have a strategic outlook. You believe in zero-sum games." To him, Russia's turn to North Korea was further evidence of this mentality. To my interjection that many people considered it humiliating, he responded: "Yes, it is humiliating, but the Russians don't care. Because they understand that to not get results in their war against us, Ukraine, is even more humiliating."

Klimkin seemed to be pointing to another example of Russian *stoykost*. While Western observers mocked what they called Putin's embarrassing reliance on Russia's poor neighbor for troops, the Kremlin was simply doing what it felt was necessary. If Russia were to come out on top against the West in Ukraine, then who would look foolish in the end?

This most pernicious of wartime trades—that in men, munitions, and military materiel—proved crucial to Russia's ability to sustain its campaign in Ukraine. The Eurasian roundabout, Nabiullina's de-dollarization efforts, Russia's drone production at Alabuga, the deployment of North Korean soldiers—all these were elements in a continuously evolving mosaic of efforts Russia undertook to prosecute its war and deprive Western states of tools to starve its economy and war machine. In this battle of wills, the balance of resources greatly favored the US and EU, whose combined GDP remained over twenty times larger than Russia's. In adapting in the most outrageous of ways, the Kremlin tilted the balance of resolve in its favor. But Putin also militarized the Russian economy in the process and made it deeply reliant on China, creating structural problems that would haunt the country for a long time to come.

Meanwhile, Russia's defense ties with Iran, China, and North Korea would evolve to have consequences far beyond the war in Ukraine. As more military gear was ferried across the Russian border, Western officials worried how Putin might compensate his partners in Tehran, Beijing, and Pyongyang. Russia concluded new strategic partnership treaties with North Korea in summer 2024 and with Iran in early 2025, to lift cooperation to new levels. Russia's defense industry became more liberal in sharing technologies and expertise with its partners, and there is evidence that Russia provided them with captured weapons and operational insights from the Ukrainian battlefield. As a result, they learned valuable lessons for their own prospective future wars against the US or its regional allies. Finally, Russia became more protective of Iran and North Korea—the former an aspiring, the latter a de facto nuclear-armed state—in international diplomacy. This marked a significant reversal for a Russia that, over decades, had worked with Western states to curb the spread of nuclear weapons.

These dynamics combined to raise alarms in Western capitals that a more complex and more dangerous phenomenon was in the making: the alignment of four formidable adversaries, intent on overturning the Western-led liberal international order, in a Russian-led "axis of upheaval." The term, first coined by US scholars Richard Fontaine and Andrea Kendall-Taylor in a *Foreign Affairs* essay in spring 2024, quickly gained traction in Washington. Others preferred to speak instead of an "axis of autocrats," an "axis of losers," or simply "CRINK"—based on the countries' acronyms.

The essential worry underpinning these analyses boiled down to this: The axis, or whatever one might call it, was benefiting Russia in its confrontation with the West, far beyond the Ukrainian battlefield. Composed of two Lilliputians—Iran and North Korea—and two giant Brobdingnagians—China and Russia—the club of four would emerge stronger than the sum of its parts. Meanwhile, it would dilute the foreign policy tools—sanctions, export controls, the nuclear nonproliferation regime—at Washington's disposal to confront them. With time, and assuming the four countries continued on this trajectory, they would be able to tie down the American Gulliver in intersecting crises—from Europe, via the Middle East, to the Indo-Pacific.

It was an alarming prospect, for sure. Yet, soon enough, the Russian-led axis would face its first critical test.

Part II

WAGING THE WAR OF NARRATIVES

CHAPTER 3

Our Friend, the Soviet Union

WHILE RUSSIA WAS SCRAMBLING TO SECURE ECONOMIC LIFE-lines, it was also trying to win support in the global information war.

At first, after Russia invaded Ukraine, the Kremlin focused on claiming it was conducting a "special military operation" against Nazis who had usurped power in a 2014 coup d'état. Ever since 2014, Russian propaganda has consistently portrayed Ukraine as an illegitimate "Nazi" state, and hence a mere construct used by the West to encircle Russia. This narrative framework served several functions. First, it elevated Ukraine to the position of formidable adversary, comparable to Nazi Germany. It also attached itself neatly to Russia's state narrative on the Second World War, in which the terror of the Stalin years and Soviet repression in Eastern Europe and Central Asia were crowded out by an emphasis on the Soviet Union's wartime sacrifices. It is a narrative in which the USSR, with twenty-seven million lives lost, was the main victim of Nazism. Foreign affairs minister Sergey Lavrov provoked outrage in May 2022 when he falsely suggested that Hitler had "Jewish blood" and that Volodymyr Zelensky's Jewish heritage meant "absolutely nothing," since the "most ardent anti-Semites are usually Jews." Eight months later, Lavrov claimed NATO was "using Ukraine to wage a proxy war against Russia with the old aim of finally solving the 'Russian question,'" just as Hitler had sought a "final solution to the 'Jewish question.'" Russia, a powerhouse nation, was comparing itself to a persecuted ethnic minority.

But soon enough, the Kremlin realized that it needed to tell a different story to garner sympathy in far-flung places like Africa, South Asia, or the Middle East. If Russia could frame its own actions in Ukraine as anti-colonial and anti-imperialist—savvily exploiting memories of past Western colonialism, hegemony, and occupation in these parts of the world—it would be a major feat.

And so Russia's spin doctors obliged, writing a script about the war that painted Russia as victim and vanguard at once, a pernicious symbiosis. Russia was a victim, the story began, because the West, in supporting Ukraine, was practicing a new form of colonialism whose final objective was to destroy Russia. The framing included an explicit warning: If the West was not stopped in Ukraine, other countries would soon enough succumb to its diktat, too. Russia was also a vanguard, both because it supported countries in the Global South against twentieth-century colonialism and imperialism and because it would lead the future fight for a more equitable world order on behalf of the "global majority." Russia presented the war as no less than a fight of global proportions, one in which Russia was challenging novel forms of Western colonialism and exploitation—what the Kremlin called "neocolonialism"—on behalf of all the world's oppressed. This framing tapped right into global grievances over an unfair distribution of power in the international system. It became the discursive foundation to Russia's effort to outlast the West.

Before long, the anti-colonial rallying cry found its way from the speeches of high-level officials into countless initiatives. A new foreign policy concept—a document that sets out Russia's official view of the world, its major interests, and how it will pursue them—was published in spring 2023, littered with references to neocolonialism. That document for the first time also defined Russia as a "unique country-civilization," underscoring its messianic global ambitions. At the United Nations, Russian diplomats tabled a suggestion to declare December 14 an annual International Day Against Colonialism. Russian history was not spared its share of anti-colonial revisionism, either. In one example, the foreign ministry's in-house journal *International Affairs* published a scholarly article that portrayed Nicholas II—who determined that Russia should not be left out of the scramble for colonial possessions and encouraged Russian expansion into Manchuria—as a global "anti-colonial" leader.

The Kremlin understood that it would find particularly receptive audiences for such rhetoric in Africa, especially in countries where resentment over Europe's colonial exploitation continued to fester. In July 2023, it hosted its second Russia-Africa Summit in St. Petersburg, where foreign ministry spokeswoman Maria Zakharova told African dignitaries theatrically that "Russian men give their lives at the (Ukraine) front so that people from the African continent are free." The subtext of this outrageous claim is that if Russia yields in the fight against Ukraine, other countries will fall victim to the dictates of Washington or Brussels next. The supposedly fairer, multipolar, post-Western order that Putin promised would then remain no more than a fleeting illusion.

In November 2024, I flew to South Africa to understand how, why, and to what extent these Russian narratives were resonating there. When Russia invaded Ukraine, the ruling African National Congress (ANC)—which has been the dominant political force in South Africa since the nineties—adopted a position infused by anti-imperialist tropes and pro-Russian leanings. It framed the war as "a conflict between the US and US-led NATO and Russia in pursuit of the objectives of the so-called Wolfowitz doctrine," further defining that doctrine as intended to "not allow that any country in the world should have the possibility . . . to challenge US interests, especially its hegemony." It was because of this doctrine, the ANC argued, that "the US provoked the war with Russia over Ukraine, hoping to put Russia in its place."

One cannot understand such ANC rhetoric without understanding the history of South Africa's own liberation struggle—and Soviet support for that struggle.

During the Cold War, the ANC led the fight against apartheid, the system of racial segregation formally established in South Africa in 1948, following the electoral victory of the White National Party. From 1960 until 1990, with many of its leaders in prison, the ANC operated underground or in exile. The South African Communist Party (SACP), an important ally, facilitated some of the ANC's connections with the Soviet Union. Those connections came in different forms. Some ANC cadres received military or political training in Moscow, in cities in what is now Ukraine, or in East Germany; others were coached by the Soviet military in Angolan camps; yet others had no direct contact, but learned about Soviet support through pamphlets or covert study groups.

Robert McBride was among those whose worldviews were shaped by Soviet support. Born in 1963, he was only a teenager when the ANC began scattering pamphlets across South Africa calling on people to resist the country's apartheid regime. The pamphlets led McBride to underground discussions that opened his eyes to the fight against apartheid, and the important role that the Soviet Union was playing in supporting it and anti-imperial struggles elsewhere, like in Korea or Vietnam. "When you're a youngster, growing up, you're not too hooked on ideology and you don't grasp it properly," he told me. "You pick up the pamphlets and you hear slogans, words, things that agitate your mind and that get you thinking."

By apartheid's shades neither Black nor white but "colored," McBride hailed from Wentworth, a bleak mixed-race township in suburban Durban. His childhood was marked by the growing pace of apartheid legislation. McBride idolized his father, Derrick, a well-educated teacher who was driven to the bottle by disappointment, and who hated whites. He started high school in 1976, the year of the Soweto uprising, a Black student protest that turned deadly. McBride joined the armed resistance in 1985. He was trained in a secret camp in Botswana and became a "special operations" guy. Today, he is best known in South Africa for his leadership of the cell that bombed a restaurant and bar in Durban in June 1986, an attack in which three white women were killed. Captured, convicted, and sentenced to death, McBride was pardoned while on death row and later granted amnesty at South Africa's Truth and Reconciliation Commission after apartheid ended in 1990.

The early 1990s were an exhilarating time for South Africans finally on the cusp of freedom, but McBride also found that era "demoralizing," as the Soviet Union collapsed. While Western governments had, at least initially, stood by the apartheid government—providing it with diplomatic, economic, and military backing—the Soviet Union had supported the armed resistance materially and morally. McBride did not visit Moscow until after apartheid ended, but the Soviet Union, or what it represented in his mind, left a profound mark on him.

When we spoke, McBride painted a sweeping picture of the nexus between the anti-apartheid struggle and the politics of the Cold War. In line with ANC thinking, he described to me a world essentially divided into two camps: capitalist imperialism, represented by the West, and anti-imperialist forces spearheaded by the Soviet Union. As our conversation pivoted to the present day, it became clear that, for McBride, this framework endured. He saw Russia's 2022 invasion of Ukraine as a war forced upon the Kremlin, the final chapter in a long attempt by the West to encircle and dismantle Russia. There seemed to be near-perfect congruence between his reading of the war and Russia's own telling.

His anti-imperialist leanings were infused with gratitude. McBride is among many for whom the history of Soviet support for the liberation struggle generated an enduring sense of appreciation toward Russia. Such feelings are perhaps most pronounced among veterans of uMkhonto we Sizwe ("Spear of the Nation," or MK), the ANC's paramilitary wing. Some of the most prominent MK veterans devote parts of their memoirs to their time spent in the Soviet Union. "Virtually all of our contingent were experiencing, for the first time in their lives, care and hospitality at the hands of white people," MK founding member and commander Ronnie Kasrils wrote of his arrival in Odesa in 1964. Kasrils recalled that within a year, Soviet instructors taught his group how to use small arms, throw hand grenades, sabotage installations, and lay booby traps. "There was a great spirit among us, and no higher than when we marched Red Army–style, goose-stepping, with arms swinging across the chest, around the parade ground, singing our national songs," he wrote.

Military training was complemented by political courses dedicated to the basics of socialism, communism, and the world revolutionary movement. Historian Irina Filatova, who has meticulously chronicled Soviet assistance to the anti-apartheid movement, argues that such support was not only indispensable for the success of the armed struggle; the Soviet mentality, values, and vision of the world also left a deep and lasting imprint on the ANC leadership. Filatova calls this imprint the "hidden thread."

Not everyone swallowed what they were served in the Soviet Union uncritically. Bheki Langa, an ANC veteran, had spent ten months in detention for his activism before being offered the chance to leave South Africa in 1976. So began nearly a decade of Soviet exile. When we met in Johannesburg, Langa told me he was attracted to the Soviet Union as a "symbol of a different dispensation," a place that represented the principles of equality and nonexploitation. He wanted, he said, to experience firsthand what it meant to live in the first socialist country.

Langa spent one year in Kharkiv, Ukraine, followed by many more years in Moscow, where he received a PhD at the Moscow Institute of National Economy. Many ANC or MK operatives experienced short sojourns in the USSR, but living there for a whole decade was unusual. When his mother passed, in February 1984, the news did not reach

Langa in Moscow until weeks after her burial. Shortly afterward, his brother Ben was killed in his home by MK operatives based on false information planted by an ANC infiltrator. A long way away from those troubles at home, Langa's immersion into Soviet society indelibly shaped his political views.

"We used to walk about, we used to go to the theater," he told me, describing his time in Kharkiv and Moscow. "In times when there were food shortages, we would be there in the queue, with them," he said. "And we experienced a lot of racism, because clearly, people were not sufficiently exposed to life in other parts of the world." These experiences did not fundamentally change Langa's views on the desirability of socialism, but he said that they made him more "realistic." When the ANC leadership parachuted on occasion into Moscow for shorter stints, it was not too keen to hear about these problems, Langa said. One had to be careful not to appear "anti-Soviet" when expressing criticism, since the Soviet Union was a friend.

After the end of apartheid, Langa served as a diplomat, including as ambassador to Russia from 2005 to 2010. After the invasion of Ukraine, he spoke publicly about the vital role that Ukraine, as a Soviet socialist republic distinct from Russia, had played in supporting the anti-apartheid movement. Still, as we discussed the origins of the war, it became apparent that Langa's views tended to be forgiving of Russia. Though he stressed that there was always an alternative to war, Langa evoked Russian apprehensions over Ukraine's movement toward NATO and Ukraine's failures in "assuring" Russia it would be a "friendly neighbor" as drivers of the conflict. Referencing what he called a "widespread view" that it was not to Russia's benefit to perpetuate the war, but rather in the interest of "certain forces" seeking "profit" from producing arms for Ukraine, Langa seemed easily inclined to adopt an imperialist lens on the conflict—one that echoed the ANC's contention that the US and Europe were "using" Ukraine as a "proxy" to keep Russia weak.

Anti-imperialism, which gave South Africa's liberation movement its ideological wrapping and a larger frame of reference, does not only live on in the hearts of veterans like Robert McBride and Bheki Langa. Today, the ANC's manifestos still commit the movement to support every effort to help "liberate humanity from the bondage of imperialism and neocolonialism." Fascinatingly, such anti-imperialism is sometimes even more virulent among a new generation of leaders who did not live through the liberation struggle and are now active in the ANC Youth Movement, the Marxist-Leninist Economic Freedom Fighters (EFF), and the SACP.

The EFF's leader, Julius Malema, was still a boy when his parents' generation broke the shackles of apartheid. He has described the war in Ukraine as a "proxy war" orchestrated by the "imperialist" West against Russia. Similarly, the SACP's Solly Mapaila has called Russia's war "defensive" and praised Putin for standing up against "the big boys of the US and European Union who are intimidating the whole world." That the SACP, an official ally of the ANC, is not a part of the government has given it greater latitude in being vocal about its admiration for Putin. It has shamelessly gone all in.

The ANC, meanwhile, is not tantamount to the South African government. The foreign ministry (DIRCO) has diluted extreme ANC positions, aware of the need for pragmatism in foreign policy. On the day of the full-scale invasion, DIRCO issued a statement in which it called on Russia "to immediately withdraw its forces from Ukraine." DIRCO and the South African presidency have also led efforts toward a peaceful settlement of the war, including through an African peace mission that visited both Russia and Ukraine in 2023.

Intimately involved in such efforts was Sydney Mufamadi, national security adviser to President Cyril Ramaphosa. Born in Alexandra Township in Johannesburg, Mufamadi was expelled from school at eighteen for participating in student protests against apartheid. He got involved in the underground resistance and cofounded the Congress of South African Trade Unions in 1985. After the end of apartheid, Mufamadi served in various roles under several South African presidents. When Russian tanks rolled into Ukraine, he had been national security adviser for six months.

When I sat down with Mufamadi in Pretoria's Union Buildings, the official seat of the South African government, I asked him who he believed was responsible for the Ukraine war. He said he saw in NATO's eastward expansion the "original causality" for the war. He asked me to put myself in the shoes of imagined ANC veterans who died just before the end of the Cold War. "One day, they find themselves alive again," Mufamadi hypothesized. "They see Moscow. They see Kyiv. And they are told that these two cities exist in two different countries now. Just imagine, this person must feel traumatized. And it's worse when the two countries are in conflict with each other."

Mufamadi's views struck me as more nuanced than McBride's, as he went on to stress that "causality" does not equal "justification," and that nothing justified Russia's attempt to redraw borders by force. At the same time, his evocation of a sense of "trauma" over the fact that Moscow and Kyiv ended up in separate countries seemed rooted in the idea that Russians and Ukrainians are essentially the same.

I encountered a similar perspective during my travels in India—another country that had benefited from Soviet support during the Cold War. Venkatesh Varma, who was ambassador to Russia from 2018 until 2021, invoked the Freudian concept of the "tyranny of minor differences" to illustrate the point to me. It relates to a phenomenon where groups with many shared similarities become hostile toward each other due to hypersensitivity to small distinctions. Western Ukrainians may not see a kinship with Russia, but the differences they invoke are overblown, he told me. "I'm not making a direct comparison. But consider the problem of communalism in India. Before partition, Hindus and Muslims, living together, were 95 percent alike. They came from the same land. They looked and dressed the same way," he said. "But when the tyranny of minor differences takes over, becomes an ideological movement, it can escalate into conflict, which can become quite intractable especially if external forces get involved."

Varma viewed the war in Ukraine, at least on some level, as a civil war. Yet he also stressed that Ukraine was, without any doubt, a separate, sovereign state. "But that does not mean that Ukraine is *any* other state that happens to be next to Russia. That would mean ignoring a reality of a thousand years," he concluded.

Whereas the South African ANC saw the world as divided into imperialist and anti-imperialist forces, the Indian perspective may be better described as Classical Realist. Powerful countries (especially Western ones) have asserted their primacy since time immemorial, the argument goes. And while a great power's claim to a sphere of influence may not be right, it reflects how nations behave. We live in a world in which might has always trumped right, and in which Western states have only ever applied the rules selectively, paying lip service to a liberal rules-based international order. It is a world in which powerful countries—Russia and India included—deserve primacy in their respective regions, given their history, strength, and size. And finally, it is a world in which Russia's weakness, let alone its defeat in Ukraine, would only benefit China, the only country both able and eager to challenge India's primacy in its own backyard—meaning, India's own interests were at stake in the outcome of the war.

Sympathy for Russia in both India and South Africa, I realized during my travels, was rooted in a complex range of emotions: deep gratitude for past Soviet support; negative attitudes toward a West seen as hypocritical and hyper-dominant; and a historical-cultural understanding of Russia and its neighborhood that tended to be dismissive of Ukrainian agency and identity. That major powers such as India and South Africa refused to join Western states in sanctioning and severing ties with Russia over the war in Ukraine had complex economic and political reasons, too. But in successfully grafting its anti-colonial framing of the war onto the sensitivities in these countries, Russia consolidated the emotional foundations for their support.

At the same time, the anti-colonial story fed entirely off external realities, sins committed in lands far from Russia, and therefore found little appeal among Russian society. It was also a narrative stuck in the past, obsessed with the West's historic wrongs, that failed to articulate a concrete and positive vision for the future. And finally, in anchoring

Russia's entire foreign policy narrative on the Ukraine war and its alleged anti-colonial nature, hyping its outcome as pivotal for the fate of humanity, Putin created a situation in which he could not easily back down in Ukraine.

IN ADDITION TO ITS ANTI-COLONIAL MESSAGING, RUSSIA resorted to other themes to win support from international audiences after its invasion of Ukraine. Its attacks on "woke" liberalism gave Russia's war propaganda a normative veil. Russia's self-portrayal as a bastion of conservative values and white male virility hardly started in 2022. After his return to the presidency in 2012, Putin published a series of essays laying out his new vision of the country's future, arguing that the West was foundering because of its lack of "traditional values," which he defined in opposition to liberal views on gender, sexuality, and reproductive rights, and as centering on the institution of the family. Through the 2010s, Russian officials increasingly portrayed the country as representing an antidote to the fractious mores of a declining West. Putin's Valdai speech in October 2021, which I witnessed firsthand in Sochi's Olympic Park, became a hallmark of that portrayal, promulgating Russia's "healthy conservatism" as a model for others to follow.

After the invasion, Russia doubled down on this messaging and skillfully attached it to its anti-colonial narrative. The attempt to isolate and "cancel" Russia, Putin claimed in a cynical rhetorical ploy, was just another example of the "woke" West imposing monothought and censuring alternative views. Only Russia's victory in Ukraine, he argued at the 2024 Valdai conference, would ensure the emergence of a multipolar world, which in turn would guarantee the survival of the globe's "diversity, variety, and complexity." Conversely, if the West prevailed, the tentacles of liberal "fascism" would soon reach everywhere. To lend further credence to its role as defender of conservative values, in September 2024 the Russian government published a list of forty-seven countries it accused of implementing policies that "contradict traditional Russian spiritual and moral values." With the stroke of a pen, the document declared citizens from these countries eligible to request temporary asylum in Russia.

In South Africa, Putin's anti-woke image won Russia an unexpected ally among Afrikaners, an ethnic group, descended from predominantly Dutch settlers, that dominated the country's politics during apartheid. By enhancing its messaging about the West's colonial legacy with other layers—the importance of conservative family values—Russia therefore managed to appeal not just to ANC and MK veterans, its natural allies, but also to the other end of the political spectrum: conservative, right-wing whites. Even though South Africa did not feature on the Russian government's list of countries from which citizens could request asylum, Moscow still came up with bespoke initiatives to appeal to Afrikaners. In 2023, Russia's Tver region established an "African village," a refuge for white Afrikaner farmers interested in resettling. In South Africa, Putin could wear an anti-imperialist face for some audiences, while appearing as a white Christian nationalist to others.

In the Middle East, the United States' unconditional support for Israel provided Russia with a new—possibly the most potent—building block for its narrative, especially after Hamas's attack on Israel on October 7, 2023. The Kremlin started to draw false equivalencies between the Ukraine war and violence in the Holy Land as purported products of US hegemony. Just as the Russian-speaking people of Ukraine's Donbas region had allegedly lived under "occupation" by the US-backed "Kyiv regime" since 2014, Russia asserted, so the Gazans had suffered from "occupation" by a US-supported Israel.

Across the Global South, Gaza's plight mobilized people far more passionately than did the suffering in Ukraine. That was true especially in South Africa. The ANC's antipathy toward Israel originated during apartheid, when Israel supplied weapons to the National Party government. "South Africa and Palestine share a common history of struggle," the ANC observed in a 2022 policy document. After October 7, the salience of the Palestinian cause would even affect South Africa's diplomatic maneuvering on the Ukraine war. Representing his country at the "High-Level Summit on Peace for Ukraine" in Switzerland in June 2024, Sydney Mufamadi criticized the participation of Israel, since the country stood accused of genocide at the International Court of Justice (ICJ). "We were sitting there in Switzerland, trying to find a solution to the Ukraine conflict, saying that all of us gathered here are committed to the UN Charter and its related instruments. And then, we're expected to sign that declaration alongside Israel, when just the previous week we were at the ICJ? It was a big disconnect," Mufamadi told me. Considered the pinnacle of Western hypocrisy and double standard by many non-Westerners, the Gaza war both eclipsed and relativized whatever injustice Russia was committing in Ukraine.

A final reason why Russia managed to appeal in some parts of the world had little to do with Ukraine, with Gaza, or with conservative values, but was much more mundane: Ruling elites were losing support and turned to Russian-inspired populism—or even got in cahoots with the Kremlin—to stay in power. A link between a growing disillusionment with domestic politics and the appeal of strongmen like Putin was palpable in South Africa, too.

Six months before my arrival in the country, the ANC had fallen short of winning an absolute majority in a national election for the first time since gaining power after the fall of apartheid. The result reflected South Africans' increasing disenchantment with the party: the lack of economic dividends, broken promises, and rampant corruption. Some voters defected to a new party named after the old MK paramilitary wing, uMkhonto we Sizwe. Founded in December 2023, it was led by Jacob Zuma, the flamboyant former president with extremely close Kremlin ties.

Zuma's presidential reign from 2009 until 2018 was marked by state capture. In 2016, a report by a constitutional watchdog investigated his relationship with the Gupta brothers, Indian-born businessmen who amassed massive wealth during Zuma's presidency through lucrative state contracts. In 2021, Zuma was found guilty of contempt for defying the Constitutional Court's order to appear at an inquiry into the alleged corruption during his reign.

With his refusal to testify and his attacks disparaging the judiciary, Zuma has challenged South Africa's constitutional system. His efforts to evade accountability, South African public intellectual William Gumede wrote in 2021, threatened the fundamental principle that all are equal before South African law. But challenges have come from other political camps, too. Lindiwe Sisulu, daughter of the late ANC Secretary-General Walter Sisulu and an MK veteran fervently loyal to Russia, has criticized the constitution as "neoliberal" and a product of "foreign inspiration." She and others in the ANC have continued to blame apartheid and white people for the country's woes, rather than admitting to their own shortcomings in governing for three decades.

During my travels, many South Africans I spoke with assured me that their democracy remained resilient, pointing to its strong courts and robust media. Yet some warned that the likes of Zuma and Sisulu were taking inspiration from Russia in their attacks on the rule of law. These South Africans worried that the political center continued to hold, but that it felt increasingly fragile. When I met Gumede in Johannesburg, he worried about the resonance of populist appeals, especially among South Africa's youth. "Among the poor, Black youths, you have a high illiteracy rate, unemployment, anger, and they get all their news on social media," he warned. To the anti-colonial, conservative, or pro-Palestinian virtues that individual South Africans might ascribe to Russia, it seemed one had to add the seductive appeal that "strong guys like Putin get things done."

As I approached the end of my trip to South Africa, I wanted to get to the heart of what, for Ukrainians, has been the most frustrating mystery. Even if ANC veterans feel a historical debt of gratitude toward Russia for its anti-imperialist support in *their* part of the world, why can't they acknowledge that Russia is currently embarking on its own project of subjugation in Ukraine? Can't they appreciate the irony? McBride found that idea preposterous, insisting it was Ukraine that had oppressed Russian speakers in its eastern Donbas region for years. Langa similarly rejected that Russia could be viewed as a colonial actor, returning to arguments about Ukraine's westward orientation as having threatened Russian security interests. Both men also dismissed the notion that Russia may be an aggressive actor with neo-imperialist ambitions beyond Ukraine. I was left with the impression, aptly captured by American historian Hilary Lynd, that "imperialism is only imperialism if Americans do it."

Serving as Ukraine's foreign minister from 2020 until 2024, Dmytro Kuleba led the uphill battle against pro-Russian sentiments in Africa. "There were two problems for Ukraine," he told me. "Legacy and instruments." Ukraine had withdrawn from that part of the world after independence in 1991, he explained, and simply was not present when war came. After February 2022, Kuleba visited fourteen African countries over the course of two years to make up for that omission. But he soon realized that Ukraine had little to offer these countries.

During his Africa tour in 2023, Kuleba tried to exploit Russia's own limitations on the continent. "In my meetings, I shared two sheets of paper with my counterparts. The first one was the list of top investors in Africa, and the second one was the list of top providers of technical and humanitarian assistance to Africa. And Russia wasn't on either of them," he recalled. One foreign minister who hosted Kuleba for lunch was candid when handed the sheets. "Dmytro, you did your homework," the minister said, "but you have to understand how we see things from here. These countries on both of your lists, from Europe and America, they owe us . . . given their sins committed here. And we don't even feel obliged to say thank you. While Russia has never done anything bad to us. In every country you go here, Russia is the one that helped us get rid of those who top both of your lists. . . . So, I'm sorry, but this argument just doesn't work here." It was a sobering moment for Kuleba.

Why do Russia's messages resonate? Like sedimentary rock, whose layers form from the natural processes of weathering, erosion, and cementation, the sources of pro-Russian affinity have formed as layers of storytelling about the past—about past rights and past wrongs. Russia appeals to some because the Soviet Union was a friend, to others because the West is hypocritical, because woke ideas unsettle them, or because democracy no longer delivers—because the status quo, however defined, is bad.

It may only be natural for humans to ignore truths that contradict their deep-seated beliefs. ANC cadres were victims of racism in the Soviet Union. This is true, but most prefer not to speak about it. The ANC and Russia experienced a period of sharp estrangement in the 1990s, after the Soviet state collapsed. This is true, but ANC veterans like to fudge that history. Russia offers little economic help to Africans today. This, too, is true, but Russia and the West are held to different standards. If gratitude toward the USSR is carved into a person's DNA, truths that might poison that gratitude have no place. They mess with the stories we tell about a people's struggle for freedom.

CHAPTER 4

Russia Cannot Be Canceled

GROWING UP IN JOHANNESBURG, PAULA SLIER FORGED A VAGUE image of Russia early in her life. Whenever she did not finish the food on her plate at school, the teachers would say that the children in Russia were starving. Whenever she was naughty, her mother would warn that she would send Slier off to Siberia.

Slier's Jewish grandmother Sarah was from Brest, a Belarusian city bordering Poland. In 1921, three years after Russia ended its participation in World War I by signing the Treaty of Brest-Litovsk, a Ukrainian Jew named Isaac Ochberg secured permission from the Pretoria government to bring two hundred Jewish orphans to South Africa, where he was living. Sarah was one of them. Though she had spoken little about her traumatic childhood in a time of rampant pogroms, Slier had picked up snippets here and there. Granny had a scar on her leg from a bullet wound she did not remember sustaining. Granny's parents had perished under circumstances no one could quite recall. Granny's friend would never wear red and white together, since that combination of colors reminded her of blood in the snow. What Slier heard as a child instilled her with a diffuse fear of Russia. It was a horrible place, and you did not want to be anywhere near it.

Slier attended Waverley Girls' High School in a Johannesburg suburb during the twilight of apartheid. Growing up in a white, middle-class household, her surroundings did not induce the kind of political consciousness that the ANC underground had cultivated in Robert McBride and Sydney Mufamadi. Though they could not afford an extravagant lifestyle, Slier's parents never had to worry about putting the next meal on the table. There was a maid in the house who lived in the back room and only saw her own children during the holidays.

Slier dreamed of becoming a journalist. When I met her in an affluent Johannesburg suburb, she struck me as the archetype of the hungry reporter always on the hunt for a story. She was affable and open, with lively eyes and chestnut-colored hair she wore in a classic pixie cut, exuding confidence and playfulness.

After starting out as a producer and anchorwoman for the *Breakfast Club* morning show at the South African Broadcasting Corporation, Slier moved to Israel in January 2005. She figured it would be easier to find a job there than it would be in Iraq, where, two years into the US invasion, many reporters were trying to break into international journalism. She hoped for an offer from CNN or the BBC, but when she went knocking on the doors of various international TV stations with no Hebrew or Arabic skills, no one gave her a job. One day in September, a lady from the Foreign Press Association phoned Slier to say a new Russian television station was looking for someone. It was called Russia Today and would broadcast in English. When Slier called her father to discuss the prospect of working for Russian television, he said, "Don't!" But Slier needed a job. She went for the interview and got an offer.

Russia Today, now known as RT, was founded in September 2005, five months after Putin declared the collapse of the Soviet Union to have been "the greatest geopolitical catastrophe of the twentieth century." Putin was five years into his reign, facing growing international criticism over democratic backsliding, including his choices to diminish the power of regional and local authorities and increase pressure on independent media. It was in this context that the Kremlin announced it was launching a nonprofit twenty-four-hour English-language channel that could explain Russia's policies to international audiences. Russia Today was to broadcast from the same brutalist-style building on Zubovsky Boulevard in Moscow that housed RIA Novosti, Russia's main news agency at the time. It would start with a minuscule budget of $30 million and five hundred employees, including two hundred Russian and international journalists, of which Slier would be one.

Hired to run the outlet as editor in chief was Margarita Simonyan, then twenty-five years old. Born in Krasnodar in southern Russia, Simonyan had spent a year living with an American family in New Hampshire before starting her career in journalism working for a local newspaper. She eventually joined Rossiya, the number two state television network, and worked in the Kremlin pool, rising to fame with her reporting on the Beslan school hostage crisis in 2004. Announcing the creation of Russia Today at a press conference in June 2005, Simonyan told reporters the channel's aim would be to offer a more balanced picture of Russia to the world. Six months later, Russia Today went live.

It was an exhilarating time for Slier. Joined by an Israeli cameraman and a producer originally from Moscow, she would go out, do stories, and then transfer the files from an internet café to Russia Today's headquarters. The small team used to joke that they were sending their stories from Israel "into the universe." "Maybe they'll end up in Russia, maybe they won't, and we aren't on air," she would think. In the eighteen years that Slier would work for RT, she would never be privy to editorial conversations back in Moscow. But in the beginning, she felt she had complete carte blanche to do any story she wanted, including on anodyne, apolitical subjects. "I could say, 'Let's do a story about falafel,' and falafel it was," Slier recalled. Catering to an audience of more than one million people hailing from the former Soviet Union who had settled in Israel, she could report on culture and "feel-good" Russia news. Slier thought she had the best job in the world.

In the early hours of August 8, 2008, Georgian forces shelled Tskhinvali, the capital of South Ossetia, a separatist region that had broken away from Georgia in the early 1990s and remained under Russian protection ever since. Russia responded with overwhelming force, pushing Georgian troops out of South Ossetia. The violence, which had been preceded by provocative Russian actions like large-scale training exercises near the border, marked the beginning of what would become a short-lived war between Russia and Georgia.

Slier got on a plane to Georgia's capital, Tbilisi, and stayed there for three months to report on the war. It was the first time she got clear editorial direction from Russia Today headquarters. She was asked to produce one story per day—but not just any story. She was to report that people in Georgia approved of Russia's actions. "That was difficult," Slier recalled, "because unless you went to Abkhazia or South Ossetia, people felt that they had been invaded." Georgian movie theaters weren't showing many Russian films at the time because Russian cinema was not very popular. "But somehow, you could twist the story to say, 'Because of what's happening, they're showing fewer Russian films,'" she told me. "That makes it sound like we were lying," Slier paused, hesitating. "We weren't lying. But to be honest, that Georgia thing was difficult, because there weren't any stories there. Nobody supported Russia."

The 2008 war was Russia Today's "crucible," as Russian-born American journalist Julia Ioffe put it. It was at that moment that the Kremlin decided to fully weaponize the channel to serve its political interests. It also marked the moment when Russia Today started producing disinformation—false information intended to manipulate. In the war's aftermath, the channel would change its name from Russia Today to RT, presumably to obscure its mission. Its coverage became less about Russia. The channel would morph into a vehicle for the Russian government to sow doubts about the West, its agenda, and its values, all under the guise of encouraging its audience to, as its motto put it, "Question More." At that time, RT further expanded its global footprint, establishing operations in the United States in

2010, Germany in 2014, and France in 2017. On the occasion of RT's ten-year anniversary, Simonyan commissioned a TV viewership survey and claimed that seventy million people were watching RT every week. RT's true audience size and influence were notoriously difficult to verify, not least because its content was spread across different social media platforms, including YouTube, Twitter, and Facebook, sometimes even unattributed. Research has shown that RT's Facebook pages were especially successful in engaging viewers in Latin America and the Middle East, whereas Western users constituted only a small minority of RT's audiences. Another data-driven study showed that most of RT's Twitter followers—more likely to be older, male, or bots than the average Twitter user—tended to be exposed to RT's content alongside other mainstream news channels and that RT was actually not a central part of their online news media environment.

Slier's reporting from that period reflects RT's changing goals. In March 2011, she was in Tripoli reporting on the NATO-led intervention into the Libyan Civil War. It was a sensitive time. Russia, in the midst of its "reset" in relations with the United States, had abstained from a UN resolution blessing the intervention rather than using its veto. With antiaircraft fire in the background, so loud one could barely understand her, Slier reported on the flurry of developments on the ground. Her ambivalent tone—on the one hand mentioning atrocities committed by the Libyan government, on the other hand alluding to discomfort with the United States and Europe spearheading an intervention—seemed to mirror the position of a Russian government that, at that moment, felt unease over the NATO intervention but was still waiting to see how things would play out. Only after the Russian foreign ministry decided that the course of the intervention was harmful to Russian interests would RT change its coverage to reflect Russia's fierce criticism of the mission.

In summer 2014, RT deployed Slier to cover the insurgency in the Donbas region in eastern Ukraine. That March, incognito Russian special forces known as "little green men" had appeared in Crimea, just days after street protests in Kyiv culminated in the overthrow of the pro-Russian government of Ukrainian President Viktor Yanukovych. Within weeks, Russia annexed the peninsula, prompting harsh Western criticism and sanctions. Soon, fighting broke out in the Donbas, as Moscow supported a separatist insurgency with money and weapons. RT coverage became even more patriotic and less interested in objectivity. The channel's management sent daily streams of directives to reporters in the field. In one dispatch, Slier interviewed soldiers and civilians, always aiming to show Russia in a favorable light. In another, Slier was shown out in a field, trapped amid gunfire in Sloviansk in eastern Ukraine. One insurgent told the RT crew to stop filming since he had a sister in Italy who would "kill him" if she watched the report. Slier retorted, "I have parents in South Africa. If they see *me*, they're going to kill *me*."

As Slier continued working, some of her colleagues started to feel the weight of the compromises that being part of RT demanded of them. With the appearance of "little green men" in Crimea, RT America anchor Liz Wahl resigned live on air, explaining she could not be "part of a network that whitewashes the actions of Putin." She went on to cite her Hungarian ancestry and the memory of the Soviet repression of the Hungarian Uprising as a factor in her decision. Slier's own heritage, her own family's connection to the painful and convoluted history of the Soviet Union, did not lead her to similar conclusions. She understood that her marching orders from Moscow were to find people who believed "XYZ" to be true—XYZ being the position of the Russian government. In some reporting contexts, XYZ could be a fringe, outlandish view one would only find by talking to marginal or offensive figures. In other contexts, like in the Donbas, XYZ could be a view that was shared more widely. Looking for the converted, Slier felt increasingly "underused" as a journalist, she told me. She regretted that RT "stopped telling stories." But she would never call what she did unethical. Hers was a crisis of boredom rather than a crisis of faith.

By the time Russia launched its full-scale invasion of Ukraine, RT had morphed into a major propaganda outlet for the Russian government, spreading disinformation and conspiracy theories across the globe on topics ranging from chemical weapons use in Syria to US domestic politics. The network had been implicated in Russia's meddling in the 2016 American presidential election, with its consistent portrayal of Donald Trump's opponent, Hillary Clinton, as corrupt, tied to Islamic extremism, and suffering from poor physical and mental health. It had amassed significant non-Western followings beyond the Anglophone mediasphere, especially among viewers of its Arabic and Spanish Facebook pages.

Long a thorn in the side of Western government officials, RT was forced into major adaptations after the invasion. US distributors took RT America off the air. Its sister channels in Canada and across Europe suffered the same fate. US satellite carrier DirecTV said the company had already been reviewing whether to renew RT's carriage agreement prior to the war, and that the invasion sped up its decision. "We are accelerating this year's contract expiration timeline and will no longer offer their programming effective immediately," a spokesperson said. The censure happened precisely at a time when Russia declared its official state policy to "consolidate its position in the international information space." Rising to the challenge, RT aggressively spread its tentacles into the non-West. In September 2022, it launched RT Hindi, and then RT Balkan the following month. RT Arabic, already well established by that point, worked hard to outperform competing channels like Al Jazeera in the Middle East, emerging as an amplifier of Russia's anti-colonial messaging. The channel also dramatically expanded its presence in Latin American countries like Mexico.

Margarita Simonyan thrived on the challenge. In her frequent appearances on Russian talk shows, her tone became more aggressive, her propaganda shriller. In July 2023, she appeared alongside Putin at the St. Petersburg International Economic Forum. Claiming sanctions were preventing Russia from exporting its grain, Simonyan said Moscow was "hoping for a famine" to bring Western states to their senses. A few months later, she caused a stir even inside her own country when she suggested Russia could produce a nuclear explosion within its borders, "somewhere over Siberia," for the purpose of issuing a "nuclear ultimatum" to the West.

In April 2024, Ukraine charged Simonyan in absentia for public calls to genocide and promoting encroachment on Ukraine's territorial integrity. Five months later, the Biden administration upped its fight against RT, sanctioning Simonyan alongside other individuals and entities over what it called malign influence efforts and illicit cyber-activities targeting the 2024 US presidential election. Showing herself defiant, Simonyan warned that RT would still find ways to reach receptive audiences in the West: "They close entry to us, and we will go through the window. Close the window and we will go through the vents." Poking fun at US law enforcement, she quipped, "What do you think—that I get orders from the CIA? Where else would I get my orders from if I head a Russian state media outlet, funded by the state?" She went on, "Repeat after me: All the employees of RT and the editor in chief only obey the orders of the Kremlin. All other orders are toilet paper."

Slier admits that she, too, obeyed orders from the Kremlin. Once RT was taken off the air in Western countries, she penned opinion pieces defending the channel's right to broadcast. "I support media plurality and believe there is value in people accessing a Russian channel that presents the Russian government's point of view, regardless of what one might think of those views," she wrote a few weeks after Russia's invasion. Two months later, Slier moved back to South Africa, having spent almost two decades in the Middle East. RT was planning to open an English-language hub in Johannesburg, and they wanted Slier to run it.

When I met Slier in South Africa, I came determined to shed the pose of easy moralizing and to probe what seemed to me two equally unconvincing myths: that those disseminating Russian propaganda must either be brainwashed believers or shallow opportunists with no morals whatsoever, in it just for the money or career advancement. I wanted to understand how a journalist, most likely driven by noble motives, could be socialized into a specific news culture, which would in turn shape her beliefs and choices. I was curious how Slier specifically—recognized by Putin for "her professionalism in covering issues of paramount importance"—would reflect on themes such as truth, propaganda, and responsibility in journalism.

Slier said she felt comfortable presenting the Russian government's point of view, because she always perceived Russia to be the "underdog" in the global information war. Russia's disadvantage, Slier thought, emanated from a diffuse animosity and suspicion people harbored toward it—perhaps of the type that had been instilled in her as a child. Slier had no qualms admitting that, in representing Russia's viewpoint, she might not have been telling the truth. "If we had said we are *the* truth, I would have had much more of a problem, but we did not," Slier told me. "We said we're Russian TV, so you understand that you're getting the Russian point of view." Slier went on to argue that RT was not unique in presenting a particular angle on reality. Everybody did it.

As we spoke, I thought to myself how, since time immemorial, humans have told conflicting and often incompatible narratives about what happened, creating different versions of history. I asked Slier about the difference between truths and facts. Shuffling in her chair, she tried to think of an example. "A missile landed. It either did or it did not land," she said, conceding there are such things as objective facts. "But if we don't report on that missile landing," she said, scribbling in her notebook, "well, did it land?" She went on to argue that journalism always involved the selection of facts, as well as of necessary background and context. And that that selection was inevitably biased and subjective.

I couldn't help but recall RT's yearslong reporting denying that the Assad regime ever used chemical weapons on its own people in Syria, and to its unsubstantiated claims that Ukraine had experimented with monstrous bioweapons. When I probed her about these falsehoods, Slier responded without seeming offended at my insinuation. "My starting point was always that I believed the Russian government," she said. "You have to have a starting point. If you are not going to give the Russian government the benefit of the doubt, then everything RT says is a lie." When I asked what inclined her toward believing the Russian government, Slier's candor caught me by surprise. "I'm open to the suggestion that I got conditioned," she said, quickly softening the weight of that admission by adding that we all are conditioned, one way or another. "My entire experience of working with RT was from the Russian perspective. . . . Something happens when, for eighteen years, you go to people's homes, you sit with them, you develop an affinity."

IN DECEMBER 2022, RT SENT SLIER TO BANGUI, THE CAPITAL OF the Central African Republic (CAR). She recalled driving roads paved with golden-reddish dust near the city's university and coming upon a massive monument depicting four armed men protecting a mother and her children. The statue pays tribute to the men of the Wagner Group, Russia's infamous mercenary outfit. She wondered how one of the poorest countries in Africa could afford that kind of extravagance. She was told the Russians had paid for it.

Wagner Group instructors entered the CAR in mid-2018, filling a vacuum left when France pulled its troops in 2016 as it ended an operation intended to stabilize the country after the outbreak of civil war in 2013. The Russians brokered a peace agreement between the CAR government and fourteen armed groups, and Wagner started providing training to the CAR's security forces. But the peace accord proved fragile. In late 2020, following elections, former president François Bozizé partnered with six of the rebel groups to form the Coalition of Patriots for Change (CPC). When the CPC reached Bangui in January 2021, Wagner forces joined the CAR's armed forces and Rwandan troops in a counteroffensive. Its mission morphed from instruction to counterinsurgency, and the group began touting itself as a military solution to conflicts elsewhere in Africa.

Among Slier's goals during her trip was to interview the president,

Faustin-Archange Touadéra. Slier told me that he initially declined the request and only changed his mind after his head of security, a Wagner operative, insisted he speak with her. In her report from Bangui, Slier characterized the CAR as a place "destroyed over the years by foreign powers jostling for its rich resources, most recently France" and as a country "teetering on the brink of collapse" until Russia emerged on the scene. While one of the poorest and most fragile countries in the world, the CAR has significant oil, gold, diamond, and timber resources. "Today, life on the streets has returned to normal, people feel safe to go about their daily routine," Slier told RT's viewers. "As a way of saying thank you, locals are learning Russian, which is being introduced as a third official language."

When we spoke, Slier let on how she really felt about that reporting trip. "It was amazing to me that people don't see that as a form of colonization, which it is," she said. "Why is Russia getting more involved in Africa? I mean, it's not because they love Africa." I was intrigued and asked her what, in her view, qualified as colonization. "If the word *colonialism* throws us, we can use another term," she interjected. "But I can't get my head around this. The people in the CAR would say, 'We're so happy that we're getting the French out,' but they can't understand that what the Russians are doing is just replacing the French." Just as I had tried my luck with Robert McBride and Bheki Langa, I put out a feeler: "Well, what about the argument that Russia is colonizing Ukraine?" Slier looked up from her scribbled page and said, "I would not agree with that." Staring into the distance, she added, "Maybe there's a contradiction."

When its leader, Yevgeny Prigozhin, inserted the Wagner Group into the African continent in 2016, he brought with him not only mercenaries but also a propaganda media wing and a group of companies known as the Russian "troll factories." For years, Prigozhin ran the Patriot Media Group, an umbrella outfit for sites and blogs that amplified pro-Russian messaging across online platforms. The troll factories gained international infamy when a 2017 US intelligence report alleged their interference in the 2016 presidential election, but they were active long before. Bloggers based in the St. Petersburg headquarters—working in teams of three, without employment contracts, paid in cash, and kept under strict surveillance—were ordered to flood social networks with anti-Western comments, often with racist or homophobic undertones. The investigative outlet the Dossier Center found that the troll factories eventually comprised roughly four hundred companies that collectively received hundreds of millions of rubles in funding to post on social media. When Russia invaded Ukraine, Prigozhin was in a prime position to promote pro-invasion narratives across Africa.

He is said to have dissolved the Patriot Media Group shortly before his death in summer 2023. But his departure from the scene hardly heralded the demise of Russian propaganda on the continent. The Russian government quickly created a new media agency called African Initiative, staffing it with former employees of the Wagner Group and other Prigozhin ventures. Elsewhere, entirely new networks sprung up, including one called Pravda ("Truth"). Back in South Africa, pro-Russian "buzzers" emerged—social media users who industriously reproduce pro-Russian content in avalanches of posts. The posts, often disguised as "breaking news," amplified pro-Russian narratives on the conflicts in Ukraine and the Middle East, while also weighing in on South African sociopolitical discussions with divisive comments. "It is unclear," media expert Hermann Wasserman wrote, "whether these accounts are real people or not. However, it is likely that they are real people who form part of the covert paid influencer industry."

After 2022, Africa became a particular focus for RT, too. "The funny thing is," Slier told me, "that I had gone to RT five years earlier, suggesting we look at an RT Africa bureau. But they said, 'No, that's not our focus.'" Until, suddenly, it was. With its demographic dynamism and resource wealth, Africa became a priority for the Kremlin after the Ukraine invasion. The continent presented an important area of potential growth for a Russian economy. And Russia could build on the legacy of Soviet-era support for the struggle against colonialism. Africa was a natural target for Russian propaganda.

Slier left RT in 2023 for reasons she called "entirely nonideological," and as of 2025, RT's plans to open an English-language hub in Johannesburg remained unclear. But RT made inroads nonetheless, finding ways to make its content available via satellite or the internet in many African countries. It established a bureau in Algeria. RT also signed partnerships to distribute its material through friendly African media outlets. Russia became especially focused on countries in Francophone Africa, like the CAR, lambasting the "old imperial power," France, and casting its own "return" as intended to help the continent throw off the colonial yoke once and for all. Among the locals there, Russia found capable influencers willing to do its bidding. One of them was a young man called Ephrem Yalike-Ngonzo.

Ephrem Yalike-Ngonzo was born in Bangui but grew up two hundred miles north, in the small town of Bossangoa, home to many Gbaya people, the ethnic group to which former president François Bozizé belonged. After studying to become a Catholic priest at a seminary in the capital, he enrolled for a law degree at the University of Bangui. It was then that he became more interested in international politics and had spare time on his hands to work for some local newspapers. Starting out as a journalist with little formal training, he looked up to the titans of Francophone African media. One was Alain Foka of Radio France Internationale (RFI), who, according to Ephrem, "revealed hidden things and put authorities into difficult positions." Another was Christophe Boisbouvier, also with RFI, who Ephrem admired because "he got people in power to say what they did not want to say."

When he received a phone call in May 2019 from the Russian mission in Bangui asking for a meeting, Yalike-Ngonzo had covered the Wagner Group's activities in the country for a while, including for the pro-government outlet *Le Potentiel Centrafricain*. He wondered what the Russians might want, but since they allowed Yalike-Ngonzo to choose the meeting place, he was not worried. The "two white guys" who showed up at Le Grand Café, a hangout popular with expatriates, were clearly familiar with his work, Yalike-Ngonzo recalled. "Relax, do you want a meal?" a man who went by "Micha" started out, before probing Yalike-Ngonzo's willingness to work for them.

Yalike-Ngonzo had no doubts as to whether or not to accept their offer. What he was asked to do—placing articles that shone a favorable light on Russia's cooperation with the CAR government—was very similar to what he was already doing for the government-financed *Le Potentiel* anyway. What's more, Yalike-Ngonzo had had a positive view of the Wagner Group when it first appeared in the country. "The Russians were seen as saviors, after the French had abandoned us during hard times," Yalike-Ngonzo said. He never signed a contract with Micha. Besides meeting in person, with an interpreter present, they usually communicated via Telegram, using Google Translate since Micha spoke little French. At the height of his collaboration, Yalike-Ngonzo was paid 500,000 CFA francs per month—around $650 and more than five times the average salary in CAR—which he collected in cash.

Eight months after their first encounter at Le Grand Café, Yalike-Ngonzo was asked to come to Camp de Roux, the Russians' headquarters, a stone's throw from the president's residence. Inside the compound, he spotted piles of T-shirts printed with the slogan *Je suis Wagner* ("I am Wagner"), a nod to the *Je suis Charlie* campaign adopted by supporters of freedom of speech after the January 7, 2015, shooting at the offices of the French satirical newspaper *Charlie Hebdo*. He also saw big printing machines for posters, likely used to produce the types of placards people raised during regular pro-Russian demonstrations, he thought. During the meeting, Yalike-Ngonzo was asked to disseminate his articles to more media outlets. He was also tasked with jobs that "went beyond what was initially agreed," he recalled—for instance, to find public figures willing to appear on the local radio with commentary supportive of Wagner's role. The Camp de Roux meeting sowed first doubts in Yalike-Ngonzo's mind and made him wonder whether and how he could quit—not because of what he was asked to do, he said, but because of what he saw. Witnessing the activities at Camp de Roux, the printers and the T-shirts, he realized for the first time just how close the CAR military and Wagner were. Yet the episode was not enough to push him over the edge.

Neither was what happened in mid-2021 at Bangui's Four Seasons hotel. Micha had picked Yalike-Ngonzo up in his car for an interview with "someone." Waiting at the Four Seasons was Ali Darassa, an infamous warlord and wanted leader of the Unité pour la paix en Centrafrique militia group. The militia stood accused of killing, torturing, raping, and displacing civilians. Darassa could not have lounged in one of Bangui's premier hotels without the government's knowledge and consent, Yalike-Ngonzo thought. "That's when I understood that all of this is a game," he told me, explaining that Darassa's forces were controlling resource-rich areas in which the Russians had mining interests. The interview, in which Darassa stated he was "ready for peace," was part of a big arrangement, a business plan, and the Russians were the facilitators, Yalike-Ngonzo thought. Afterward, he became even more certain he wanted to quit—but not without a chance to denounce the Russians. He thought his only vehicle to do so would be Radio Ndeke Luka, an independent outlet, and he looked for ways to collaborate with them. Once he got involved with the station, he quickly realized no one there dared to air anything critical of Russia.

When Yalike-Ngonzo met up for drinks with other local journalists doing similar work for the Russians, he tried to probe their views. His doubts were not shared, so he made sure to keep them to himself, scared that Micha might find out. "They had families to feed," Yalike-Ngonzo said when I asked him why these other journalists wanted to keep going. "But also, the Russians have their ways of showing you the positive side of what they are doing. They'd say, 'Wagner and the government stand for peace. Those who are against us are the enemies of peace.'" Wagner's claims were not without merit. Though some local communities suffered from its operations, others felt that, thanks to

Wagner, security had improved and commerce picked up. Central African views on Wagner were far from monolithic.

Though Yalike-Ngonzo became more distrustful of Wagner, he knew he had to be patient before turning his back on his employers. He continued to work for the Russians through 2021. At one point that year, Micha told him Russia needed seventy-five students from the CAR to come for a study program and asked Yalike-Ngonzo whether he was interested. One year before the launch of Alabuga Start, intended to lure young African women into the production of Shahed drones in Tatarstan, Russia was already ramping up its efforts to recruit students from Africa. Mentioning his wife and existing employment, Yalike-Ngonzo politely declined.

Soon, Yalike-Ngonzo got the courage to seek ways to quit. Three days after Russia launched its invasion of Ukraine, Micha asked Yalike-Ngonzo to join him on a small plane bound for Bouar, a market town in the west of the CAR. Allegedly, rebel groups had massacred local Peulh people (an ethnic group also known as Fula) and stolen their cattle, and Yalike-Ngonzo was supposed to write an article about it. When they got to the local health center, two surviving Peulh herders lay severely injured. Even before speaking with them through an interpreter, Micha told Yalike-Ngonzo his article should chronicle how the men had been attacked by rebels and how Wagnerites had saved them. "I didn't believe it," Yalike-Ngonzo told me, "because I could not believe that the Russians would charter a private plane to go to Bouar just for me to do that kind of story."

Through the interpreter, the two Peulh men said they were so thankful to the Wagner Group, whose members had been "right on time" to save them from the "enemies of peace." Looking at their expressions, Yalike-Ngonzo came to believe "they were saying things they did not mean." He worried that the men had not told the truth out of fear, and that the interpreter had further embellished the account of the heroic Russian saviors. After landing back in Bangui, Yalike-Ngonzo, overcome by doubt, confronted Micha. "If you want my article to be good, please tell me the truth. Did you feed that interpreter with talking points?" he asked. At that point, Micha admitted his "Russian brothers" had killed and injured several Peulh by error. He urged Yalike-Ngonzo not to share a word about the episode with anyone. Yalike-Ngonzo, appalled, did not even believe that admission to be true. He was convinced the Russians must have attacked the Peulh deliberately. Still, he wrote his article, repeating the official story he had been asked to tell.

When a rival newspaper broke the real story one month later, the Russians panicked. Micha picked Yalike-Ngonzo up at his house, drove him out of Bangui, stopped the car, and asked him to admit he had blown the whistle. "I will ask you only once," Micha said coldly. "Why did you do this?" Agitated by Yalike-Ngonzo's denials, he got out of the car, made a long phone call in Russian, then turned back to Yalike-Ngonzo. "I will kill you right here! Your government won't do anything to protect you! You will just be abandoned here!" Yalike-Ngonzo continued to insist on his innocence and Micha, having checked Yalike-Ngonzo's phone, eventually gave up and drove off, leaving him abandoned on the side of the road, some fifteen miles outside the city. After the Bouar incident, Yalike-Ngonzo told me, the Russians kept in touch with him, and even offered him continued payment, but did not give him any further tasks. They never trusted him again, Yalike-Ngonzo felt, but wanted to control him, to ensure he would not denounce them.

Though Yalike-Ngonzo's fears had grown over time, what happened in Bouar was decisive because he witnessed how the Russians caused his people to suffer, "how they took advantage of the CAR," he told me. It would take Yalike-Ngonzo nearly two more years to find a way to flee the country, with the help of the Platform to Protect Whistleblowers in Africa. In February 2024, after being prevented from leaving the country by air—apparently on the order of the Russians—he crossed the Ubangi River and escaped into the neighboring Democratic Republic of the Congo. "I fled . . . with my bare hands, taking nothing with me. All I could do was save my body," Yalike-Ngonzo told the outlet *Forbidden Stories*, which first broke the story about his escape and his work for the Wagner Group. When we met in April 2025, in a safe location in France, Yalike-Ngonzo did not want to talk about his arduous journey out of the country again. Too painful were the memories, too narrow the escape from death.

As harrowing as Yalike-Ngonzo's story is, he was just one of many cogs in Russia's propaganda machine. Micha, and other dubious Russian operators like him, set up a media machine across several African countries, recruiting local journalists and media figures to produce pro-Russian content that would dominate the front pages of newspapers, flood radio airwaves, and saturate social networks. They were the frontiersmen in a cultural battle waged by Russia—a battle that often exploited memories of the past in order to elevate Russia in the present.

In September 2022, three months before her trip to the CAR, Paula Slier became an agent of such "memory diplomacy." Having returned to South Africa, she presented a new documentary at a movie night hosted by the Russian embassy. It was entitled *The Questions I Never Asked*, and its subject was the Holocaust. It tapped into Slier's family history of suffering under Nazism, telling the story of her grandmother Sarah and of Ukrainian Jew Isaac Ochberg, who had brought the Jewish orphans to South Africa. But in doing so, the documentary also subtly sprinkled in the Kremlin's claim that Ukraine is a Nazi state. "There will be people who will revive Nazism. It's already happening," Vladimir, a Holocaust survivor interviewed by Slier, says in the movie, his voice accompanying historical footage of German Nazi Heinrich Himmler. "What's going on in Europe and Ukraine today is horrifying," he adds. Seconds later, another survivor, Frida, is featured, ominously warning: "I think that the West is making a mistake. They're trying to hide what is happening today, but it will backfire on them." Welcoming the audience on the night of the film's screening, Russia's ambassador to South Africa, Ilya Rogachev, regretted that members of the Jewish Board of Deputies of South Africa had declined the invitation to attend. "Russia cannot be canceled," he said. "We are ready to be your guides in your journey into the world of Russian culture."

The film screening marked an example of memory diplomacy, one of the devices in Russia's toolbox to build a pro-Russian echo chamber. British linguist and historian Jade McGlynn defines "memory diplomacy" as a state's export of commemorative practices and historical narratives, in an effort to link them with those of the target audience. The practice leverages symbols, activities, and core national myths for international use. The Russian government and media have practiced it for years, but stepped up their efforts from 2022, with the anticolonial framing of the Ukraine war providing new ingredients.

In addition to its embassies, a venue Russia has used is the "Russian House," a center of cultural and educational cooperation. Since 2022, Russia has opened more and more Russian Houses across the world, including in many African cities. At first glance, Russian Houses may seem similar to their international equivalents, like the German Goethe Institutes. But their activities go beyond benign cultural promotion. Russian Houses screen RT films like Slier's *The Questions I Never Asked* in the evenings to entertain young Africans. They train local journalists on how to recognize and expose "fake" Western news in cooperation with RT Academy—RT's program of online courses and live workshops for journalists. And they offer opportunities to young people to travel and train in Russia.

The Russian echo chamber is not a phenomenon unique to Africa. Trying to outlast the West, Russia has sought to infiltrate the West, too. The United States has its own version of the echo chamber, dominated by prominent right-wing media figures like Tucker Carlson. Russian state media must have discovered Carlson's utility soon after the invasion, when the TV personality parroted Russia's conspiracy theories about America developing bioweapons in Ukraine. After he and Fox News agreed to part ways in April 2023, Russian state media portrayed him as a victim punished for his fearless commitment to speaking the truth. Since then, Carlson has published interviews with Putin, Lavrov, and even Russian alt-right ideologue and nationalist

Alexander Dugin, airing their views unchallenged and in ways that appeal to America's hard-right factions.

It is easy to gravitate to what many consider the attention-grabbing, blatant pandering of the Tucker Carlsons of the world when we think of pro-Russian propaganda. But doing so risks losing sight of the many unknown, less sensational individuals, those like Ephrem Yalike-Ngonzo, who form part of an interlocking pro-Russian messaging machinery. As an individual, an Ephrem Yalike-Ngonzo is far less consequential a voice than a Tucker Carlson. Yet many Ephrems—embedded in their communities and framing pro-Russian views in ways that resonate locally—make for a humongous and potent force. And their reach can't just be called a product of disinformation that is spread among the "misinformed." Russia's messaging is effective because it taps into real grievances—and then contextualizes and explains them within a broader worldview that demonizes the West and extols Russia. And it is also effective simply because it is everywhere, drowning its audience with so many "buzzes" and counterintuitive claims—meant to encourage the viewer to "Question More"—that it becomes harder for the average audience to tell the truth from a lie, the essential from the excess noise.

If their tool kit is diverse, so are the moral compasses of Russia's agents. Paula Slier, fearful of Russia as a child, joined RT on a whim and then found her calling in doing Russia's bidding. She conceded that journalists were no longer neutral purveyors of news, that they had become "information soldiers." She called it a reality that was regrettable. Yet, whenever I confronted Slier with uncomfortable truths about the propagandistic or deceitful nature of RT's coverage, her cop-out tended to be that Western journalists were just as bad. Ephrem Yalike-Ngonzo wanted to be a priest, not a journalist, and had little formal training when he came across Micha. Both Yalike-Ngonzo and Slier convinced themselves that their motives in working for Russia were justifiable, even noble. But Yalike-Ngonzo was ready to question Russia's goals—and his own role in advancing them—in ways that Slier never was.

Part III

PLAYING CLOSE TO HOME

CHAPTER 5

The Art of Survival

BARDAK WAS A PLACE WHERE STRANGERS BECAME FRIENDS. Azat Adamyan ran the small pub, whose name means "mess" in Russian, on the outskirts of Stepanakert, the capital of the Nagorno-Karabakh enclave that Armenians like him call Artsakh. Instruments, graffiti, and mural art decorated the walls of what had previously been a garage. Foreign visitors, rare in this remote mountainous region peppered with churches and villages, especially loved Bardak. An old van outside, refurbished as sleeping quarters, was readily available for travelers who wanted to stay overnight.

Adamyan was a pub owner, but by necessity, he was also a warrior. Born in 1990, he had fought in two wars against Azerbaijan and witnessed three. Always prepared for the fourth war, he kept a cache of weapons in Bardak's backyard.

On September 25, 2023, Adamyan was home taking a bath when he heard his mother and wife, Anna, crying. He hurried downstairs to learn that a fuel storage facility had exploded on a nearby highway. The explosion set a busy gas station ablaze, killing more than two hundred people. Adamyan rushed to the hospital, where he was told that several relatives had died. He set off to the morgue to search for his cousin, but couldn't identify him among the burned bodies. It only sank in later, when he returned to inspect the dead once more, that one of the corpses was his cousin's.

With the blast, Adamyan lost all remaining hope. He had joined the fighting against Azerbaijan in previous outbursts of violence. Now, nearly one week into Azerbaijan's latest military offensive—this one with explicit designs to take control of Nagorno-Karabakh—he knew his options were different. The explosion had killed many of his comrades, the Armenian government was not going to send reinforcements, and the Russian peacekeepers stationed in the enclave were not stepping in, either.

Three days later, Adamyan put Anna, who was pregnant, and their eighteen-month-old boy in the car, and whatever belongings they managed to take in the trunk. Adamyan's mother, father, and other relatives followed in the car behind, while a third vehicle took Anna's family. Leaving behind everything, they joined thousands of others fleeing Nagorno-Karabakh. To their left and right, they could see tractors, trucks, cars, buses, children and pets squashed together inside vehicles with belongings tied to the roofs, all driving into an unknown future. Adamyan was petrified at the sight, but he also found some solace in the feeling that he and all these people shared the same fate.

Because of the intense traffic, the journey to Yerevan, the Armenian capital, took them almost twenty hours. On the road, they passed a group of Russian peacekeepers who were looking to exchange some goods; they offered a pack of cigarettes in return for Adamyan's thermal imaging camera. The encounter only deepened his bitterness toward Russia. His family had lost their home, he thought, and here were the Russians, trying to make deals.

The mass exodus marked the crushing end to nearly two decades of conflict between Armenia and Azerbaijan over Nagorno-Karabakh. The first war between the two nations, from 1992 to 1994, saw tens of thousands killed and displaced and ended with Armenian forces taking control over seven regions adjacent to Nagorno-Karabakh. The enclave gained de facto independence while remaining reliant on Armenia, yet legally within Azerbaijan's internationally recognized borders. Then, as in the many rounds of fighting that followed, Moscow typically supported the Armenian side.

But in 2023, Russia stood by as Azerbaijan took over Nagorno-Karabakh. Demanding the Kremlin's undivided attention and resources, the war against Ukraine had also shifted Putin's political calculus. He recognized the growing importance of Azerbaijan, a close ally of Turkey, which, in the wake of Western sanctions, became crucial for Russia as a conduit for its Eurasian roundabout trade. Russia's strategic tilt toward Azerbaijan preceded the Ukraine invasion and was driven by a desire to explore trade and transport routes to the Middle East and India via Azerbaijani territory. But after February 2022, the shift intensified. Enhanced Western efforts to implement the so-called Middle Corridor—a transport route from western China and Central Asia to Europe that bypasses Russia—made Moscow's alignment with Azerbaijan in the complicated corridor diplomacy even more urgent. Entangled in Ukraine and increasingly reliant on good relations with Azerbaijan and Turkey, Russia no longer cared much about Armenia's security. Its lackluster performance amid the tragic events of September 2023 presented the clearest evidence yet that Russia had to fear for its enduring primacy in the South Caucasus. And Karabakh Armenians like Adamyan had to fear for their future.

Russia's conduct may have come as a shock to outside observers, but it didn't really surprise Adamyan. As far as he was concerned, there had been growing signs over the years that Russia's commitment to supporting Armenia was waning.

The connection between Armenia and Russia goes back centuries.

The Russian Empire advanced into parts of the Caucasus beginning in the early nineteenth century. In the 1830s, the Russians built the Black Fortress, or Sev Berd, atop a hill in the western part of Armenia's second-largest city, Gyumri. The fortress was meant to defend the Russian Empire against the Ottomans. At that time, there was no Armenian political state at all. Instead, the heartland of historic Armenia—the area south of the Black Sea, between Turkey on the one hand and Georgia and today's Armenia on the other—had been under the rule of others for centuries.

During the First World War, the Ottoman Empire's Young Turk government drove hundreds of thousands of Armenians from their homes. Many were massacred or forced to march until they died in what became known as the Armenian Genocide. In 1920, Armenia became a constituent republic of the USSR, with its borders finalized in the 1921 Treaty of Kars. Starting in the early 1940s, Russia deployed several thousand soldiers near Sev Berd at what later became the 102nd Russian Military Base. It would be an enduring symbol of Russia's military clout in its extended neighborhood. When Putin visited the base in 2013, three years after Armenia and Russia agreed to extend its lease until 2044, he said: "Russia is never going to leave here. On the contrary, we are going to strengthen our positions here." Moscow, according to Putin's message at the time, maintained a proprietary view not only of Ukraine, but also of neighboring countries like Armenia, and would go to some length to preserve its dominion.

After 1990, Armenia continued to rely on Russia as its strategic partner and security provider. Besides hosting the 102nd base, it became the only country in the South Caucasus to join the Russian-led Collective Security Treaty Organization (CSTO). It procured the vast bulk of its weapons from Russia. Moscow also played a leading role in mediating over Nagorno-Karabakh. It offered to deploy peacekeepers on several occasions, and it was the most active player in the OSCE Minsk Group, which was mandated to find a peaceful solution for Nagorno-Karabakh and cochaired by Russia, France, and the United States.

When fighting broke out between Armenia and Azerbaijan in fall 2020, it exploded into a six-week war that killed over seven thousand people. Russia helped broker a ceasefire that went into effect in November, signed by Putin, Armenian Prime Minister Nikol Pashinyan, and Ilham Aliyev, Azerbaijan's longtime president. While the truce did not settle Nagorno-Karabakh's final status, nearly two thousand Russian peacekeepers were deployed in the territory, tasked with protecting the local Armenian population.

Adamyan remembers that period vividly—not just because he fought on the front line, was wounded by shrapnel, and returned to a Bardak badly damaged by the fighting, but also because it was then that he began to nurture an intuition that the Russians could not really be relied upon. Shortly after the November ceasefire went into force, Azerbaijan took over a village in Nagorno-Karabakh and the Russian peacekeepers did nothing, Adamyan told me. Disappointed, he took down Putin's portrait from the wall in Bardak.

Adamyan observed firsthand how Russia's commitment to fulfilling its role as guarantor of the truce waned further after the invasion of Ukraine. To be fair, the Russian peacekeepers deployed to Nagorno-Karabakh lacked a clear mandate; their role was spelled out with just a few sentences in the 2020 ceasefire statement. But after 2022, their impotence became increasingly exposed as Azerbaijan tested Russia's resolve. In September 2022, Baku provoked fighting at several spots along its border with Armenia, with the violence spilling over into towns on the Armenian side. The fighting left 207 Armenian and eighty Azerbaijani soldiers dead. In early November, there was another shootout at the eastern border, and again, the Russians failed to step in.

The Armenian prime minister's anger with Russia became clear later that month, when he hosted a CSTO summit. As leaders gathered for a final photo, Pashinyan could be seen awkwardly shuffling away from Putin. Pashinyan's relationship with Russia had been rocky from the beginning. He had come to lead Armenia in the peaceful Velvet Revolution of 2018. Though the Russian government refrained from intervening in the events, it has never liked Pashinyan, nor the way he came to power, nor his desire to develop ties with the West.

To Adamyan, Russia's deliberate passivity became most painfully apparent a few weeks later, in December 2022, when Azerbaijan-backed activists started blocking the sole road connecting Armenia to Nagorno-Karabakh, known as the Lachin Corridor. Residents couldn't even access necessities like food and medicine. Russian helicopters would drop deliveries for the Russian peacekeepers, he said, but not for the local population. People lived from one day to the next, sometimes queuing up for hours to get basics. The first word Adamyan's infant son learned to say at the time was *bread*. "But the hardest thing was the feeling of isolation," he told me. "We were cut off from the world." What gave Adamyan solace was the sense of order and solidarity that prevailed in Stepanakert. Since there was no fuel, the streets went completely dark at night, and still, people took their children out for a walk, their steps and voices filling the dreadful silence. "Despite everything, life went on," he recalled.

Notwithstanding the resilience of the Karabakh Armenians, by summer 2023, the situation had become catastrophic. Locals were angry at the Russian peacekeepers for failing to force Azerbaijan to end the blockade, yet at the same time they thought those peacekeepers were the only factor still standing between them and ethnic cleansing. When Azerbaijan took full control over Nagorno-Karabakh in September, it seemed like Russia had abandoned them for good.

THE LOSS OF NAGORNO-KARABAKH THREW ARMENIANS INTO A state of crisis. Divided over who was responsible for their predicament, they also disagreed over the right way to navigate their future in a dangerous region.

Some Armenians were convinced that Russia had betrayed them—that Azerbaijan's surprise assault was preceded by some sort of deal between Baku and Moscow. Those displaced from Nagorno-Karabakh harbored mixed feelings. Despite their dramatic escape, some still felt some fealty to Russia for historical reasons. During the Soviet period, Nagorno-Karabakh had been an autonomous region within the Azerbaijan Soviet Socialist Republic. As in other enclaves with ethnic minorities—such as Abkhazia, South Ossetia, or the Georgian region of Javakheti, which all differed in legal status—the Soviet Union had promoted Russian language and culture to facilitate the integration of these distinct communities. As a result, most of Nagorno-Karabakh's ethnically Armenian residents, Adamyan included, understood and spoke Russian. Some blamed the Armenian government first, Russia second for the tragic events of September 2023. The Pashinyan government had long failed to negotiate the final legal status of Nagorno-Karabakh, instead kicking the can down the road—and then, in May 2023, it stated that Armenia was prepared to recognize Nagorno-Karabakh as part of Azerbaijan.

Pashinyan's government, meanwhile, scrambled to contain the damage and chart a path forward. It looked south and west to diversify Armenia's international security partnerships. India emerged as a major new weapons provider, complementing France, which hosts a large Armenian diaspora and has long-standing ties with the country. Armenia broadened its diplomatic ties, too, opening new embassies, strengthening its relations with countries in the Middle East and Latin America, and accelerating efforts to become a member of the EU.

Most urgently, however, Pashinyan needed to deter further Azerbaijani aggression. Seven months after the events of September 2023, his government reached a preliminary agreement with Baku on parts of the Armenian-Azerbaijani border, which would involve the official transfer of four small Armenian border villages in the province of Tavush. It was a gesture intended to quell Baku's appetite for more. But many Armenians were angry, feeling that ever since the 2020 war, they kept losing one thing after another to Azerbaijan, while Armenian concessions produced no stability.

In May 2024, protesters shut down streets in Yerevan and blocked roads throughout the country, demanding that Pashinyan step down rather than keep appeasing Azerbaijan. The protests united refugees, families of fallen soldiers, and opposition figures and were led by Bagrat Galstanyan, a prominent archbishop from Tavush, who channeled public backlash against the village transfer into weeks of anti-government demonstrations. Catering to conservative audiences, Galstanyan painted the Armenian church as the last defender of Armenian identity and accused Pashinyan of serving external interests. Unmoved by the protesters, the government went ahead with handing over the villages. By the summer, the protests had fizzled out, and it was clear there would be no next steps—at least for now. The rallies had, however, been indicative of a deteriorating mood in Armenian society. People worried that Armenia was losing territory piecemeal, essentially accepting Azerbaijani blackmail.

To some, it therefore seemed only prudent to prepare for the next round of war. Since Russia could no longer be counted upon, everyone had to contribute to the nation's defense, and organizations like VOMA stepped up their efforts to ensure civil preparedness. VOMA is a nongovernmental organization that trains civilians in combat and survival skills. Its name is an abbreviation of an Armenian phrase that means "the art of survival." VOMA was created in 2014, separate from the government, and initially focused on "active tourism"—for instance, alpine exercises in extreme weather conditions—rather than military training. After clashes with Azerbaijan in 2016, the organization shifted its focus toward security and defense. By the time of the 2020 war, half of the training offered by VOMA was military in nature, and the organization assisted with recruitment into the Armenian armed forces.

The events of September 2023 marked the biggest turning point, I learned when I visited a VOMA training hall. The number of people who signed up for training courses surged, just as it had after the 2020 war. "It is always hot on our border, and the army cannot sufficiently prepare everyone, so we help," Vaghinak Vartanov, VOMA's deputy head, told me as we walked through the entrance hall toward his office. One wall was lined with guns that fire rubber bullets, the other with photos of a VOMA training camp in Armenia's mountains. A group of people was just getting ready for a training session. Armenians of all ages showed up after work hours, between 7 and 10 p.m., to attend such courses in one of VOMA's twelve centers across the country. Upon completing three months of basic training, they could opt for courses offering specialized instruction in first aid, or how to operate artillery. Over ten thousand people have been trained by VOMA since its inception.

When I asked Vartanov whether many Karabakh refugees had signed up for training courses since September 2023, he told me they were not ready psychologically.

Indeed, the Karabakh Armenians remained preoccupied with the more mundane challenges posed by life after displacement. Adamyan settled down in Yerevan, where he fought bureaucratic hurdles in trying to reopen the new Bardak. We sat on the terrace of his pub one night, Yerevan's midsummer night sky swimming with stars. As we talked over glasses of Ararat, the famous Armenian cognac, Adamyan told me about his daily struggles. It had been difficult to get a license to operate past midnight, and paying utility bills in Yerevan was more complicated than it had been in Stepanakert, a small town with less bureaucracy. The Armenian government wasn't cutting those displaced from Karabakh any slack, he said. One of his sisters stayed in the Armenian capital, too, while a brother had started over in Los Angeles. Strange as it may sound, two other sisters had moved to Russia—one to Moscow, the other to Sochi—because it was easier for them to find work there. His family may have been disillusioned by a Russia that abandoned them, but they also needed to survive.

Adamyan's story recounts just one among innumerable lives that were upended by Azerbaijan's 2023 offensive. Masis, a small town southwest of Yerevan, saw a particularly big influx of Karabakh Armenians. Close to the Armenian capital, Masis had been a refugee town for over three decades, accommodating those displaced by all the waves this conflict had seen since its start. Many had temporarily fled there during the 2020 war. But the sudden arrival of huge groups of people in fall 2023 required makeshift arrangements and a lot of improvisation, the Masis city administrator, a middle-aged woman called Hasmik, told me during my visit. People were put up wherever there was space, including on the floor of the town hall. An old school was repurposed as sleeping quarters. The biggest challenge was getting enough diapers, considering how many small infants were among those arriving.

While locals offered much support to the displaced, the government also tried to help, giving every adult arriving from Karabakh a one-off payment of $250, followed by a $185 monthly stipend to cover rent and basic needs. But Olesya Vartanyan, a seasoned South Caucasus analyst, warned in spring 2024 that in the absence of more funding and a clear plan for integration, social problems could increase. "Resentment may take root among locals if they see refugees being helped into jobs and housing that others might struggle to find, or bringing down wages," she wrote.

That an already polarized Armenian society could see growing fissures between local Armenians and those from Karabakh did not seem far-fetched. Sociological surveys showed that Karabakh Armenians, having lived in isolation for several decades, formed a particular cultural identity that differed from that of the Armenian titular nation. That may partially explain why so few have taken on Armenian citizenship since September 2023, notwithstanding their entitlement to it. Without citizenship, their possibilities remained limited: Men cannot serve in the Armenian military, workers cannot apply for certain types of jobs, and people cannot apply for better housing. When I asked a group of women at the Masis community center why they chose to forgo citizenship, one showed me her passport: "Look, it's the same blue passport that all Armenians have—but here is the 070 code," she said, pointing to a line below her personal information. "It confirms the fact that we are from Artsakh." Since I looked confused, she continued to explain: "If we give up this passport, we are afraid of losing the connection to our land." Her voice cracked and she paused for a moment, then said, "Our bodies may be here, but our souls are in Artsakh."

Armenians were not alone in having to navigate the chaotic situation that Russia's preoccupation with Ukraine created in the South Caucasus. Russia's pivot of attention opened space for new hostilities between some regional players but also moves toward peace between others.

Long embroiled in a proxy confrontation in the South Caucasus, Iran and Israel took their rivalry in the region to a new level. Israel stepped up its engagement with Azerbaijan, to whom it had exported weapons for years. Iran, in turn, viewed that engagement as part of a broader strategy to counteract its influence. It also feared that Azerbaijan and Turkey, no longer deterred by Russia, could proceed with their vision for the Zangezur Corridor, a projected road and rail link that would undermine Iran's regional clout by sidelining its importance as a transit route. Eight months after Russia's invasion of Ukraine, Iran held military exercises on its border with Azerbaijan, prompting Baku to conduct its own maneuvers across the border. Azerbaijan evacuated its embassy in Iran after a fatal shooting in January 2023, and two months later the Azerbaijani foreign ministry expelled four Iranian diplomats while also opening its first embassy in Israel. Russia's distraction had created a power vacuum, and Iran and Israel were busy filling it with blows and counterblows.

Between other players, Russia's waning clout improved the prospects for peace. For nearly a century, Turkey and Armenia have had almost no relationship and a closed border due to the legacy of the Armenian Genocide, the Cold War—during which Turkey acceded to NATO while Armenia was part of the Soviet Union—and the conflict between Azerbaijan and Armenia. The war in Ukraine opened a window of opportunity for Turkey to push for the normalization of its relations with Armenia. After the loss of Nagorno-Karabakh, Armenia became ever more eager to reduce its dependence on Russia and to deepen its alignment with the European Union—efforts that could be served by better ties with Turkey, which enjoys a customs union with the EU. And normalization with Armenia could expand Turkey's influence in the South Caucasus at a time when the regional order remained in a state of fragmentation.

When I drove to the Armenia–Turkey border in summer of 2024, there appeared to be moves toward accommodation. Pashinyan visited, and weeks later special representatives from both countries convened a meeting at the border crossing. But after that, the peace process stalled, with Turkey saying its relations with Armenia would improve only if Armenia and Azerbaijan signed their own peace treaty. Propelled by Azerbaijan's takeover of Nagorno-Karabakh, talks between Armenia and Azerbaijan proceeded through 2024. Then, in March 2025, the foreign ministries announced they had finally agreed on a peace agreement. Baku, however, laid out several requirements that Armenia had to complete before the deal could be signed. Those included an amendment to the Armenian constitution to "eliminate claims against the territorial integrity and sovereignty of the Republic of Azerbaijan." Armenia and Azerbaijan were moving toward peace, it seemed, yet the road was still long.

Azerbaijan's growing confidence posed challenges not just for Armenia, but also for Russia. When Russian air defenses inadvertently shot down an Azerbaijan Airlines plane in December 2024, Aliyev picked a rare fight with Putin, insisting that Russia publicly recognize its guilt. Then, after two Azerbaijani men died in police custody in Yekaterinburg in summer 2025, Aliyev's government lashed out with retaliatory actions, canceling cultural events tied to Russian institutions and scrapping a visit by a Russian parliamentary official. Announced by Azerbaijani state-owned media as a "special security operation," a police raid of the Baku office of Russia's state-run news agency Sputnik sent Margarita Simonyan into a tailspin. "Special operation—Wow," she mocked on social media before sharing videos of handcuffed Russian journalists. Having let the "special operations" genie out of the bottle, the Kremlin had to watch an emboldened neighbor turn the framing against Russia's own interests.

Handling a disappointed Armenia was even more urgent. The

Kremlin tried to deflect criticism of its abandonment of the Karabakh Armenians onto others. Russian diplomats asserted that Armenians only had themselves to blame, since Pashinyan had recognized Nagorno-Karabakh as part of Azerbaijan in May 2023. At the same time, they decried Armenia's growing turn toward the West as a strategic blunder. "Armenia is ready to exchange the time-tested alliance with Moscow for some vague promises from the West, not even concrete assistance," Lavrov lamented in December 2023. Russian officials also sent not-so-subtle signals to Armenia that it should not stray too far and that Russia could still hurt the country. Showing what was possible, Moscow had temporarily banned Armenian dairy imports in spring 2023. Eight months after the International Criminal Court (ICC) issued an arrest warrant for Putin over his actions in Ukraine, Russia warned Yerevan there would be consequences for its accession to the court.

The reality is that, amid Russia's waning military clout in the South Caucasus, Armenia's economy has remained deeply dependent on Russia. Russian businesses continue to dominate significant parts of Armenia's energy, mining, transport, and telecommunications sectors. Armenia imports heavily subsidized natural gas from Russia. On occasion, Russian officials have threatened that the benefits Armenia receives from Russia should not be taken for granted. Speaking at the 2024 Primakov Readings, an annual policy forum in Moscow, Russian Deputy Prime Minister Alexey Overchuk warned that the entry of non-regional players—a not-so-subtle jab at Western states—into Armenia would have consequences. He reminded Yerevan that the advantages Armenia accrued from its proximity to Russia should be seen as payment for Russia's security and strategic depth.

Armenia tried to deter such bullying and show it had cards of its own to play. In February 2024, Pashinyan announced that Armenia's participation in the CSTO was "basically frozen" since the grouping's refusal to come to its aid in the face of Azerbaijani attacks "could not have gone without consequences." Three months later, an agreement was reached to withdraw Russian border guards from Tavush, Syunik, and several other regions along the border with Azerbaijan. Armenia also concluded the decades-long presence of Russian border guards at Yerevan's Zvartnots International Airport and even joined the ICC, notwithstanding some huffing and puffing from Moscow.

Still, breaking free from a Russia that had shown apathy toward them in their darkest hour did not strike Armenians as a viable option. Reflecting on the relationship, Armenia's ambassador to the EU told *Politico* in April 2024 that "Armenia's geography means it historically and practically has so many connections with Russia that only phantasmagoric people think Armenia would take the suicidal step of trying to undermine Russian interests in the region." Russia's shifting priorities cost Armenians dearly, but antagonizing their neighbor would be unwise. Despite organizations like VOMA, Armenia was vulnerable; real peace with Azerbaijan and Turkey remained a distant prospect; and new partners could be counted upon only so much. What's more, the country needed to prepare for the eventuality that Russia would emerge victorious in Ukraine and could then return more of its attention and resources to the South Caucasus.

Trying to come to terms with what happened to them, the Karabakh Armenians would continue to dream of returning home one day, but in the meantime build new lives as best as they could. Azat Adamyan wants to open a restaurant adjacent to Bardak, he told me when we last spoke in winter 2025. He is also embarking on a series of side hustles: He wants to buy eight to ten hectares of land somewhere outside the city and develop a village—a place where life follows a natural rhythm, with pastures, small houses, and a watering place, he said. I couldn't help but wonder whether this was Adamyan's way of keeping alive his memories of Nagorno-Karabakh, with its lush hilltops and fertile lowlands, its tranquil lakes and bucolic settlements. In case he would never be able to see it again.

CHAPTER 6

The Oligarch's Plan

UNLIKE ARMENIA, WHERE THE KREMLIN HAS NEEDED TO FEAR for its enduring influence after invading Ukraine, neighboring Georgia presented Russia with an unexpected opportunity. The Ukraine war gave the ruling elite—a conservative political party called Georgian Dream, or GD—an excuse to move further into Russia's orbit. In a stark political reorientation, GD adopted Russian-inspired legislation cracking down on civil society groups, which took to the streets in response. These dramatic developments would all come to a head in the October 2024 parliamentary elections, which the political opposition to GD framed as an existential choice between Georgia's European path and a growing alignment with Russia—and between democracy and authoritarianism.

I flew into Tbilisi, Georgia's capital, on October 25, 2024, the night before the polls opened. The streets buzzed with nervous energy. "It could get messy tomorrow, be careful," my cab driver from the airport warned. He dropped me off in front of an imposing building that had once served as the headquarters for a Soviet printing press. Now it was the Stamba Hotel, its brutalist facade draped in an EU flag. When I had visited in summer 2023, a Ukrainian flag had been hanging in its place.

In the months since, GD had instrumentalized the war for its election campaign, erecting placards depicting a devastated Ukraine—collapsed bridges, the ruins of Mariupol's theater—that created a stark contrast to Tbilisi's pristine buildings. It was a not-so-subtle warning to Georgians: Ukraine's fate would befall them should the opposition win.

GD portrayed itself as the sole political force resisting attempts by the "global war party"—its domestic opponents, NGOs, and Georgia's Western allies—to drag the country into war. The party combined this with an appeal to conservative values, seen most starkly in new bills to crack down on "foreign influence" and "LGBT propaganda." "It is this global force that first forced the confrontation of Georgia with Russia, and then put Ukraine in even worse peril," GD founder Bidzina Ivanishvili, the country's richest oligarch, said of the "global war party" in April 2024 in a landmark speech replete with conspiracy theories. "The laws that we are proposing are there to expose those dark linkages."

The campaign struck at the heart of organizations like Tbilisi Pride, a prominent LGBTQ advocacy group, which in turn represented a small but very visible part of the opposition to GD. After dropping off my bags near the Stamba, I made my way to Tbilisi Pride's office down a narrow alleyway to Giorgi Akhvlediani Street, their location easy to find thanks to the rainbow flag—one of the few left openly on display in the city—hanging from the balcony. Inside, I found Tamar Jakeli, the group's twenty-eight-year-old director. Called Tata by her friends, she had a pixie cut and kind, knowing eyes that sized me up through oversized glasses. She was on the phone with fellow activists making final preparations to accompany others from Georgia's LGBTQ community to the polls the next day. Many were too scared to go by themselves.

GD had already passed the two laws Ivanishvili had mentioned in his speech. The "foreign influence law," enacted in August 2024, required NGOs that receive 20 percent or more of their funding from abroad—meaning, almost all NGOs—to officially register themselves as "pursuing the interests of a foreign power." The law against "LGBT propaganda" was enacted two months later. It banned same-sex marriage (which had never been legal anyway), adoption by same-sex couples, changing one's gender on identity documents, and depictions of LGBTQ people in the media. The law put intense pressure on Tbilisi Pride. "That is why our office is so empty," Jakeli told me, "in case we get raided by the police."

Jakeli double-checked that she had properly locked the balcony before we headed to a nearby bar for drinks. I asked her what she would do if GD won the election the next day. "As long as there is resistance, I will stay," she said. "But if thousands of people are put in jail, if it gets hopeless, then I will probably have to think of my own survival."

At eight o'clock the next morning, over three thousand polling stations opened across Georgia. A light rain fell as I strolled down Rustaveli Avenue, taking in its eclectic atmosphere—the stray dogs, the luxury shops, the vintage book stalls, the babushkas selling fresh pomegranate juice. Small clusters of voters waited outside Tbilisi First Public School and the Georgian National Academy of Sciences, which were serving as polling stations. I had wondered if the drizzle would affect voter turnout, but this election was far too consequential to miss.

My afternoon visit to a key election watchdog called the International Society for Fair Elections and Democracy (ISFED) hinted at a long day ahead. The ISFED staff looked worried: Almost 10 percent of its 1,500 election observers had already reported incidents at polling stations. What's more, the types of violations seemed to be more serious than those observed during the 2021 vote. There was ballot stuffing, incidents of mobilization for vote buying, and observers being intimidated. There were also allegations that voter privacy was being compromised, with cameras installed in some polling stations and ballots so thin that one could see a colored circle on the back, revealing who someone had voted for. The TV running in the background showed live coverage of a violent incident erupting at a polling station in Tbilisi, and those holding the fort in the office started making calls to find out whether any ISFED staff were affected. I saw myself out quietly, leaving the monitors to get on with their work. *Going OK. With other activists now, and waiting,* Jakeli responded by text when I messaged to check in on her, worried that she, too, might have got caught up in some of the chaos.

A couple of hours later, I watched the election results come in at the headquarters of the Coalition for Change, an informal alignment of pro-Western parties created a few months prior to the election. Alongside the United National Movement (UNM), Strong Georgia, and Gakharia for Georgia, the Coalition had signed the Georgian Charter, a call to action by Salomé Zourabichvili, Georgia's pro-European president. In it, she called on the parties to help remove GD from power. The curious situation in which the president opposed the ruling party was a product of constitutional changes approved in 2010. With those changes, Georgia transitioned from a presidential to a mixed parliamentary system. As a result, much government power would lie with the newly created office of the prime minister, determined by the parliamentary majority, while the president remained directly elected by the people.

The Coalition headquarters were crowded, filled mainly with Georgian journalists glued to their laptops. The atmosphere was tense, plates with cold pizza slices mostly untouched. Just before 8 p.m., the Coalition's leadership arrived to take in the results. A few minutes later, the room burst into intense cheering and clapping—the opposition's TV channel was reporting the first exit polls, showing the opposition victorious. But minutes later, the mood shifted as another exit poll, this one commissioned by pro-GD broadcaster TV Imedi, indicated the government would win. By the time Georgia's Central Election Commission released the final vote count two hours later, giving about 54 percent of the vote to GD, the room had settled into a quiet disbelief. Serious pollsters had expected GD to win the largest share of seats in parliament, but with a tally of between 42 and 47 percent.

Reactions from abroad came quickly. Viktor Orbán, Hungary's conservative prime minister, did not even wait for the exit polls to congratulate GD on its victory. Margarita Simonyan took to social media just after 8 p.m. "The Georgians won! Well done!" she wrote. Russian politicians soon chimed in, expressing relief that the West's "neocolonial project" in Georgia, its effort to engineer regime change, had failed.

The crystal blue sky and sunshine that dawned on Tbilisi the next day did not befit the somber mood in the city. Overnight, opposition parties had come out with statements declaring the election and the official results illegitimate. ISFED staff told reporters that, based on the evidence gathered, "the results of the October 26 parliamentary election cannot be seen as truly reflecting the preferences of Georgian voters."

Tbilisi's liberal political scene was in a state of intense impatience. They wanted to know what the opposition would do and wondered why no one had been called to the streets. At 9 p.m., Salomé Zourabichvili finally addressed the nation in an emergency statement, calling the election a Russian operation. "I do not recognize these elections—to do so is to accept Russia's entry into Georgia and the submission of our country to Moscow." She implored Georgians to protest.

When Georgians finally hit the streets, some forty-eight hours after the first exit polls, they did so in full force. Thousands rallied outside the parliament, accusing GD of stealing the election, and Russia of playing a part in it. *We are trying to be resilient, to protest, and to see what might happen*, Jakeli wrote me. *I have no idea whether we even have a chance—but I try to remain hopeful.*

POST-SOVIET RUSSIA AND GEORGIA HAVE HAD A TROUBLESOME, at times tortured, relationship. After Georgia regained its independence amid the breakup of the USSR, it could barely be called a functioning state. It lost control over part of its province of South Ossetia following a separatist conflict. In 1992–93, another Georgian province, Abkhazia, fought a war of secession with Georgia and, in 1999, unilaterally declared its independence. Russia deployed peacekeepers to both regions—in Abkhazia alongside unarmed UN observers, in South Ossetia as part of joint peacekeeping forces monitored by an OSCE mission.

The Second Chechen War, waged by Russia from 1999 until 2009, exposed the enduring fragility of the Georgian state. Thousands of Chechen fighters found refuge in Georgia's restive Pankisi Gorge area, giving Moscow a pretext to hype the terrorist threat emanating from its neighbor. On several occasions, it even bombed the gorge. The Rose Revolution of 2003 marked another pivotal moment in Russian–Georgian relations. In November 2003, opposition leader Mikheil Saakashvili and his allies stormed Georgia's parliament in protest over elections whose results they deemed fraudulent. A day later, President Eduard Shevardnadze resigned, notwithstanding efforts by Russian foreign minister Igor Ivanov to mediate. A myth would later take hold, especially in Russia, that the US government had actively planned and supported the revolution. But US-funded NGOs played a supporting role at best, and the dynamics leading to Shevardnadze's departure were extremely improvised.

The Rose Revolution briefly electrified the world. Meanwhile, after a brief thaw, Georgia's relations with Russia turned sour, as Saakashvili courted the West and vowed to resolve the secessionist conflicts and seek NATO membership. At a summit in Bucharest in April 2008, NATO allies stated that Georgia would become a member, provided it met all necessary requirements. Four months later, Russia fought a short war with Georgia and recognized Abkhazia and South Ossetia as independent. As Paula Slier found while covering the events for RT on the ground, by that point, most Georgians harbored a deep antipathy toward Moscow.

In the years that followed, Russia would remain an important factor in Georgia's messy political trajectory. After GD came to power in 2012 as the democratic alternative to the authoritarian-leaning UNM,

Saakashvili left the country. Even though Georgia and Russia had cut all diplomatic relations after the 2008 war, GD started a slow process of restoring economic ties with Moscow—while also continuing to engage the West. Saakashvili warned of the country's gravitation into Russia's orbit, labeling Ivanishvili "Putin's errand boy." In later years, Saakashvili would go into exile in Ukraine, smuggle himself back into Georgia in 2021, and call for mass anti-government demonstrations. He was arrested and has remained behind bars ever since.

Beneath the drama of national politics, Georgia's population remained overwhelmingly pro-Western. They reacted with outrage when Russia invaded Ukraine in 2022. Visiting Tbilisi in summer 2023, I saw Ukrainian flags everywhere, dangling from balconies and windows. One hung from atop the entrance gates to Bassiani, Tbilisi's largest nightclub, another from the Stamba Hotel. Anti-Russian graffiti was omnipresent, and—unlike in Armenia—people were increasingly uncomfortable using Russian as a lingua franca.

While Russia's invasion evoked strong feelings across Georgian society—itself traumatized by war with Russia—it also fueled a growing polarization between GD and the opposition. Early into the invasion, GD rejected the idea of expediting Georgia's EU application, while President Zourabichvili met in Brussels with EU officials to advance the country's admission into the union. GD made a surprise U-turn only days later, applying for EU membership alongside Moldova. But it continued to navigate cautiously vis-à-vis Russia and made clear it would not participate in any economic sanctions against Moscow. Zourabichvili lamented that decision, saying that "in this battle between Russia and the free world, Georgia has a government that stands on the side of Russia."

I asked Tamar Jakeli what she thought was behind GD's appeasement of Russia. The party's priority, she believed, was domestic. Before the invasion, Ivanishvili saw merit in pursuing Georgia's slow alignment with the West and so embarked on superficial reforms. After all, the country had benefited greatly from this growing closeness over the years. The West had supported Georgia's state-building, the professionalization of its bureaucracy, and, through investment and trade, its economy. It had also helped build Georgia's defense sector through assistance for the military and intelligence sharing. After the invasion of Ukraine, the EU, desperate to avert the gravitation of other countries into Russia's orbit, became eager to embrace Georgia.

For Ivanishvili, however, proceeding on the European path would require genuine governance reforms, which would in turn threaten his assets and his hold on power, Jakeli said. "For him personally, to maintain his power, being aligned with Russia is better. Because Russia is not going to ask him for democratic reforms." Cognizant that it could no longer maintain Georgia's slow, superficial move toward the EU, but that the country—once embraced for fast-track membership—had to go all in, GD had no choice but to shut the door for good. It did so by passing anti-democratic and homophobic legislation that it knew was unpalatable to Europe.

Other Georgians believe that GD's maneuvering may also have been sustained by a newfound self-confidence, a belief that Tbilisi enjoyed increased leverage. Because of the Ukraine war, Georgia's "price tag" in the geopolitical competition for influence in the Caucasus went up. This gave GD greater room to maneuver vis-à-vis both Brussels and Moscow—or so the reasoning went.

Though Ivanishvili is considered close to the first generation of Russian oligarchs, who made their fortunes in the 1990s, there is no conclusive evidence that he has ever taken direct orders from the Kremlin. The Russian government did, however, support GD's Putin-friendly tilt through its own actions and words. While it threatened the Armenian government with coercive measures should it stray too far from Russia, it showered GD with praise for its planned foreign influence and anti-LGBT legislation. In 2023, it proceeded with visa liberalization for Georgians and resumed direct flights between Georgia and Russia. Moscow also applauded Tbilisi's position on the Ukraine war and on Western sanctions as evenhanded. While these moves signaled an appreciation for GD, they also served as tacit recognition of Georgia's importance as a node in Russia's Eurasian roundabout trade.

Still, Russia also took measures to ensure that it retained levers over Georgia that could be activated in case the October 2024 election took an undesirable turn and brought anti-Russian forces to power. On the eve of the election, Bloomberg published an investigation that exposed the extent to which Russian agents had penetrated Georgian government agencies, major companies, oil terminals, and media platforms. The yearslong spying campaign gave Russia the necessary access to tamper with Georgia's vital infrastructure services in case the Georgian government drifted in unwelcome directions. Subtle hints by Russian officials and intercepted messages by Russia's Foreign Intelligence Service (SVR) suggested Moscow may even have been prepared to intervene militarily to keep GD in power—something the Kremlin vehemently denied. Still, Andrey Klimov, deputy chairman of Russia's federation council (the upper house of its parliament), implied Russia would be prepared to help GD retain power if requested. Aware of its power to revive Georgian trauma over the loss of Abkhazia and South Ossetia, Russia also warned, ten days before the election, that potential "provocations" near these regions could "escalate on the ground."

When the election results came in, Russia's relief was palpable, its warnings to the West not to interfere sharp. The sentiment was understandable. Cognizant of its waning influence in the South Caucasus after its abandonment of the Karabakh Armenians, the Russians did not want to lose Georgia, too. Especially since Georgia presented a rare opportunity for Russia to recruit a country once celebrated as a vanguard of democracy into the front lines of autocracy.

Georgia's tumble toward autocracy gave Tamar Jakeli purpose. She had a happy childhood, spending her early years in Hanover, Germany, where her parents studied at university. She recalls singing Georgian songs with them before bedtime and idolizing female role models like Joan of Arc and Mulan. By the time she was a teenager, she was living in the United States. But she remembers clearly how antigay activists, some of them Georgian Orthodox priests, disrupted an LGBTQ rally in Tbilisi on May 17, 2013. Watching footage that showed anti-LGBTQ protesters hurling obscenities at gay rights activists, pursuing them and beating them, Jakeli felt despair. She had not yet come out, and the images confirmed that people like her were outcasts, hated by the majority of her society. Her sorrow was compounded by the fact that, for the first time, she had fallen in love with a girl who did not reciprocate her feelings. All these hardships led Jakeli onto the path of seeking support from others and, eventually, coming out. In 2017, she decided to move back from America to Georgia, eager to join progressive circles and get involved in feminist and queer activism in her home country.

It was a time of social change, with new movements emerging and queer spaces opening up. But an early sign of democratic backsliding came in May 2018, when police raided Bassiani, the famous nightclub, in an anti-drug operation. The club had become an important safe space for LGBTQ Georgians, hosting a monthly queer party called the Horoom Nights (derived from the celebrated Georgian war dance, the khorumi). Activists were convinced the anti-drug mandate was merely a pretext for the raid, which became the first in a string of polarizing events that outraged the young and liberal-minded, while enjoying support among religious and conservative Georgians.

The next setback came with what Georgians would remember as Gavrilov's Night. In June 2019, GD had allowed Russian MP Sergey Gavrilov to address the Georgian parliament from the Speaker's chair. Many Georgians were appalled. Ensuing protests were brutally dispersed by police who fired rubber bullets into the crowd. Mako Gomuri, a girl younger than Jakeli, lost an eye, and many others were injured. "This was the first time that Russian influence became really visible, that people realized our government may be pro-Russian," Jakeli said. That summer, Tbilisi Pride was planning to hold Georgia's first-ever pride march, but the protests following Gavrilov's Night, and the government's response to it, complicated those plans. A pride march was attempted again in July 2021, after the COVID pandemic, and it turned violent. The Tbilisi Pride office on Giorgi Akhvlediani Street was smashed. When she told me the story, I understood why she had locked the balcony doors twice. Back in July 2021, anti-pride activists had climbed up the building facade to force their way into the office.

Georgia has long had a conservative streak—same-sex sexual activity was only legalized in 2000, while gay marriage remained illegal. Religion occupies a central place in society and the Georgian Orthodox Church, which is accorded special status by the constitution, is among the country's most trusted institutions thanks to the role it played in the formation of Georgian statehood and the preservation of the country's cultural and spiritual identity. Just over 83 percent of the population is Orthodox Christian and, according to a 2018 survey by the Pew Research Center and the 2018 Caucasus Barometer survey, almost 50 percent of Georgia's population considers itself highly religious.

The trajectory of anti-liberal and anti-LGBTQ activity in Georgia accelerated with GD's appeasement of Russia following the Ukraine invasion, Jakeli told me. The charged geopolitical context allowed GD to combine antiwar, anti-woke, and anti-Western sentiments in one narrative that said, "The West is trying to open a second front against Russia, using Georgia. And it is trying to make Georgian people gay. Russia, in contrast, is not morally corrupt." Georgia's government promoted propaganda that fit seamlessly within Russia's own anti-woke and conservative narratives.

Then, on July 8, 2023, the attack on LGBTQ rights became even more personal for Jakeli. She had spent weeks looking forward to a festival that Tbilisi Pride was due to host at Lisi Wonderland, the city's premier open-air venue. The government had promised solid police protection, showing Jakeli and her colleagues exactly where they would deploy and where they would put up barriers in case protesters from Alt-Info, an ultraconservative movement with pro-Russian affinities, showed up. They even had water cannons, which they threatened to use in case Alt-Info got violent.

Jakeli and her friends realized something was off shortly before the festival was due to open. All of a sudden, the entire area was encircled by Alt-Info activists. The police started shouting, asking everyone to evacuate immediately. Within two minutes, buses appeared, as if out of nowhere, to move the festival organizers from the site. It was all preplanned, Jakeli thought. Just half an hour before the evacuation, the police had asked her how many people were at the venue, and at what time Western ambassadors were expected. "We connected the dots later," Jakeli told me, "but it was pretty clear. They wanted to evacuate us, and do so before all these ambassadors arrived." Many of Jakeli's friends were crying as they were shuttled away from Lisi Wonderland, with Alt-Info activists throwing stones and empty bottles at the buses.

Once they were in safety, they watched videos posted to social media showing Alt-Info raiding the festival area, destroying props and placards, and drinking the champagne organizers had stored for the festivalgoers. Some of the videos showed policemen and Alt-Info activists hugging, Jakeli recalled. "The government wanted to take a middle ground," she said. "They did not want blood to be shed, or LGBTQ activists being beaten up by the ultraright, because that would have caused tensions with Western countries. But on the other hand, they did not want the festival to go ahead, either, because they wanted to please their conservative electorate."

GD's legislation against foreign influence and against LGBT propaganda passed the following year. The party had first introduced the foreign influence law in spring 2023, before withdrawing it under public pressure and then steamrolling it through in 2024, notwithstanding renewed protests. Some Georgians I spoke with believe that the messy approach might have been part of the plan: GD wanted to exhaust civil society prior to the parliamentary elections, believing that if people protested the foreign agent law over a protracted period, they would be worn out by the time the polls opened. Another explanation was that Ivanishvili wanted to take a step drastic enough for the EU to have to freeze Georgia's accession process. Indeed, after the Georgian parliament passed the foreign agent law in May 2024 and endorsed the anti-LGBT law in a first reading one month later, the EU announced its suspension of a tranche of financial aid to the Georgian military.

"Russia's influence is very visible in the laws passed by GD," Jakeli told me on the night before the October 2024 election. Russia's own anti-LGBTQ legislation had evolved over the years, she explained, starting fairly soft, with a 2013 law ostensibly aimed at protecting minors from information that could "entice them into a homosexual lifestyle." But by 2022, the ban was extended to prohibit "gay propaganda" among all citizens, not just minors, and Russia also introduced bans on the "propaganda of pedophilia" and the "promotion of gender reassignment." "There was all that regression in Russia over a decade, things became worse and worse," Jakeli reflected, "and the Georgian government just took the final version and adopted it." Several countries struggling with Russian influence have gone down the same path, she added.

Natalie Sabanadze, a former head of Georgia's mission to the EU and now a senior fellow at Chatham House, a British think tank, considers that point worth further unpacking. She has argued that, in passing its legislation, GD has been emulating Viktor Orbán's increasingly illiberal Hungary rather than Russia. Unlike in Russia, she said, Orbán had perfected state capture by legal means and without blowing up the democratic facade, and GD had followed that example. Leveraging its absolute parliamentary majority to push through controversial laws, GD was able to maintain the appearance of legality and legitimacy, just like the Hungarian government. And like in Hungary, GD's dominance over Georgia's information space ensured that the political playing field disadvantages the opposition. The Georgian and Hungarian practices occupy a gray zone, Sabanadze said. Observers look at both countries and wonder: Is this still a democracy?

Should GD continue to stay in power, she warned, there is a risk of Georgia eventually moving beyond the Hungarian model and fully emulating Russia. That is because Georgia is not susceptible to the same reputational pressures and institutional constraints that come with Hungary's membership in the EU and NATO. What's more, the Hungarian model for undermining the rule of law and eroding democracy might appeal to others. Russia, Sabanadze said, stands to gain from the emergence of other illiberal imitators chipping away at the idea of a united, liberal, democratic West.

In the weeks following Georgia's October 2024 parliamentary election, there were signs that such worries were not unfounded. In response to the European Parliament calling for a rerun of the election in late November, GD decided to suspend EU accession talks until 2028. One month later, the installation of GD ally Mikheil Kavelashvili as president marked Ivanishvili's full state capture, the completion of a process whereby GD would bring all the country's institutions, including the presidency, under its control.

Its invasion of Ukraine had cost Russia dearly in Armenia, since it no longer had the wherewithal to perform its original role as guarantor of the country's security. To the Kremlin's delight, the situation in Georgia was quite different. The invasion threw that country back into Russia's clutches, giving GD a convenient pretext to pull off an astonishing political about-face. In turning away from the West and toward Russia, Georgia embraced an authoritarianism that both increasingly emulated its long-reviled Russian neighbor and acted in service of its geopolitical agenda. Georgian Dream had become Putin's dream.

Unwilling to accept Georgia's fate as sealed, Jakeli and countless others took to the streets tirelessly through winter 2024 and spring 2025 to protest against a stolen election and for a different future. Rustaveli Avenue remained in a state of agitation. The protesters were determined to ruin the oligarch's plan. In an increasingly violent standoff, the police deployed water cannons and tear gas, while demonstrators threw fire crackers. "We all knew that, at some point, we would have to take to the streets and stay there for a long time, if we really wanted to get our country back," Jakeli called on her supporters on social media. "This is a struggle for all of us," she wrote. "After this experience, we will be a better society."

CHAPTER 7

Geography Is Everything

ON MARCH 19, 2023, AN ODD SPECTACLE TOOK PLACE IN PETROPAVLOVSK, a city in northern Kazakhstan near the border with Russia. A group of nineteen men and women crammed together in a sparsely furnished conference room. Their grand aim stood in contrast to the modesty of their attire and abode: to proclaim the foundation of a people's soviet. "We, men and women, laborers, able and free," a middle-aged woman read out listlessly, "hereby declaring our self-rule, our independence and sovereignty from the national corporation that is 'the Republic of Kazakhstan' . . . are reviving the People's Soviet of Workers of Petropavlovsk in the North Kazakhstan province." In the low-quality footage of the meeting, which lasted around twenty minutes, the woman's voice is muffled by the buzzing of what seemed to be an air conditioner unit.

Initially, the bizarre scene went barely noticed. The video posted to the Petropavlovsk People's Soviet page on Vkontakte, a Russian social media platform, garnered a meager twenty-two likes. But once it went viral, some Kazakhs were troubled by the state's administrative and criminal inaction against the group. This was a time when Russia was waging war against Ukraine—a country where Russian-engineered separatist movements had cropped up in 2014, giving Moscow a pretext to intervene on behalf of Russian-speaking minorities. Surely, Russian fingerprints were all over the Petropavlovsk spectacle, too. What did such rogue activities foreshadow for Kazakhstan, a country which Russia tried to keep on a tight leash, and with which it shared the second-longest border in the world?

Ever since Russia's annexation of Crimea in 2014, the Kazakhstan government led by President Kassym-Jomart Kemeluly Tokayev had cracked down on any activity that smelled of separatism. Three months after the invasion of Ukraine, a court in Petropavlovsk had sentenced a married couple to five years' imprisonment. Their crime: calling on Russia to absorb the region. As lawmakers and civil society groups came out to condemn the Petropavlovsk People's Soviet, the police finally reacted, announcing an investigation. By April 2, two of the nineteen assembly members had taken to social media to offer a meek half-apology. Then, the episode disappeared from public view.

Dimash Alzhanov, a political activist and analyst critical of the government, believed there was more to the story. In remarks two weeks after the incident, he alleged that Kazakhstan's own security services were involved in the Petropavlovsk People's Soviet. The video was released on the same day Kazakhstan held early parliamentary elections, and the government was keenly aware of suspicions that those elections weren't going to be fair. "How can you drown out that noise? Of course, by creating a feeling among people that there are threats to territorial integrity," he argued.

To Zarina Akhmatova, the fear of a Russian overlord was no joking matter. Born in Almaty to an ethnically Chechen family in 1986, just a few years before Kazakhstan became independent, Akhmatova was the heir to a family history steeped in pain and entangled with Russian influence.

The lands and people inhabiting the territory of modern-day Kazakhstan were ruled by the Russian Empire from the eighteenth century, when czarist forces conquered the Kazakh steppe. Through the 1920s and 1930s, when Kazakhstan became part of the Soviet Union, Moscow tried to mold Kazakhs into a modern nation, eliminating nomadism and other practices it considered backward. During Stalin's reign, a program of forced collectivization in the countryside caused a devastating famine that led to the death of 1.5 million people between 1930 and 1933. Just over ten years later, Stalin ordered hundreds of thousands of Chechens and Ingush, ethnic minorities, to be deported to the Soviet empire's outer reaches, including Kazakhstan.

Akhmatova's grandparents were among them. In an operation code-named Chechevitsa (Lentil), Chechens and Ingush were picked up by soldiers, barely allowed to pack any belongings, and taken away in cattle cars destined for the Kazakh and Kyrgyz Soviet Socialist Republics. It was not until Akhmatova was at university, studying to become a journalist, that her maternal grandmother, Zara, shared the full story with her.

Zara was five years old when the soldiers came. During the arduous journey, her mother, Khazimat, exchanged some gold jewelry to get a few breadcrumbs for her children. They were traveling with Zara's brother Andarbek, who was nine years older, but not their father, who had died just before the Second World War. On the rare occasion they were fed, soldiers handed them some smelly slop and crackers. If they managed to break the crackers, midges would fly out. One day, Zara and Andarbek waited in line for a photographer who had come to the labor camp to which they had been brought, just outside Semipalatinsk in eastern Kazakhstan. Andarbek wanted a photo with his little sister, but when it was their turn, the photographer ran out of film. "Come back tomorrow, I'll take your picture first," he assured the siblings. But Andarbek would not live to see the next morning. He fell off a horse later that day, and because of a curfew in the camp, medical help arrived too late to save him.

Because Andarbek's photo was never taken, Zarina Akhmatova felt it was up to her to keep his memory alive. For decades, the fate of her ancestors was a taboo topic. The tragedy remained undiscussed, the stories untold. Only Akhmatova's generation started to ask questions. "It scares me that we did not reflect on this in a way commensurable with the scale of the tragedy," she wrote in early 2024, "and that there are so few living witnesses left to remember the dates, the colors, the smells and the faces." Akhmatova felt a moral obligation to speak about the injustice her grandparents' generation endured. In 2016, as the managing editor of *Vlast*, one of Kazakhstan's few independent media outlets, she began publishing a diary section featuring the personal stories of people deported to Kazakhstan during the Soviet era.

Though Akhmatova is Chechen—ethnically and culturally distinct from Kazakh—she considers Kazakhstan her homeland. When we met on a crisp November morning in 2024 in the city of Almaty, she sat—dressed fashionably, with immaculate makeup and dyed-blond hair worn in luxurious long waves—and recalled one of her early childhood memories. It was a rainy, cold day in November 1993 and her parents were in a state of agitation. They had only a couple of days to exchange all their rubles and pick up new shiny banknotes called tenge. Kazakhstan was introducing its own currency. It was the dawn of a new age.

Some twenty years on, Russia's invasion of Ukraine provoked a surging interest in what Kazakh elites refer to as decolonization—a not-uncontroversial concept that, to some, means a greater interest in Kazakh historiography and a new reckoning with the past, whereas to others, decolonization connotes the replacement of the Russian language with Kazakh in everyday life. "In Kazakhstan, decolonization is practiced mostly through a Kazakh lens, which is fair," Akhmatova told me. "But it has also been a vehicle for us Chechens to deal with our trauma. There are more platforms now to share our story. And more people listen."

WHILE CALLS FOR DECOLONIZATION PRECEDED THE RUSSIAN invasion of Ukraine, the war gave those calls greater heft. Young, urban

Kazakhs worried that their country, home to a sizable ethnic Russian population in places like Petropavlovsk, could be next on the Kremlin's list. They also felt Kazakhstan remained stuck in its past. Whereas the Ukraine war reminded average Georgians of the trauma of their 2008 war with Russia, the wounds it opened among Kazakhs were older, dating back to the Soviet period. Considering Ukraine's fate, it was high time to undo the final vestiges of Russian and Soviet colonialism in pursuit of a Kazakh identity.

Language became the main target. The USSR had promoted Russian as a unifying language, which meant Russian was the primary language of instruction in Kazakhstan's urban schools before 1991. Kazakh, a Turkic language, was given the status of "state language" in 1995, when the country adopted a new constitution, but Russian remained an official language. According to the 2021 census, just under three million Russians lived in Kazakhstan prior to the invasion of Ukraine, accounting for 15.5 percent of the population. In 1991, Kazakhs had accounted only for 40 percent of the overall population, an indication of how advanced the Russification of this Soviet republic had been.

After February 2022, young Kazakhs advocated for the abandonment of Russian in favor of Kazakh in everyday life. Bibarys Seitak, founder of the popular Kazakh-language Instagram channel Kazakh Bubble, framed the issue as one of national security. "We realized that we urgently need to speak Kazakh when we are bordered by a belligerent, imperial country," he said in an interview.

Aigerim Pazylbekova, a university lecturer in Astana, became interested in language pedagogy because of her own family's experience. Her father hailed from a southern region in which the Kazakh language dominated, but her relatives in the north faced mockery and job limitations due to their lack of Russian-language skills, she recalled. While her father refused to speak Russian on principle, her mother was more pragmatic, viewing mastery of the language as necessary for success. Aigerim's parents sent her to a school in which Russian was the primary language of instruction so she would enjoy greater opportunities in life. From an early age, she felt like a Russian soul captured in a Kazakh body, feeling an attachment driven by deep cultural immersion. She loved Russian music, science, and especially Russian books. But after February 2022, the language suddenly felt alien to her. Both because of a compassion for Ukraine, but also because the invasion reignited the historical trauma of what had been done to Kazakhstan in the past, she said. Russia's actions brought back memories of the 1930s famine.

"The Ukraine invasion did more for the Kazakh language than ten years' worth of government programs and millions spent on language policy," Aigerim told me. Going out to restaurants, Kazakhs suddenly felt entitled to order in Kazakh. Going to the cinema, they would watch movies with Kazakh subtitles. Surfing on their phones, they would find more apps available in Kazakh. The popularity of Kazakh-language schools and clubs exploded. Aigerim vividly remembered watching President Tokayev speak Kazakh in a meeting with Putin in November 2023, forcing top Russian officials in attendance to reach for their translation devices. She felt proud.

The decolonization trend captured spheres beyond language. It generated a growing interest in the complexities of Kazakh history. Tales about the Soviet past—especially about its ugly sides—had existed mostly as oral histories, told from generation to generation, just like in Akhmatova's family. But now those hidden histories were becoming more mainstream. After Russia attacked Ukraine, Kazakhstan's booming domestic film industry churned out a growing number of movies about the country's history, its warriors, and writers. Updates to the curriculum resulted in revisions to textbooks that included the idea that Kazakhstan had a long history as a political nation—contradicting Putin's claim in 2014 that "the Kazakhs never had any statehood."

The idea of Russia, or the Soviet Union before it, as a colonial power was rejected by those I had spoken with in India and South Africa. ANC veterans like Robert McBride or Bheki Langa could not fathom that what Moscow had practiced in its neighborhood, whether during the Soviet period or more recently, could be understood through a colonial lens. That assessment from afar clashed with the convictions of some of the young Kazakhs I met during my travels.

And yet, I was left wondering how deeply and widely ideas of decolonization resonated. Some Kazakhs assured me decolonization was not merely a buzzword for Western-educated activists and artists. They said people in the countryside shared the same sentiments, the same longing that underpinned calls for decolonization, though they would never use that term—and neither would the country's political elite, wary of antagonizing Moscow. Aigerim Pazylbekova conceded that Kazakh perspectives on the Soviet past remained diverse. Her own parents would never think of themselves as having been colonized. Though they hailed from southern Kazakhstan, far from the Soviet heartland, and though they had endured repression and privations, they still remembered the Soviet past with a certain nostalgia.

In Moscow, Kazakh decolonization efforts hit a raw nerve, causing the ruling elite to worry that Russia's clout was slipping in a country it regarded as part of its traditional sphere of influence. Pro-Kremlin media railed against what it said were initiatives driven by Russophobia. The Russian House in Almaty became active, organizing events about the famed Russian poet Alexander Pushkin and about the Russian language. Other Russian institutions joined the fray. In October 2024, the Moscow State Institute of International Relations organized a roundtable at Al-Farabi Kazakh National University in Almaty. Some in attendance warned that the decolonization discourse was creating problems for the historical friendship between Kazakhstan and Russia. One speaker argued that what the West did in other parts of the world was colonialism, whereas what the Soviet Union did in Central Asia was a blessing.

Three weeks later, foreign affairs minister Sergey Lavrov visited Astana to meet Kazakh officials. He announced the creation of a joint group of historians, both Kazakh and Russian, tasked with the custody of historical memory. Russian scientists had conducted a review of Kazakh textbooks and bemoaned that "a tenth-grade history textbook described the Russian Empire's policy toward Kazakhstan as 'territorial expansion' and 'colonial policy.'" Leading Kazakh historians pushed back. "When we start reacting to what Russian scholars say about our textbooks, that's a postcolonial mindset symptom," Yerkin Abil, historian and deputy in the lower house of Kazakhstan's parliament, said.

For some Kazakhs, the Russian concerns were understandable. Attitudes toward Russia have always been mixed in Kazakh society—not just split by ethnic lines, but also across generations and across a rural-urban divide—and became even more polarized after the invasion of Ukraine. According to a survey-based report by the Kazakh research center PaperLab, attitudes toward Russia overall deteriorated with the onset of the Ukraine war, and few people saw the invasion as justified. But older Kazakhs, and those more oriented toward Russian media content, tended to adopt pro-Russian narratives. When I spoke to PaperLab's director, sociologist Serik Beissembayev, he suggested that some segments of society were becoming more consolidated as they unified in their quest for a Kazakh identity distinct from Russia. But across society as a whole, he said, views on Russia had become more divided.

Just like in Armenia and Georgia, Russia's aggression against Ukraine deepened fissures in Kazakhstan. Yet average people felt the impact quite differently: The war left Armenians feeling abandoned by Russia, and then disagreeing over the right way forward; it left Georgians sharply divided between adherents of an authoritarian government that took advantage of the moment to both mimic and move closer to Russia, and the young and liberally minded; and it left Kazakhs reexamining their own history with Russia, with some calling on the country to throw off the yoke of Soviet legacy once and for all, while others argued for caution.

CONCRETE SLABS SHOOT OUT OF THE GROUND JUST OFF THE Akimat, the seat of Almaty's mayor. Engraved with quotes by Kazakh thinkers, some steles are black, some white, and others are dressed in different shades of gray. Called Tagzym ("Reverence"), the composition stands in Republic Square, the epicenter of events that the government calls an attempted coup and that Kazakhs remember as Bloody January. In early January 2022, barely two months before Russia's invasion of Ukraine, small protests over fuel prices in western Kazakhstan spread to other cities. By January 5, Almaty, Kazakhstan's biggest city, was in a state of chaos. Protesters forcibly entered government buildings and set fire to the city's main administration office. Deadly clashes with the police and military ensued. The government described the protesters as terrorists supported by foreign forces and called on the CSTO to send peacekeepers. In response, Russia and other CSTO members deployed two thousand troops in a matter of hours. They would stay for seven days.

At least 238 people lost their lives. The events remain a hushed topic in Kazakhstan. To journalists at *Vlast*, Akhmatova's old employer, Tagzym's architecture affirms the taboo of Bloody January. "Republic Square is not an accessible area, with its uneven grounds and without proper walkways, (and) the Akimat sits on a hill, literally cut off from the people," the news portal wrote in a damning editorial soon after Tagzym's inauguration in December 2022.

I dropped by the memorial on my way to a café to meet Dimash Alzhanov. With his goatee and black hair buzzed very short at the sides, Alzhanov, thirty-nine, looked more like a rock star than an analyst. The British university–educated political scientist-turned-activist participated in the Bloody January demonstrations, but his political and protest activity started long before. Alzhanov was detained on June 12, 2019, the day Tokayev was first inaugurated as president, amid widespread resistance to the power transition. As he was being pushed into a paddy wagon, he shouted, "*Oyan Qazaqstan!*" (Wake up, Kazakhstan!)—the name of the protest movement he had recently cofounded. "We want to declare the need for profound political reforms in Kazakhstan," he had told a news conference a week prior to his detention. In subsequent protests, he was arrested twice more and has remained an uncomfortable critic of the government ever since. Masked men tried to attack him in front of his house in July 2024, likely because of his political activity.

The lack of political reform and growing repression against civil society became even worse after Russia's invasion of Ukraine, Alzhanov said. In March 2022, the government announced a program to deliver a "New Kazakhstan," promising the liberalization of the party system and electoral reform. But in fact, the government further restricted the right to peaceful assembly. In one instance, a feminist march planned in Almaty for March 8, International Women's Day, was banned on the pretext of another group having already booked what was the only street on which marches were allowed. Snap presidential elections in November 2022 and parliamentary elections in March 2023 were accompanied by pressure on independent observers. During the March elections, for instance, monitors complained they were expelled from voting stations and obstructed from having a full view of ballot boxes. Ahead of the elections, the government loosened electoral legislation to generate the impression of greater political competition, making it easier for new parties to register, allowing some independent candidates, and permitting the discussion of sensitive topics during the campaign. In the end, however, the election—marked by record-low turnout and some electoral fraud—resulted in the ruling party effectively retaining complete control of parliament.

Then, in June 2024, the government passed a new media law that was widely criticized for enhancing government control rather than making journalism more independent. Notwithstanding some positive provisions, it empowered authorities to carry out "mass media monitoring" and gave the government expansive power to interfere with and suspend the work of foreign journalists. In fact, the media landscape had started to deteriorate years earlier, as Akhmatova told me. She described how, as editor in chief of an independent news website called Hola News, starting in 2020 following her five years at

Vlast, she faced growing pressure from the authorities. At first, the intrusion came in the form of requests to edit or delay stories due to what the government called "national security" concerns. Then, in October 2021, Hola News reported on the Pandora Papers investigation, a leak of almost twelve million documents that revealed hidden wealth, tax avoidance, and, in some cases, money laundering by some of the world's rich and powerful. Their story focused on the unofficial third wife of former president Nursultan Nazarbayev. In response, the authorities blocked the website for ten days. "We removed the story and replaced it with a Soviet cartoon," Akhmatova told me. "And after that, I quit." Whereas Paula Slier could rationalize RT's increasingly intrusive editorial meddling, the top-down guidance Akhmatova experienced was more than she would put up with. Three months before Bloody January, she decided she could no longer lead a newsroom where she had to break her own editorial rules.

Alzhanov and other opposition-leaning analysts I met saw Kazakhstan's democratic backsliding as endemic. Their account is one of a kleptocratic governing elite that refused to move toward genuine political pluralism out of fear of losing their assets. But in clinging to power, this elite—much like GD in Georgia—benefited from the changed geopolitical environment produced by Russia's invasion of Ukraine. The Ukraine war allowed the Kazakh government to divert the domestic conversation from the need for political reform to the need for "stability." At the same time, Western states became more lenient vis-à-vis Tokayev, worried that if they pressed him too much on reforms, they would drive him further into Putin's arms. Liberal observers also accused the Kazakh government of having looked toward Russia as a model for implementing increasingly authoritarian measures, albeit in a "lite" form—again, just as GD has mimicked Viktor Orbán's Hungary. In rhetoric, Tokayev certainly began to emulate Putin. After Bloody January, he shifted from talking about the "rule of law" to the "dictatorship of law and order." It was Putin who coined the term "dictatorship of law" when he first rose to power.

Eight hundred miles north of Almaty sits the capital, Astana, a city crawling with government functionaries, former diplomats, and experts devoted to working with the state. Outside liberal circles, observers there reach a different verdict about how Tokayev has led the country amid the war in Ukraine. They usually start with the basics, noting that Kazakhstan is the world's largest landlocked country, with no direct access to the sea and a land border with Russia that spans more than 7,800 kilometers (4,890 miles). Geography determines the country's fate and mandates accommodation with Russia. Over the long run, Russia's aggressive conduct may well strengthen the Kazakhs' ethnic and national identity, just as it turbocharged the evolution of statehood in Ukraine. But Kazakhstan needs to get there without risking conflict with Russia. It needs strategic patience, these observers say. Gossip that Tokayev "owes" Putin, because of the assistance the CSTO provided during Bloody January, has only reinforced that view.

As in Armenia, Kazakhstan's economic dependence on Russia has given the Kremlin levers to retain its influence, despite its diversion of resources to Ukraine. Kazakhstan exports around 80 percent of its oil through Russian territory. Its main crude oil export route is the 1,511-kilometer (939-mile) Caspian Pipeline Consortium (CPC) pipeline, which originates at Kazakhstan's giant Tengiz oil field and ends at a terminal located near the Russian port of Novorossiysk. After the invasion of Ukraine, Russia temporarily disrupted exports from the CPC terminal on several occasions. Though it cited technical and regulatory issues, Kazakh elites understood these acts as a political signal, an attempt by Moscow to remind Astana of its leverage. At the beginning of the war, Russia also temporarily banned sugar and flour exports to Kazakhstan, fueling inflation that was already skyrocketing due to Kazakhstan's dependence on the ruble exchange rate.

While the war in Ukraine drove up food prices and rents in Astana and Almaty, it also reinforced Kazakhstan's economic interdependence with Russia, giving the neighbor to the north additional footholds to project influence. Russian businesses like Wildberries, the largest Russian online retailer, and Yandex, a Russian technology company, expanded their Kazakh operations. Polymetal, one of Russia's largest gold miners, redomiciled in Kazakhstan. The Eurasian roundabout trade made 2022 and 2023 record years for Kazakh–Russian economic cooperation. The interdependence also enhanced Kazakhstan's vulnerability to shocks in the Russian economy, generating a Kazakh stake in how Russia would fare in its efforts to outlast the West.

Kazakhstan's plan to build its first nuclear power plant in the village of Ulken, near Almaty, illustrated the myriad sensitivities surrounding this interdependence with Russia. The plan has long been controversial in a country scarred by the legacies of Soviet-era nuclear testing. During the Cold War, the Soviet Union conducted more than 450 nuclear tests at the Semipalatinsk nuclear test site, near where Akhmatova's relatives had suffered in a labor camp. The radioactive fallout from the tests resulted in elevated rates of cancer, congenital disabilities, and other health issues that persist to this day. The invasion of Ukraine compounded concerns over whether a plant should be built at all, with apprehensions over who should build it. Russia's Rosatom was a primary contender. Preferred by Kazakhstan's nuclear lobby for logistical and technical reasons, the company reminded ordinary Kazakhs of the legacy of Semipalatinsk. Some elites also worried about the political risks inherent in proceeding with Rosatom. Confronted with these conundrums, the government held a nationwide referendum on the plant in October 2024. While Kazakhstan's central election commission announced a 71 percent approval rate for the new reactor, critics alleged that the referendum was not fair. After the vote, Tokayev promised that a multinational consortium would build the plant. It was his way of accommodating Moscow—since Rosatom would most likely lead the consortium—while also appeasing Russia's critics.

Keen to loosen the bonds tying Kazakhstan to the former imperial hegemon, yet at the same time cautious not to antagonize Russia, Tokayev has pursued a fine balancing act on the cultural and political fronts, too. He accelerated plans to Latinize the Kazakh alphabet, while also declaring 2023 the year of the Russian language and supporting the opening of new Russian-language schools. Under his watch, Kazakhstan abstained from major UN General Assembly resolutions on Russia. Essentially, the war in Ukraine gave Kazakhstan's "multi-vector foreign policy" a new meaning. Initially intended to put the country on the international map and attract foreign investors from around the world, it became a vehicle for reducing Kazakhstan's dependency on Russia. To that end, Kazakhstan—much like Armenia—strengthened its relations with a host of other countries, including Turkey, Iran, the Arab Gulf countries, and, above all, China. The Ukraine war also gave further impetus to Kazakhstan's efforts to spur integration among Central Asian countries, bypassing Russia. In October 2024, just days before Russia hosted a BRICS summit in Kazan to great fanfare, Kazakhstan announced it had no intention of joining the club, in a further snub to Moscow.

Opposition-leaning analysts dismissed Tokayev's tiptoeing as window dressing, arguing that displays of neutrality were de facto endorsements of Russia. Still, they gave Tokayev better marks on foreign policy than on his domestic governance. Akhmatova conceded that "Kazakhstan has the longest land border with a country run by a crazy man. You need to be careful and maintain some balance."

Indeed, the crazy man across the border has regularly reminded Kazakhstan of its vulnerabilities. Meeting Tokayev in November 2023, Putin mispronounced the Kazakh president's name several times, in what was seen as a display of disrespect. That was after Russian Telegram channels became more active in criticizing Kazakhstan—its multi-vector foreign policy, its decolonization efforts, the referendum on the nuclear power plant.

Russian rhetoric reignited fears over the fate of places like Petropavlovsk that were close to the border and host to incidents including the people's soviet. Russian officials had insinuated for years that northern Kazakhstan was not, in fact, part of Kazakhstan. But after the events of Bloody January and the invasion of Ukraine,

Russian pundits turned up the temperature. In June 2022, Russian member of Parliament Konstantin Zatulin raised the question of Kazakhstan's future territorial integrity, referencing those parts of the country with a predominantly Russian population. He warned that "if we have friendship . . . then no territorial questions are raised. But if that does not exist, everything is possible. As in the case of Ukraine." Similar attacks on Kazakhstan were echoed by other Russian MPs. Russia telegraphed that, even though it was preoccupied in Ukraine, it was watching Kazakhstan carefully and would not allow its neighbor to stray too far from a pro-Russian course.

It was December 26, 2024, two weeks before Orthodox Christmas, and the Tagzym memorial was being cleaned up for the three-year anniversary of Bloody January. On that occasion, Margarita Simonyan outdid herself again. In an interview with a Russian blogger, she insinuated that the Russian military could again deploy to the country to deal with some "bogeymen," just as it had under CSTO auspices during Bloody January. The Kazakh Telegraph Agency asked Simonyan to clarify, but received no reply.

The idea that Russia poses a threat to their country is one that ordinary Kazakhs find hard to shake. Surveys co-conducted by PaperLab showed that 26 percent of Kazakhs, polled in November 2022, thought a Russian attack on Kazakhstan was either "probable" or "probable under certain circumstances." That figure increased to 39 percent in May 2023. The analysts and elites I interviewed were more sanguine. Ethnic Russians in northern Kazakhstan are not politically organized, they argued, dismissing the Petropavlovsk People's Soviet episode as a prank. A Russian military operation into northern Kazakhstan was extremely unlikely, they said. Given the two countries' deep interdependence and Astana's accommodative stance, there was no need for Russia to invade. Their concern was rather about Russia's creeping cultural, economic, and political takeover; about Russia's ownership of strategic assets in the country; about the continued entanglement of business and political elites; and what it all meant for Kazakhstan's future.

They feared that that diffuse threat could increase, depending on the future course of Russia's confrontation with the West. If the Russian Army collapsed in Ukraine, the consequences for Kazakhstan's elites would be unpredictable and there could be chaos. But if Russia prevailed, Kazakhstan would slowly see its sovereignty erode. Countervailing forces—efforts to decolonize or to pursue a balanced foreign policy—would then prove too marginal and too weak to withstand the pulls and pushes of a Russian colossus that emerged victorious in Ukraine. And domestically, Russia's perseverance would likely accelerate Kazakhstan's authoritarian descent, much like in Georgia.

Aspiring to a kind of dominion over post-Soviet Eurasia, Russia—with its resources stretched thin because of Ukraine—has used different tools to retain influence over its neighbors. It has flexed its muscles vis-à-vis Armenia and Kazakhstan, while praising GD's agenda in Georgia. Russia's war has put these countries before formidable yet very different challenges: It forced all Armenians into greater self-reliance, and the Karabakh Armenians into the ultimate sacrifice; it forced young, liberal Georgians into the struggle of their lifetime against a Georgian Dream-turned-dictator; and it forced Kazakh political elites into a cautious balancing act. But as much as their fates are unique, the Kremlin's ideal future playbook for these countries—and others in its neighborhood, like Belarus and Moldova—follows the same broad contours: entrench their economic dependencies, encourage them to mirror Russia's domestic illiberalism, lean on them to join Russian-backed regional and international bodies, and possibly accept a Russian military presence within their territories. In Putin's effort to outlast the West, the future of post-Soviet Eurasia would remain of special importance—and Russia would not yield its privileged position without putting up a fight.

Part IV

PLAYING FARTHER AFIELD

CHAPTER 8

Too Much Upheaval

A MAKESHIFT MEMORIAL STANDS IN THE CENTER OF MAJDAL Shams, a quiet town on the rugged edge of Mount Hermon in the Israeli-occupied Golan Heights. Twelve faces—young, smiling, carefree—shine from photographs attached to the damaged fence of a soccer field, its wires speckled with black ribbons. These are children who were killed in a rocket attack while playing soccer on July 27, 2024, nearly ten months after Hamas attacked Israel, unleashing a furious Israeli response that would decisively change the Middle East and expose the limits of Russia's throw weight in the region.

Majdal Shams is mainly home to the Druze, a roughly one-million-strong Arab minority spread across Syria, Lebanon, Israel, and the Golan Heights. Exploring the town in January 2025, I stumbled upon traces of its troubled history everywhere. There were trenches from the 1967 war, when the Golan Heights first came under Israeli occupation. A nearby ridge was known as the "Shouting Hill," where Druze on the Israeli side would yell news at their relatives on the Syrian side, before the internet made video calls possible. On the town's outskirts,

I peeked across a security fence onto the Alpha Line, the western edge of a buffer zone that separates the Israeli-controlled area of the Golan Heights from Syria.

The deadly attack on Majdal Shams, which Israel blamed on Hezbollah, became a turning point in the country's campaign against members of the anti-Israeli and anti-Western "axis of resistance," a network of Iranian partners that included Hamas in Gaza, Hezbollah in Lebanon, Syrian and Iraqi militias, and the Houthis in Yemen. First, Israel killed Ismail Haniyeh, the political leader of Hamas, in the Iranian capital. Then it unleashed a sophisticated campaign against Hezbollah in Lebanon, which began with an operation exploding the group members' pagers and culminated in the killing of its leader, Hassan Nasrallah. Israel's goal was to deal Iran and its partners a defeat so serious that they would not be able to recover.

As iran suffered blow after blow, Russia was unable or unwilling to do much of anything about it, preoccupied as it was with Ukraine.

Putin was far from the carnage when Hamas attacked Israel on October 7, 2023. He was celebrating his seventy-first birthday in Moscow. As news of the attack unfolded, rumors spread on social media that the Kremlin could be behind the attack. Putin had always shown a penchant for marking important dates with acts of violence. Anna Politkovskaya, the Russian journalist who spoke truth to power in the early days of his reign, was shot dead on October 7, 2006, Putin's fifty-fourth birthday. Russia must have instigated Hamas to fuel conflict in the Middle East in order to broaden Moscow's battlefield with the West, the rumors went. It would be the perfect birthday gift.

Evidence of Russia's involvement never emerged. Still, it took Putin nearly ten days to dignify Israeli Prime Minister Benjamin Netanyahu with a phone call to express condolences for the attack, which was unusual, given their cordial relationship. As Israel unleashed its inhumane military campaign on Gaza, Russia lamented the war's civilian casualties and pressed for a humanitarian ceasefire at the United Nations. Meanwhile Russia continued to rain destruction on Ukrainian cities on an almost daily basis. By emphasizing the suffering of Palestinian civilians and distancing itself from Washington's unequivocal support for Israel, Moscow was tapping into grievances about Palestine across the Middle East and Global South.

Many in these regions felt appalled by what they viewed as the West's asymmetric responses to the conflicts in Ukraine and Gaza. The West, in their perception, helped the predominantly white and Christian Ukrainians, while it denounced and sanctioned the aggressor, Russia. Yet, despite the rapidly growing number of Palestinian civilians killed by Israeli attacks in Gaza, the West remained tepid in its criticism of Israel and even continued to sell it weapons. Western elites tended to understand the war in Ukraine in a broad historical perspective that foregrounded the legacy of Soviet and Russian imperialism. But they tended to tell a story about the Gaza war that started with Hamas's heinous attack on October 7, de-emphasizing the decades of Israeli occupation that preceded it. The West, in this telling, opposed the violation of human rights in some places, but not in others. What mattered was the color of your skin.

At the United Nations, Russia skillfully grafted its own messaging onto these perceptions. "For the West, Palestinians are second-class people," Russian diplomats asserted at the Security Council, using their appearances to describe the devastation wrought by Israel in Gaza in minute detail. It was impermissible, they argued, to compare the wars in Ukraine and Gaza, since "almost nothing" had been destroyed in Ukraine, whereas Israel was razing Gaza to the ground. At the same time, Russian diplomats saw utility in linking both wars as products of US hegemony. According to Russia's diatribes at the UN, the wars in Ukraine and Gaza were and weren't the same—depending on what point it was trying to impress.

Besides such diplomatic posturing, Russia took its military collaboration with members of the "axis of resistance" up a notch in the wake of October 7. After invading Ukraine, it had already relinquished to Hezbollah and other Iran-backed militias several of the military positions it had maintained in Syria since intervening in that country's civil war in 2015. It also ramped up intelligence sharing with these groups. Such collusion was doubly convenient. It allowed Russia to shift some of its burdens from Syria at a time when its priority was Ukraine, while also enabling forces hostile to the United States. Russia also funneled some weapons to Hezbollah and provided targeting data to the Houthis, enabling the group's drone and missile attacks on international shipping in the Red Sea. It combined this military aid with diplomatic assistance and invited Hamas and Houthi representatives to Moscow. The message was that these groups were at the forefront of challenging the mighty Israel, backed by the West, and they could count on Russia for support. At the same time, Russia's backing for its dangerous new friends would always have limits. The Kremlin remained careful to maintain ties with the Arab countries in the Persian Gulf—and even with Israel.

It initially appeared that this skillful maneuvering could only help Russia with its overarching priority: outlasting the West in the confrontation over Ukraine. As Israel started fighting in Gaza and then had to fend off attacks from Hezbollah in Lebanon, from Iran, and from the Houthis, the United States moved Patriot missile batteries and other weapons to the Middle East to aid its ally. Washington also sent one senior diplomat after another to the region to negotiate ceasefires in Gaza and, later, Lebanon. Moscow, it seemed, could watch gleefully from the sidelines as these conflicts put extra pressure on finite Western air defenses, while stirring resentment across the Global South of the double standard people perceived in the West's responses to the wars in Gaza and Ukraine.

But the dynamics that first seemed to benefit Russia turned into a strategic headache. As Israel's response to October 7 escalated, direct confrontation with Tehran moved ever closer. Iran attacked Israel directly in April and October 2024, but its strikes yielded minimal damage and exposed its missile capabilities as less formidable than previously thought. Through it all, Russia expressed concern about the spiraling violence but was unable or unwilling to provide meaningful assistance to an increasingly vulnerable Iran. In the Middle East, Russia suddenly seemed like the emperor with no clothes. It had extolled itself as a reliable ally to Iran, as protector of the Palestinians, as a power to be reckoned with. But distracted in Ukraine, Russia proved profoundly limited in what it could do, beyond rhetoric, to steer the regional turmoil. And the starkest examples of Russia's reduced ability and appetite to shape Middle Eastern events were only yet to come.

DURING THE COLD WAR, THE SOVIET UNION REGARDED ISRAEL as the linchpin of Western imperialism in the Middle East. It severed diplomatic relations with Israel after the 1967 war—fought between Israel and a coalition of Arab states—and contacts were minimal, though not altogether absent. After the collapse of the Soviet Union, there was great optimism for a different kind of relationship, recalled Natan Sharansky as we settled down in his small and humbly furnished office at the Jewish Agency in Kiryat Moriah, a stone's throw away from the US embassy in Jerusalem.

Born in Donetsk, Ukraine, in 1948, Sharansky was educated in Moscow and later became a refusenik—a Soviet Jew who applied for permission to emigrate to Israel but was refused. In his case, Sharansky was punished and spent nine years in Soviet prisons and labor camps, separated from his beloved wife, Avital. Freed in 1986, he joined her in Israel and emerged as a powerful moral voice and a symbolic reminder to many of the raison d'être of the Israeli state as a haven for persecuted Jews.

"Russia saw in Israel a bridge to the West, and it wanted to show the world that it was not anti-Semitic," Sharansky told me. When he visited Russia in the mid-1990s, as the Israeli minister of industry and trade, he held a secret meeting with then foreign minister Yevgeny Primakov to complain about what Israel believed was the leaking of sensitive missile technologies to Iran. The Russians initially denied the accusations, but a day later, they pulled him aside to admit a private Russian firm had transferred the technology. They assured Sharansky it would not happen again. The Russians, it appeared, were attentive to Israeli concerns.

"When Putin came to power, it seemed that relations would be even better," Sharansky said. Sharansky first met Putin when the latter was still head of the KGB, and has refused to meet with him since 2005, given his authoritarian tilt. But he recalled a lunch in the Kremlin soon after Putin became president. On that occasion, Putin told Sharansky he believed the USSR had committed a big mistake in fighting against Jewish identity. "He told me stories about how good Jews were to him during his difficult childhood, how his most beloved teacher was Jewish," Sharansky said.

He thought Putin was sincere. "He's definitely not an anti-Semite," Sharansky emphasized several times in our conversation. "But when it comes to Putin pursuing his real interests, if he needs to use anti-Semitism, of course he will use it!"

The Middle East became a point of focus for Putin early in his rule. In the early 2000s, he and Israeli Prime Minister Ariel Sharon shared a common enemy in the fight against what they called Islamist terrorism, as Russia fought its second war in Chechnya, a Muslim-majority region, and Israel battled the Second Palestinian Intifada. Russia became a member of the Middle East Quartet, which comprised the UN, the EU, the United States, and Russia, with a mandate to help mediate Middle East peace. Russia and Israel were also interested in developing trade relations.

Ehud Olmert remembered that period vividly. When we met, he echoed Sharansky's contention that Putin was benevolently predisposed toward Israel. Sharp and gregarious, Olmert served as deputy to

Prime Minister Sharon from 2001 until 2006, and then as prime minister until 2009. Putin had repeatedly assured him of his fondness of Jews, he told me, sharing anecdote after anecdote. "Putin would say to me: 'Do you know how many times I came to Israel to visit my childhood friends? We used to lie on the beautiful sands on the beaches of Eilat, watching the beautiful young Israeli girls march past.'" Olmert paused for dramatic effect: "'It's inconceivable even to *think*,' Putin told me, 'that I would ever jeopardize the existence of the state of Israel.'"

Notwithstanding that fundamentally friendly attitude, Olmert harbored no illusions as to Putin's Middle Eastern maneuverings. Russia's strategy was one of having its fingers in many pies. When Hamas won parliamentary elections in Gaza in early 2006, Putin invited the chairman of its political wing, Khaled Mashal, to Moscow. "I called Putin and said to him, 'How can you meet with this terrorist?'" Olmert told me, his voice agitated. "Putin pondered for a couple of seconds, then said to me, 'What do you want from me, Prime Minister? He's alive—I meet with him. He won't be alive—I won't meet with him.'" Olmert encountered a similar obstinacy when confronting Putin over Russian support for Iran and Syria over the years. He felt that whenever he leaned on Putin, it would result in Russia refraining from giving the most sensitive support—S-300 air defenses to Iran, or the Yakhont anti-ship cruise missile to Syria. But Putin was unwilling to fundamentally rethink his partnership with those countries.

During those years, and after Netanyahu came to power in 2009, anti-Semitism was largely absent from Russian official rhetoric. Instead, Russia and Israel took great pains to show sensitivity to each other's cultural, historical, and religious heritage. As prime minister in 2008, Olmert facilitated the transfer of the property of Sergei's Courtyard in Jerusalem, initially built at the end of the nineteenth century to accommodate Russian pilgrims, back to Russia. "Never since then has Putin failed to mention that he will always hold me in very high esteem for keeping my word to him about Sergei's Courtyard," Olmert told me. The two countries also aligned in remembrance of the Second World War. In January 2020, when Putin visited Israel for

Holocaust Remembrance Day and to mark the seventy-fifth anniversary of the Red Army's liberation of Auschwitz, he and Netanyahu jointly unveiled a memorial honoring the defenders of besieged Leningrad in the Second World War. For Putin, the Leningrad siege was personal. His father had been seriously wounded during the battle to defend the city, and his older brother, Viktor, had died from diphtheria during the siege at just one year old.

Ze'ev Elkin was the one who advised Netanyahu to focus on the importance of the Leningrad siege in order to strengthen his rapport with Putin. Born in Ukraine, just like Sharansky, Elkin emigrated to Israel as a young man and emerged as one of the most pivotal politicians cultivating Israel's friendship with Russia. He headed the Israel-Russia Parliamentary Friendship League for years and accompanied Olmert on his trips to Russia. Later, he served as Netanyahu's top adviser and translator in talks with Putin, sharing the room with both men on many occasions. Elkin told me Netanyahu had cultivated close ties with Putin by focusing on several "keys"—their shared past as men with a military background; their alignment in the war on terror; and, most important, their shared disposition in remembering World War II, in particular Israel's acknowledgment of the important role the Soviet Union played in defeating Nazism.

When Russia invaded Ukraine in February 2022, that alignment was put to the test. Once the war started, the Israeli government—led by Prime Minister Naftali Bennett, who had taken over from Netanyahu in June 2021—had an immediate priority: to ensure the safety of Jews in both Russia and Ukraine. Yomtov Kalfon from the Yamina party was put in charge of a Knesset committee to facilitate aliyah, the immigration of Jews to Israel, from Russia and Ukraine. With Russia, the imminent worry was that the Kremlin would not allow Jews to leave. With Ukraine, the prime minister's office had not developed close relations prior to the war, and there was a concern that the infrastructure to get Jews out quickly simply wasn't in place.

After the invasion, thousands of Russian Jews came to Israel, joining the hundreds of thousands who had already settled in the country in prior waves of aliyah in the 1990s and after the 2014 annexation of Crimea. Those who arrived for pre-consular checkups at Ben Gurion Airport were usually young, liberal, highly educated Russians who saw no future in their country. The Nativ agency, a special branch of the Israeli Prime Minister's Office, had the mandate to check these Russians' eligibility for aliyah, pursuant to the Law of Return, a 1950 law that granted every Jew in the world the right to settle in Israel. In fall 2022, another wave of Russians would follow, once Putin announced a partial military mobilization.

Another immediate Israeli priority was to mediate between Russia and Ukraine. Unlike Europe and the US, Israel avoided harshly criticizing Russia after the invasion and refused to join sanctions. Bennett had built a good rapport with Putin. When the two met in Sochi in October 2021, Bennett was accompanied by Ze'ev Elkin, who recalled the men spending five hours together and taking a stroll in the park. Putin even invited Bennett to his private house. On his travels back to Israel, Bennett got stuck over Shabbat and had to spend an extra twenty-four hours in Russia. The incident fueled speculation back in Jerusalem that the Russians had caused delays on purpose in order to obtain more face time with him.

Bennett eventually pulled himself away from the mediation over the war in Ukraine. The Israeli opposition argued both sides would blame Israel should he fail. Strains on Bennett's eight-party governing coalition increased, for these and other reasons. All efforts at peace stalled anyway in the wake of the Bucha massacre in March 2022, when Russian soldiers slaughtered civilians in the Ukrainian town of Bucha, opening up accusations of war crimes. Western pressure on Israel to take sides against Russia increased. Yair Lapid was sworn in as prime minister—replacing Bennett, who became his "alternate" in Israel's rotation government—in July 2022, and Russian–Israeli relations soured. Lapid had condemned the Bucha massacre as a "war crime" and aligned with center-left parties in Europe in their criticism of Russia. In response, Russia's attitude toward Israel cooled. During the second half of 2022, its language vis-à-vis Israel at the UN became harsher, its criticism of Israeli strikes against Iranian proxies in Syria more pronounced.

These developments provoked intense debate in Israel. While public opinion overwhelmingly supported Ukraine, the country had also absorbed more than a million Russian immigrants since the 1990s, a demographic that produced some leading politicians, most notably Avigdor Lieberman. A majority of Israelis thought the government was right in staking out a neutral position on the war. The view shared in policy circles was that this was not Israel's war and it had little to gain from choosing sides. There was also the view—to which Netanyahu and those close to him adhered—that Israel needed to navigate cautiously because of Russia's partnership with Syria's Assad and Iran. When Russia intervened in Syria in 2015, the two countries had installed a deconfliction channel—a phone line between Russia's Khmeymim base and the Israeli Air Force. Israel used the mechanism to give the Russian military a heads-up shortly before it would strike Iranian positions in Syria. Israel's pragmatists believed that by maintaining a dialogue with Russia, they ensured they had some influence over Putin—over how far he would go in assisting Iran in return for the Shahed drones; over how much trouble Russia would cause Israel in Syria; over the extent to which he would leave Russian Jews in peace.

Sharansky considered such accommodation a mistake. Viewing the invasion as a "struggle for the future of the world," he argued Israel should stand "clearly and unambiguously on the side of Ukraine." In October 2022, he met with Zelensky in Kyiv, expressing his "embarrassment" over the Israeli government's position on the war. The Ukraine invasion, and Israel's response to it, seemed to divide the refuseniks. On one end of the spectrum, Sharansky had grown increasingly wary of Putin from the mid-2000s and emerged as one of Israel's most vocal critics of Russia's war. Ze'ev Elkin, who had labored tirelessly for amicable Israeli–Russian relations through the decades, pivoted sharply against Russia, but only after the invasion. In early 2023, Elkin joined Yuli Edelstein, another Ukraine-born MP from Netanyahu's party, on a visit to Ukraine, where they were shown Iranian drones used by Russia.

On the other end of the spectrum, figures like Yakov Kedmi—one of the first refuseniks to battle for the right to emigrate to Israel—defended the Russian president in regular appearances on Russian state television. Kedmi told me he had no interest in whether a state's goals were "just" or "moral"—what mattered were the consequences of its actions. Russia's war in Ukraine, he argued, had no bearing on Israel and therefore should not affect Israel's attitude toward Russia. On the one-year anniversary of the invasion, the Council of the European Union imposed personal sanctions against Kedmi, accusing him of disseminating Russian official propaganda intended to justify the invasion of Ukraine. Speaking to the press, Kedmi called the decision a "cheap attempt" to silence him.

Meanwhile, anti-Semitism reared its ugly head in Russian state media and official parlance. Putin alleged that Zelensky was "not Jewish but a disgrace to the Jewish people" and that Zelensky's "Western handlers put an ethnic Jew in charge of Ukraine" to mask the country's "antihuman nature." The invocation of such tropes was meant to give credence to the idea that Ukraine was run by a "Nazi regime," notwithstanding the fact its people had freely elected a Jewish president. Russian propaganda did not end there. Anti-Semitic rhetoric morphed into anti-Israeli actions. In summer 2022, the Jewish Agency—the largest Jewish nonprofit organization in the world, which facilitates aliyah and runs social programs for Jewish communities abroad—came under growing pressure in Moscow over what were purportedly administrative violations. Russia's justice ministry demanded its closure, claiming that it had illegally collected and transferred data about Russian citizens. In July 2022, the Jewish Agency in Russia put a press release on its website, saying that all its activities and programs continued as planned, and that it was studying the issues raised by the Russian government.

With the onset of the Gaza war in October 2023, the situation worsened. Russia fanned the flames of anti-Israeli and anti-Western sentiment, hoping to score points in its broader anti-Western campaign. In December, Sergey Naryshkin, director of Russia's Foreign Intelligence Service, published an article in the service's magazine. It featured a cartoon that displayed BRICS countries—the Russian bear, the Chinese dragon, the Indian elephant, and so on—fighting the collective West. In the caricature, the US was shown as an eagle, leading the Western camp. Clinging to the eagle's wing was Israel—pictured as a parasite.

Wherever there was vitriol, Margarita Simonyan was sure to chime in. After October 7, she mocked antiwar Russians who had emigrated to Israel. "The country that isn't at war with its neighbors is at war with its neighbors again. Let's welcome the exodus of Russian pacifists. Actually, no, they're not welcome," she wrote. Putin himself revived the anti-Semitic cliché of Jews as "rootless cosmopolitans" in a press conference in late 2024.

As much as Russia's instrumental anti-Semitism was meant to serve Russia's international interests, it was not without its domestic repercussions. In late October 2023, three weeks after Hamas's massacre, the Kremlin watched in disbelief as riots spread in Russia's predominantly Muslim North Caucasus region. Following a particularly nasty incident, in which hundreds of angry men stormed the airport in Makhachkala, Dagestan, to look for Jews from a plane arriving from Israel, the Russian authorities clamped down hard on those involved, eager to deter potential imitators. With the Russian military preoccupied in Ukraine, the last thing Putin needed was unrest at home.

Russia's pro-Palestinian tilt had limited success abroad, too. It registered as cynical and opportunistic among some Arab constituencies. And it did not even give Russia much leverage over Hamas. Among the dozens of hostages Hamas had taken on October 7 were several dual Russian-Israeli citizens. Moscow had to lobby continuously, and hard, to secure their release.

Russia's chill toward Israel impacted the bilateral relationship. Engagement in areas like science, technology, and culture atrophied, also in part due to the effects of Western sanctions against Russia. Yet, at the strategic level, the dialogue continued. Even after October 7, Israel's embassy in Moscow remained fully staffed. Simona Halperin, the ambassador, while vocal in her critique of Russia's position on the Gaza war, attended Putin's fifth presidential inauguration. Most critically, Israel's deconfliction mechanism with Russia in Syria—the phone line between Russia's Khmeymim base and the Israeli Air Force—continued to function. Though the relationship with Russia was turbulent, the Israeli government always thought it paramount that no Russian be harmed by Israeli military action, even as it upped its campaign against the "axis of resistance" after the Majdal Shams attack. The phone line stayed open until December 8, 2024—the day that Syrian leader Bashar al-Assad fell.

SOVIET TIES WITH THE ASSAD FAMILY GO BACK TO THE 1970S, when Hafez al-Assad—Bashar's father—solidified Syria's place in the USSR's orbit. The younger Assad, who came to power in 2000, benefited from Russian military support over the years. When he met a peaceful uprising in 2011 with a violent crackdown that escalated into a bloody conflict, Russia shielded his regime from sanctions at the UN Security Council. Putin was determined that Assad not suffer the same fate as Libyan dictator Muammar al-Qaddafi, who was killed by militias after a UN resolution authorized air strikes against his regime in 2011. In 2015, when Assad's forces controlled barely 20 percent of Syria's territory, Russia launched a military intervention to save him. In 2017, it established what it called the Astana process with Iran and Turkey, negotiating temporary "de-escalation zones." Russia deployed military police from the North Caucasus to help Assad control recaptured areas and collaborated closely with Iran, while maintaining deconfliction channels with Israel, Turkey, and the United States.

Russia's military support for Assad was complemented by patient political backing. Two years prior to the military intervention, Putin had headed off the prospects of US air strikes against Syria, vouching for the destruction of its chemical weapons. Russia stood by the Assad regime in the UN peace process that attempted to negotiate a settlement to the conflict. In January 2018, Russia hosted a Syrian congress in Sochi to great fanfare, where the opposition's hope for an ambitious political transition was dashed; henceforth, it was decided in Sochi, the peace process would focus on rewriting the country's constitution. Many Syrians rightly feared that such an exercise would yield little more than cosmetic political changes. Once the fighting in Syria subsided, Russian diplomats tried to rehabilitate Assad internationally and attract financial support for the country's reconstruction. Through it all, Russia was often frustrated with the Assad regime's refusals to make even the smallest concessions, but it never threw in the towel.

Its investment in Syria brought the Kremlin handsome dividends. Russia expanded and upgraded its bases on Syria's coast, Khmeymim and Tartus, a military footprint right on NATO's southern flank. Its backing of Assad gave it leverage with a host of actors that had a stake in Syria's endgame: the Gulf Arab states, Iran, Israel, Turkey, and, of course, Europe and the United States. Faithfully standing with Assad and showing it to the Americans, Putin cultivated respect across the region and beyond, even among those who loathed the Syrian dictator.

Once the 2022 invasion of Ukraine eclipsed all other foreign policy priorities, Russia's Syria policy acquired an even stronger anti-Western tilt. Russia became less interested in cooperation with Western states, even on humanitarian issues. In summer 2023, it ended its support on the UN Security Council for the continuation of cross-border aid into northwest Syria. Progress toward a genuine political solution to the conflict screeched to a complete halt, with Russia stonewalling the convening of Syria's constitutional committee. Russia also became more aggressive against the US military presence in the country's northeast, harassing US aircraft.

Meanwhile, Moscow, stretched thin because of Ukraine, seemed to calculate it could maintain an acceptable status quo in Syria with limited efforts. It somewhat reduced its military presence, which since 2020 had already morphed into a smaller force suitable to managing low-level conflict. It continued to lobby for Assad's regional rehabilitation, but hit a wall with the Syrian leader's refusal to yield an inch in normalization efforts with Turkey. Syria was suffering from severe economic crisis and dismal governance, but it seemed Russia could live indefinitely with a frozen conflict.

When Russian diplomats descended onto Astana on November 11, 2024, for routine talks on Syria with their Iranian and Turkish counterparts, they expected smooth sailing. Speaking to journalists on the meeting's sidelines, Putin's special representative, Alexander Lavrentiev, delivered Russian talking points with soporific predictability: Western states should drop their unilateral sanctions against the Assad regime. Hayat Tahrir al-Sham (HTS), the opposition group dominating Syria's northwest, was a terrorist organization. The country's constitutional committee would hopefully reconvene soon.

Two and a half weeks later, the Kremlin experienced a rude awakening. On November 27, rebels in Idlib, the last opposition enclave in northern Syria, launched their first major offensive since 2020. Led by HTS, they advanced with speed, entering Syria's second-largest city, Aleppo, for the first time in eight years. Videos circulating online showed military vehicles driving into the city and fighters chanting "Allahu Akbar" ("God is greater"). By the next day, the rebels had already cut off the M5 highway connecting Aleppo with the capital, Damascus, and taken over the junction between two highways, including the M4, which links Aleppo to the Syrian coast—the regime's stronghold and home to Russia's military bases in Khmeymim and Tartus.

Syria's armed groups—or what was left of them, after more than a decade of resistance against Assad's brutal dictatorship—were on the march, and it seemed there was no stopping them. The world watched the dramatic developments unfold with bewilderment, as did Russia. Once the initial shock subsided, Russia intensified its air strikes on Aleppo and Idlib, but failed to significantly slow the rebels' advance. Putin got on the phone with the presidents of Iran and Turkey to discuss the situation. Was Russia about to lose a decade of investment in Syria?

By December 3, the rebels were closing in on the city of Hama in west-central Syria. Once they broke through the government's defensive lines, they released hundreds of inmates from Hama's central prison. "Guys, my country is being liberated. I swear to God, we are inside Hama city," a fighter shouted as he filmed himself by the Alaarbaen Roundabout. Nearby, the rebels mounted the opposition flag—a horizontal triband of green, white, and black with three red stars in the center—as young men cheered, holding their heads in disbelief.

By December 6, the cities of Homs and Deraa came into the rebels' crosshairs. "Our heroic people in Homs, your time has come," a spokesperson for the rebels announced. That day, Russia's foreign ministry advised its citizens to leave Syria. On December 7, with the rebels close to breaking through the outskirts of Damascus, Lavrov gathered with other regional diplomats in Doha. In an interview with Al Jazeera afterward, he tried to put on a brave face. HTS were terrorists, he said, and Russia called for an immediate end to the hostilities. There should be dialogue between the government and the "legitimate opposition."

But the writing was on the wall, and Lavrov seemed to know it. "I am not in the business of guessing what is going to happen," he said, twice. When the journalist compared the unfolding situation in Syria to the Taliban overrunning Afghanistan in summer 2021, Lavrov got frustrated. The Americans had abandoned Afghanistan even more hastily than the Syrian military had caved to the rebels, he blurted out angrily, urging the interviewer to move the conversation to a topic Lavrov would much rather talk about: Ukraine.

It took less than twenty-four hours for the unimaginable to happen. In a statement broadcast live on Syrian national TV, a rebel leader announced in the early hours of December 8 that Syria was free and Assad had been toppled. At the time, I was attending a Middle East conference in Manama, Bahrain, and the Syrian attendees were ecstatic. So were the scenes that I watched from my hotel room, glued to the live dispatches broadcast by Arabic TV channels from Damascus and cities across the country. The rebels opened the prisons, freeing thousands who had languished in inhumane conditions for years, sometimes decades. "It was the best day of my life. An unexplainable feeling. Like someone who had just escaped death," a man called Adnan, freed that day from the notorious Saydnaya prison, said. People rushed to Umayyad Square in Damascus, their chants drowned out by bursts of celebratory gunfire. Some toppled statues of the Assad family; others walked through the empty halls of the presidential palace, taking selfies. Thousands of cars jammed the roads to Damascus as Syrians from all over the country rushed to the capital.

Russia let the Syrian earthquake run its course. With its military capacity consumed in Ukraine, its calculus had changed. If Assad's persistent obstinacy had laid the groundwork, the momentum generated by the rebel offensive did the rest. The Syrian regime's own forces failed to fight, and the weakened Iranians weren't coming to Assad's rescue, either. Putin decided it was time to cut Assad lose and to prioritize negotiating arrangements that might ensure the retention of some Russian influence in a new Syria.

Russia's spin doctors pivoted quickly to distract from Moscow's passivity. Overnight, they stopped calling HTS or other opposition forces "terrorists." Russia would engage with all political forces in Syria, Russian officials said, and focus on ensuring the safety of Russian citizens and assets in the country. Military bloggers panicked that Russia might lose access to its military bases in Khmeymim and Tartus, which had become critical to Russia's military operations in Libya, the CAR, and the Sahel. Few dared to reflect publicly and with candor on Russia's failures in Syria. In one example, Russian military expert Ruslan Pukhov wrote that, in the modern world, victory was only possible in quick and fleeting wars, and that Russia did not have the military resources to intervene effectively outside the former USSR.

Russian state TV seemed eager to draw as little attention as possible to the Syrian debacle. Putin himself made his first comments on December 19, eleven days after Assad had fled to Moscow. He said he wished Syria "peace and calm." He had not yet met with Assad, but Russia had accomplished its mission, he quipped. It had come to Syria ten years earlier to fight terrorists. Since Western countries were now developing relations with the forces that had toppled Assad, Russia must have succeeded. Surely, these forces must have changed and could no longer be "terrorists" if Europe and the United States were extending an olive branch to them, Putin said.

Fifteen months prior, in September 2023, Russia had been able to explain its abandonment of the Karabakh Armenians on the basis of shifting regional realities, while hoping that few would take note. But the Syrian earthquake was of a different order of magnitude. No amount of rhetorical gymnastics could distract from the fact that the jilting of Assad represented the clearest proof, since the invasion of Ukraine, of the limitations of Russian power projection. The anti-Assad Syrians were the little boy in Hans Christian Andersen's tale, pointing out the truth: The emperor had no clothes. With his nakedness exposed, others would henceforth think twice before admiring the beauty of the emperor's garments.

WHEN I VISITED MAJDAL SHAMS JUST WEEKS AFTER ASSAD'S ouster, in January 2025, its residents were still grieving the attack on the children playing soccer, but also feeling a sense of hope from events across the Syrian border. For the first time in many decades, the Druze of Majdal Shams could dream of seeing their relatives across the border again.

"When Assad fell, some people here could not believe it at first," Dolan Abu Saleh, the town's mayor, said while offering me some tea and baklava. "Once it became clear that Assad was really gone, everyone came out into the streets and celebrated, despite the trauma of the attack last summer." Asked what the Russian presence in Syria over the years prior had meant to the people in Majdal Shams, Dolan had mixed feelings. "Russia supported a dictator, a tyrant," he said. But he also conceded that the Russian military intervention had produced some calm and stability across the border in southern Syria.

"The people here are Syrian in their souls," Dolan said. "They felt every spike in the conflict, every casualty in Syria, acutely."

As I headed south from Majdal Shams after a long day in the hills, the sunset engulfed the sky in gorgeous red and gold. Passing ashen ruins of villages abandoned by Syrians in the 1967 war, I spotted a road sign. It read "Trump Heights," in English, Arabic, and Hebrew.

During his first term, Trump had become the first and only foreign leader to recognize Israel's sovereignty over the Golan. Israel thanked Trump by rebranding a settlement after him. I drove on, pondering how Trump's impending second presidential term would impact the United States' position on a post-Assad Syria and its relationship with an Israel that remained embroiled in a war in Gaza and at loggerheads with Iran.

As the world awaited Trump's inauguration, the Israeli government seemed cautiously optimistic. Iranian influence had been pushed out of Syria. The Israeli security establishment, in dealing unprecedented blows to the "axis of resistance," had recovered some credibility after the October 7 debacle. Still, it was not going to take any chances. And so, by January 2025, Israeli forces were steadily advancing from the Golan Heights into the Syrian side of the buffer zone, adamant that Syria's new army never be able to pose a threat to Israel.

Though Russia had been considerably weakened, Netanyahu and those close to him thought it important to remain on speaking terms with Putin—who could still choose to harm Israel, given Russia's defense ties with Iran. Since Trump was ready to reengage Russia, the thinking also went, Israel could surely do the same. And it might actually be better if Russia held on to its bases on the Syrian coast. The other option was a Syria exclusively dominated by Turkey, which would not be in Israel's interest.

That thinking aligned with Russia's priorities. Once Moscow had recovered from the shock of Assad's fall, diplomats scrambled to ensure that Russia would retain its bases. Officials traveled to Damascus in January to negotiate with Syria's new leaders about an array of topics, including the repatriation of funds that Assad had previously transferred to Russia, investments in gas fields and ports, and even a request for Assad's extradition.

The Russians had good reason to believe Syria's new leader, Ahmed al-Sharaa, would be amenable to a compromise. After all, Russia was a veto-yielding member of the UN Security Council and could provide much-needed commodities, like fuel and grain, and potentially weapons for Syria's new national military. And as al-Sharaa looked to consolidate power, he faced many challenges: Notwithstanding his promises to protect Syria's religious minorities—chiefly the Christians, Druze, and Alawites—sectarian killings sent shock waves through the country. In March 2025, Sunni militants killed many Alawites on Syria's coast, and in July, hundreds of people died in fighting between Bedouins and Druze in the country's southwest. Islamic State militants continued to pose a threat. Al-Sharaa also clashed with the Syrian Democratic Forces, a Kurdish-led militia in the northeast, which feared losing its autonomy in the new Syria. Trying to stabilize the fractured domestic landscape, al-Sharaa and his entourage decided it was best to strive for "zero problems" with foreign powers—including Russia, their former nemesis.

Still, Russia's influence in Syria—and the regional clout that came with it—would not be what it was before Assad's fall. The collapse of the Assad regime exposed the limits of Russia's ability to shape events in faraway theaters. And the attacks on October 7 and in Majdal Shams had become part of a string of developments—and would not be the last—to erode Russia's strategic position in the Middle East. Keeping its eyes on the biggest prize, Ukraine, Russia had to exercise some restraint.

And so, the long-carved-up Syrian lands, stretching out from Mount Hermon in the west to the Iraqi border in the east, entered their latest chapter of fragmentation. With the Iranians out and the Russians down, it seemed that Israel, Turkey, and the Gulf Arab states would henceforth be the ones to shape Syria's future.

CHAPTER 9

Phoenix from the Ashes

WHILE RUSSIA WAS SLOWLY LOSING ITS GRIP ON CONFLICTS IN the Middle East, tensions at home were coming to a head.

On June 24, 2023, a Saturday, the staff in the Moscow mayor's office received word that a column of military vehicles was on the move from Rostov-on-Don in southern Russia. It was headed toward the capital on the orders of Yevgeny Prigozhin, head of the Wagner Group, Russia's preeminent mercenary outfit. Prigozhin announced that he would continue his "march of justice" unless he was allowed to confront his detractors in Russia's defense ministry. Moscow's mayor, Sergey Sobyanin, urged residents to stay inside. He suspended outdoor events and tightened security in the capital. Roadblocks were set up to prevent Prigozhin's men from entering the city. A mutiny was underway, the greatest internal challenge mounted to Putin in his twenty-four years in power.

Prigozhin's conflict with defense minister Sergey Shoigu and chief of the general staff Valery Gerasimov had been brewing for some time. Wagner forces had become indispensable in their support for the Russian military campaign in Ukraine. But Prigozhin claimed, increasingly loudly, that the Russian military was starving Wagner forces of ammunition. The blame game escalated through spring 2023, with Prigozhin eventually taking umbrage at Putin himself. "Our soldiers are being killed, and the happy grandpa thinks that everything's fine," he lamented in a video recorded on May 9, Russia's Victory Day. Though he later claimed that by "grandpa" he had meant someone else, he could not fool anyone.

Prigozhin's issues with the defense ministry reached their apogee on June 10, when Shoigu ordered all Wagner forces to sign official contracts by July 1, effectively absorbing them into the ministry. With the stroke of a pen, Shoigu ended Prigozhin's career as mercenary in chief. In a last-ditch effort to win over Putin, Prigozhin launched his "march of justice" one week before Shoigu's deadline. Just hours earlier, Russian expert Dmitry Trenin had told US pundit Ian Bremmer that Putin had given Prigozhin great latitude because he wanted to keep the defense ministry on its toes. "The idea that somehow Prigozhin is a challenge to Putin is just ludicrous," Trenin said.

Ludicrous as it might have been, Putin was no longer amused by Prigozhin's tantrums. And the people of Moscow weren't taking any chances. As the Wagner Group column rode north from Rostov, flights to Istanbul and Astana were selling out quickly. Officials hastily dug antitank ditches into federal highways and deployed military vehicles on the streets. Around 10 a.m., Putin delivered an emergency address to the nation, vowing that "all those who deliberately stepped onto the path of treachery, who prepared an armed insurrection . . . will have to answer before the law and before our people."

Those watching the developments unfold live via social media from abroad were flabbergasted. Erdogan called from Turkey, urging "common sense." India's Prime Minister Modi was on a plane, asking his staff to keep him up to date on the events unfolding in Russia. In Armenia, Prime Minister Pashinyan got on the line with Putin, requesting an update on what was happening in the "friendly country." The Iranians wasted no opportunity to sow conspiracy theories alleging the West was somehow behind Prigozhin's actions. Most circumspect in its reaction was China. Though a couple of tweets by Chinese commentators expressed worry, the government avoided taking an overt position.

Then, the action ended as suddenly as it had started. In the early evening, Prigozhin announced Wagner was standing down. "Right now, the moment has come when blood could be spilled. Therefore . . . we are turning our convoy around and going back to our base camps, according to the plan." Belarus's strongman leader, Alexander Lukashenko, emerged after consulting with Putin to take credit for having convinced Prigozhin to come to his senses. Prigozhin would leave Russia for Belarus, and Wagner fighters who did not take part in the uprising would sign contracts with the defense ministry, he said.

Later that night, Prigozhin could be seen driving away in an SUV from the Russian Army HQ in Rostov, chased by a smattering of adoring fans. "Was this it?" some wondered. "Would he get away with it?"

Conspicuously quiet was Margarita Simonyan, who had showered Prigozhin with praise for months. She reappeared two days later, claiming she had missed all the drama because she was on a boat cruising the Volga. Simonyan issued a belated "thank you" to her "*nachalnik*" (boss) for having dealt with the mess so efficiently. It came in response to another speech by Putin, in which he praised Russia's armed forces for having averted the tragic outcome that Russia's enemies—"the neo-Nazis in Kyiv, their Western patrons and other national traitors"—had hoped for, namely for "society to break up and perish in a bloody feud." That was an exaggeration. Prigozhin had no intention of challenging Putin's hold on power. His "march of justice" had been a last-ditch effort to prevent the defense ministry from subordinating Wagner—a move that would have greatly diminished his own power. To achieve that, Prigozhin had taken a massive gamble, and it ended in a crushing failure.

The Kremlin was eager to sweep the episode under the rug. Within days, Russian newspapers read as if it had never happened. Yet Prigozhin's fate remained the source of intense speculation. At first, he vanished, only to resurface on social media and at the Russia-Africa Summit in July. Wagner forces, relocated to Belarus, continued their training.

Then, on August 23, a plane carrying Prigozhin and some of his closest entourage crashed en route from Moscow to St. Petersburg. Putin claimed that the plane went down because the Wagner leadership was drunk or on drugs and then set off hand grenades during the flight. Prigozhin's funeral in St. Petersburg was held in private, with police stationed outside the cemetery to keep away nosy onlookers. Prigozhin's death marked the dramatic finale in the downfall of a man who had overseen the rise of a massive mercenary force, accompanied by a sprawling business and media empire whose tentacles reached from Libya, across Africa, into the Middle East.

Before Prigozhin, Russia had a long mercenary tradition. Czars used private and semi-state forces for centuries to quell internal unrest and protect Russia's borders. The most famous example are perhaps the Cossacks, a people that played a key role in extending Russia's imperial frontiers. The Soviet Union continued that legacy, enlisting "volunteers," partisans, and guerrillas to fight its wars. Putin's reliance on Wagner thus built on centuries-long Russian practice. Yet no individual mercenary in modern Russian history had amassed as much power as Prigozhin. An avatar for Putin's expansionist agenda, he knew how to wield informal influence while making himself useful to the Russian state—even indispensable in the war against Ukraine. That is, as long as he knew his place and didn't challenge Putin.

Going forward, Russian mercenaries would need to be kept on a much tighter leash; of that much, the Kremlin was certain. The appearance of business as usual between Prigozhin's attempted mutiny and death had been a facade. Behind the scenes, the Kremlin was scheming over how to retain its military ventures in Africa once it decided to rid itself of Prigozhin. The defense ministry would henceforth be in charge. For Africa's strongmen in cahoots with Russia, that was just as well. "If Moscow decides to withdraw [the Wagners] and send us the Beethovens or the Mozarts . . . we will have them," Fidèle

Gouandjika, a top adviser to CAR President Touadéra, said a few days after Prigozhin's death.

HAILING FROM ST. PETERSBURG, PUTIN'S HOMETOWN, PRIGOZHIN spent most of the 1980s behind bars for robbery and theft. Once out of prison in the lawless 1990s, he set up several restaurants. They were, as Russia watchers Anna Arutunyan and Mark Galeotti write in their biography of Prigozhin, a "time of networking and opportunistic deal-making . . . when nothing was certain and everything was up for grabs." One of the restaurants, New Island, became so acclaimed that Putin celebrated his birthday there in 2003. Years later, Prigozhin's catering company, Concord, was contracted to supply food to the Kremlin.

Eventually, the prisoner-turned-Putin's chef embarked on more daring business ventures. In 2013, employees of a conventional Russian private security company, the Moran Security Group, set up a new entity in Hong Kong called the Slavonic Corps. It deployed to Syria to assist regime forces in recapturing oil facilities from the Islamic State. Suffering from logistical and operational problems, the Slavonic Corps was soon dismantled and its commanders transitioned into a new entity called the Wagner Group. Wagner then took part in Russian operations in Ukraine in 2014. Over time, Prigozhin created a sprawling business empire as part of the group, which he oversaw while letting field commanders run operations. But as a military outfit, the Wagner Group was tethered from the beginning to the GRU, Russia's military intelligence service, relying on Russian military infrastructure and GRU-issued passports. Prigozhin tacitly carried out Putin's bidding while enjoying a great deal of latitude.

After Russia's intervention in the Syrian civil war in 2015, the Russian government brought in Wagner as an assault force and to reinforce the militaries of local allies—tasks that allowed it to morph, over time, into an elite infantry of sorts. It took on a leading role in the recapture of the Syrian city of Palmyra from the Islamic State in

March 2016. Wagner's role proved lucrative. Like its predecessor, the Slavonic Corps, Wagner signed contracts with the Syrian government for commercially attractive ventures such as guarding oil and gas fields and phosphate mines.

Wagner also started operating in Libya in 2015, keeping a relatively low profile as it engaged in training and demining services for the Libyan National Army (LNA) in the country's east. Its position became more prominent in 2019 when Wagner took on an active combat role to support the LNA's stalled advance toward the capital of Tripoli. After the conclusion of a ceasefire in 2020, Wagner focused on guarding oil facilities in central and eastern Libya, and companies affiliated with it secured contracts in a range of sectors. Over the years, Wagner also came to use its Libyan bases as a logistics hub for its expanding activities elsewhere in Africa.

Wagner's involvement in the Tripoli offensive shined unprecedented light on its cruelty. In September 2019, armed men from the Wagner Group kidnapped thirty-three-year-old Mohammed Enbis, his father, two brothers, and brother-in-law after days of fierce fighting near the capital. They were blindfolded and taken to a Russian "base camp." Throughout the ordeal, Enbis and his relatives were tortured. Their hands were bound, they were regularly doused with water, and they were accompanied to the bathroom at gunpoint. The morning after they were taken, the men drove them to a concrete house on a farm, bound and blindfolded them, and ordered them to kneel. As bullets rained down, Enbis could hear his relatives fall to the ground. He threw himself down, pretending to be dead, an ingenious reaction that would save his life. After a short while, he heard the Russians' car leaving. One of his brothers survived, too, with a gunshot wound to the leg, but the others were dead. Enbis was sure the men were from Wagner, because of their blue eyes, advanced weapons skills, and, most important, the fact they all spoke Russian.

By the time Mohammed Enbis suffered his ordeal, Wagner was busy consolidating its foothold in the Central African Republic, too. The group had arrived in the CAR in 2018 and played a major role in bringing the government and armed groups to sign a peace agreement a year later. In Mali, Wagner emerged on the scene after a 2021 coup brought to power a military junta that pivoted away from the country's traditional international partners, chiefly France. It also built a presence in Sudan and tried to expand elsewhere. At one point or another, Wagner operated in Botswana, Burundi, the Democratic Republic of the Congo, Lesotho, Madagascar, and Nigeria, the Ukrainian open-source intelligence agency Molfar has claimed.

Across these different Africa operations, Wagner's services ranged from military training and advice, via providing personal security for leaders and protecting natural resources and mines, to higher-risk counterinsurgency operations. Each mission set carried its own risks, but across the board Wagner always relied on the Russian defense ministry for equipment, logistics, and materiel.

With the invasion of Ukraine came the Wagner Group's chance to prove its utility to the homeland like never before. Needing manpower and skills, the defense ministry turned to Prigozhin for help one month into the war. Wagner forces first appeared in Ukraine's Mariupol. While Wagner often deployed alongside Russian airborne forces, its decisive role in the battle for Popasna in May became a turning point, elevating the group's importance to the Kremlin.

No stranger to Russia's prisons, Prigozhin soon started an aggressive recruitment drive, touring Russia's penal colonies and luring thousands of convicts with the promise of plentiful payments and pardons. He also took Wagner's advertising to massive billboards across Russian cities, with slogans like "Motherland, Honor, Blood, Bravery. WAGNER." The outfit even posted ads on Russian porn sites. In one example, an ad showed a woman licking a lollipop as a female voice says, "We are the most fucking amazing private army in the world."

Wagner's activities in Africa always remained separate—and therefore largely insulated—from its Ukraine operations. Whereas in Ukraine, Wagner rapidly expanded by taking on tens of thousands of untrained convicts, in Africa, it relied on experienced field commanders who oversaw a manageable number of highly trained fighters. By

March 2023, one year into the war, Wagner retained an estimated total of 3,500 to 4,500 mercenaries in Africa.

Notwithstanding his successes, Prigozhin's relationship with the Kremlin remained informal and, therefore, fragile. Unlike Sechin, who had been close to Putin for a long time, or Nabiullina, who impressed the president with her technocratic skills, Prigozhin never truly made it into Putin's entourage. "He never made the crucial jump from servant of the czar to friend," Arutunyan and Galeotti write. Russia's involvement in Ukraine's Donbas, in Syria, and across Africa opened space for savvy operators who knew how to wield informal influence and be useful to the Russian state, while being allowed to amass a fortune for themselves—as long as they did not threaten the Kremlin.

After the failed mutiny, the Kremlin moved quickly to ready Russia's sprawling mercenary business for a post-Prigozhin future.

The Central African Republic was a special case. When Prigozhin died in late August, Touadéra's government declared a day of national mourning, as journalist Ephrem Yalike-Ngonzo, at that point still in Bangui, recalled. It went to show just how powerful the Wagner Group had become in the country. In September, Touadéra gave an interview at the presidential palace in which he confirmed that Russian fighters would stay in the CAR and continue to provide security at a "difficult moment." The CAR would be the only country where little changed after Prigozhin's death.

Elsewhere, the situation was quite different. In July and August, Russian officials traveled to other Wagner playgrounds to lay the groundwork for a new structure called Africa Corps. Russia's military intelligence was to provide the legal mechanisms for Wagner fighters to join the new corps. Unlike Wagner, Africa Corps would have official state-to-state relations with its host countries, and forces would be put under the military's chain of command. While putting Africa Corps in place, the Kremlin also cracked down on Wagner domestically, raiding its offices and usurping its social media infrastructure. Africa Corps started recruiting for a wide range of positions and promised that those serving would receive the same benefits as Russian troops fighting on the frontlines in Ukraine.

The nature of Wagner's rebranding into Africa Corps differed from country to country. In Syria, the Kremlin asked Assad to oust Wagner forces unwilling to sign new contracts with the defense ministry. In Libya, where the LNA had become increasingly wary of Wagner's overconfidence, the hosts seemed happy for Africa Corps to take charge.

The Sahel became a particular area of interest for the Russians. The US had for years fought terrorist groups in this strategically important, yet impoverished strip of land stretching from the Atlantic coast to the Red Sea. It was joined by European countries eager to hem in mass illegal migration from Africa to the EU. Western countries' failures in stemming militants and improving security, compounded by growing resentment of France as a former colonial power, provided an opening for Russia—which came armed with its aggressive anticolonial rhetoric and hundreds of Africa Corps troops.

In Mali, Africa Corps would for a while operate alongside the Wagner Group, which Prigozhin had inserted into the country back in 2021. In July 2024, Wagner made a disastrous push into separatist territory at Tinzaouten, their forces ambushed in what would mark one of the deadliest attacks against Russian forces in Africa in years. The ambush gave Africa Corps an opportunity to assert itself in Mali—and ammunition to those Russian military officers who argued Russia should scale back its participation in such high-risk operations and focus instead on training local host forces.

That is precisely what Africa Corps was already doing in neighboring Niger and Burkina Faso. In Niger, a military coup occurred one month before Prigozhin's death, opening a window for Russia to make a play for an additional African stronghold. At that point, the United States kept more than a thousand soldiers in Niger and operated a drone base in the country's north to surveil extremist groups across the Sahel. After the coup, as Niger's military junta tilted closer to Russia, that partnership with the US became increasingly precarious. Through fall 2023 and spring 2024, Russian military delegations met with Nigerien counterparts on several occasions. The US scrambled to turn the tide, but a visit by an American delegation in March went awry. On state television, the junta denounced the Americans' "condescending attitude" and declared the military relationship with the US over. Meanwhile, the first Africa Corps troops arrived, setting up camp at the same military base that still housed the soon-to-depart US forces. Africa Corps also deployed to Burkina Faso and, eventually, Equatorial Guinea. When Burkina Faso, Mali, and Niger announced the formation of the Alliance of Sahel States, a mutual defense pact, in September 2023, Russia welcomed the move and promised arms and training to their newly formed joint force.

Russia indicated appetite for more. Through 2024, it worked hard to reopen consulates, embassies, and Russian Houses in a number of additional countries—activities that usually forebode an interest in a military presence. It also laid the groundwork for military cooperation agreements with Togo and Benin, both located on the Gulf of Guinea.

The emergence and expansion of Africa Corps hinted at a broader Kremlin strategy aimed at giving Russia a sustainable presence in West Africa. Resentment over the legacies of Western colonialism and more recent interventions gave Russia a convenient entry point. Not only was the region rich in minerals but permanent port access in the Gulf of Guinea would allow Russia to project maritime power into the southern Mediterranean and Atlantic Ocean. The Kremlin likely recognized that Russia would lack the bandwidth to build up a serious presence while it remained bogged down in Ukraine. But it could establish a foothold on which to build something more ambitious in the future. Africa, it seemed, had become Putin's new frontier.

It was critical to the new effort that Africa Corps adopt a low-risk strategy that could be accomplished with a modest footprint—not engage in the kinds of dangerous counterinsurgency operations Wagner had conducted. It would focus predominantly on training local forces. And it would be tethered closely to the Russian state. No one would ever be allowed to become as powerful as the mercurial Prigozhin.

But whether the Russian defense ministry could make do entirely without Prigozhin-type entrepreneurial figures remained an open question. Surely, someone would need to pay for an expanding Africa Corps business. Prigozhin's commercial enterprises had made Wagner's Africa operations self-financing, at least to an extent. There were signs that Russia would try to translate Africa Corps's presence into commercial gains, too, seeking access to gold mines in the Sahel, for instance. With time, new mini-Prigozhins might appear on the continent to help Russia advance such commercial ventures.

ON DECEMBER 4, 2024, A FESTIVE CEREMONY TOOK PLACE IN Bangui, the CAR's capital. Under the watchful eye of the CAR's top military brass, a new bronze statue went up. It was the second statue erected in honor of the Wagner Group, complementing the one Paula Slier had spotted on her reporting trip two years prior. Only this one was of the man himself: Prigozhin, in bulletproof clothing and holding a walkie-talkie, standing next to his right-hand man Dmitry Utkin, who held an AK-47 rifle.

Four days later, events some 2,300 miles north would throw Russia's Africa operations into a state of crisis. As rebels in Damascus toppled the government of Bashar al-Assad, it became unclear if Russia would be able to retain its two most important military sites in the country, which served as logistics bases supporting Africa Corps's activities. By mid-January 2025, initial panic in Russia's military blogger scene gave way to cautious optimism that Moscow would probably strike a deal with Syria's new leaders. Still, to hedge its bets, Russia continued to invest in expanding its bases in Libya, the next refueling hub for Russia after Syria. Around the same time, videos showed a large Russian convoy composed of one hundred military vehicles rolling into Mali. The movements suggested that Moscow was determined to not let this second calamity in eighteen months—first Prigozhin's mutiny, now Assad's ouster—derail its play for Africa.

Amid the intense scrutiny of Africa Corps's adaptation to Syria's shifting realities, one man was determined to not let the Wagner Group's atrocities be forgotten. In Washington DC, a far distance from Russia's African playgrounds, lawyers were busy readying a pile of paperwork. Mohammed Enbis, the victim of Wagner's cruelty and torture, was taking Yevgeny Prigozhin's son, Pavel, to court.

Enbis had initially filed a lawsuit against Yevgeny Prigozhin in July 2023, just weeks before the Wagner chief died. With his civil case, brought under the 1991 Torture Victim Protection Act, Enbis sought accountability for the slaughter of his relatives. After Yevgeny Prigozhin's death, the lawyers shifted their focus to Pavel. The twenty-five-year-old inherited most of his father's assets, and Enbis's lawyers saw in him the rightful heir to his father's legal problems. On February 4, 2025, Enbis's lawyers sent a summons in civil action to Pavel Prigozhin electronically and explored alternative means to service him through 2025. "We want justice for Mohammed Enbis's family," Omar Tabuni of the Libyan American Alliance, which supported Enbis, told me, "and we want to deter others from acting with such impunity in Libya."

Just as the son had inherited the father's treasures and troubles, Africa Corps had inherited much of what the Wagner Group used to be—while morphing it into something new. Confronted with unforeseen circumstances, Russia had repeatedly proven able to adapt its military ventures in Africa. Launching its invasion in February 2022, Russia had managed to insulate its Africa operations from the carnage in Ukraine. Once its mercenary in chief, dizzy with success, launched a mutiny, the government midwifed a new structure, Africa Corps, to take over and even expand Russia's Africa operations. Like a Phoenix from the ashes, Russia's mercenary enterprise had emerged from Prigozhin's death more controllable—though perhaps also less nimble and less good at making money.

In adapting its business model, it is possible that Moscow fueled the fragmentation of the security assistance landscape in Africa. As of 2025, players like China, Iran, Turkey, and even Hungary were stepping up their own games in and around the Sahel, spreading their soft power, selling their weapons, and, in some cases, sending their mercenaries. With Africa Corps refocusing on training and routine security assistance—and eschewing the types of higher-risk missions that had marked Wagner's baptism of fire—it remained an open question whether these other players would henceforth step in more aggressively to compete with Russia.

More than anything, Russia's deployment of Africa Corps went to show how an obsessive anti-Western agenda dictated its foreign policy. Russia's modest foothold in Libya, in the Sahel, and on the Gulf of Guinea would give it a pressure valve on NATO's southern shores, but it was not strictly required for Russia's own security. At best, it was economically attractive to a handful of individuals in the Russian military. Their activities of dubious benefit to the Russian people, Africa Corps mercenaries had become the latest frontiersmen in Russia's battle to outlast the West.

Part V

FRAGMENTING INTERNATIONAL ORDER

CHAPTER 10

When the Elephants Fight . . .

DURING WORLD WAR II, THE UNITED STATES, THE SOVIET UNION, and Britain took a fateful decision: to build the atomic bomb. By 1964, France and China had joined the nuclear club, and the science of fusing and splitting the atom was becoming more widely accessible. These developments raised the specter that nuclear weapons might appear elsewhere. Eager to nip that threat in the bud, Washington and Moscow led an effort to negotiate an international nonproliferation treaty, the NPT. Signed in 1968, it would stand on three pillars: preventing the further spread of nuclear weapons, encouraging nuclear disarmament by the existing five nuclear-weapons states, and promoting the peaceful uses of nuclear energy to the benefit of all.

To take stock of the progress achieved on the NPT's pillars, its adherents convene every five years for a review conference whose success is measured against a simple standard: Can participating states agree on a final document, sign off on a text that summarizes their shared assessment of the treaty's current health and of what efforts are needed going forward? Past conferences failed to meet this bar on several occasions, including in 2015, given disagreements over language regarding the establishment of a zone free of weapons of mass destruction (WMD) in the Middle East.

When Gustavo Zlauvinen started preparing for the 2022 conference, which was originally scheduled for 2020 but was postponed several times due to COVID, expectations were modest. The multilateral nuclear order—a kaleidoscope of organizations, treaties like the NPT, and regional nuclear agreements—had been under stress for years. The NPT, in particular, suffered from a growing legitimacy crisis because of stalled progress on the second pillar, nuclear disarmament. The failure to produce a consensus document at the 2015 conference had left a bitter aftertaste. Now, Zlauvinen faced the difficult task of steering the conference, convened in August 2022, six months into Russia's invasion of Ukraine.

"I knew that the invasion was a game changer," Zlauvinen told me when we met at Vienna's iconic Café Central in fall 2024. Few were better suited to preside over the review conference at such a delicate moment. A career diplomat, the Argentinian had considerable experience working through difficult problems related to nuclear weapons in intricate international settings. In the 1990s, Zlauvinen was chief of staff to the executive chairman of the UN Special Commission for the Disarmament of Iraq, tasked with ridding Saddam Hussein's Iraq of WMD. When the Iranian and North Korean nuclear problems took diplomatic center stage in the early 2000s, he represented the International Atomic Energy Agency (IAEA) at the UN in New York.

Once representatives from 151 countries arrived in New York's ungodly August heat and humidity braced for four weeks of marathon diplomacy, Zlauvinen tried to manage expectations. The most important thing, he told everyone from the outset, was to have a meaningful exchange on all substantive issues related to the NPT. Worried that Ukraine might overshadow the entire agenda, he suggested, "Let's have those fireworks during the first week. And then, let's get to work!"

But this year, US and Russian diplomats were not much on speaking terms because of Ukraine—as representatives of "depository states" of the NPT, they carried a special responsibility for the treaty and had in the past coordinated on sensitive issues during review conferences. On top of that, Moscow sent only a low-level delegation to New York, telegraphing a reduced interest in the negotiations. Senior US diplomat Tom Countryman, asked to come out of retirement in 2021 to support the US delegation, likened his Russian counterparts to "the junior varsity team."

As the conference got underway, polemics between Russia and Ukraine polluted the atmosphere. At one point, Countryman recalled, Russia demanded the expulsion of the head of the Ukrainian delegation, who wore a T-shirt that read *Russkiy voyenny korabl, idi nakhuy* ("Russian warship, go fuck yourself"). But the overwhelming majority of non-Western states focused on the treaty, just as Zlauvinen had hoped.

In the second week, delegations moved into three main committees (which were open to observers) and three closed-door subsidiary bodies. Diplomats sparred over issues like naval nuclear propulsion, nuclear sharing, commitments to disarmament, and language emphasizing gender—for instance, the gender dimensions of the effects of nuclear weapons testing, or the important role women can and must play in nuclear abolition. But it soon became clear that draft wording related to Ukraine was especially contentious, causing friction among the committee tasked with discussing the peaceful uses of nuclear energy. Russia objected to language related to Ukraine's Zaporizhzhia Nuclear Power Plant, which Russian forces had occupied days into the invasion. At the time, there were constant reports about the plant being shelled, which exacerbated fears of a nuclear accident. Many parties in New York pushed for explicit language referencing Russia's responsibility for the deteriorating safety at the plant, something Moscow vehemently refused.

Zlauvinen checked in with the Russian delegation on a daily basis. Had it been up to them, he told me, there would have been no reference to Ukraine in any of the discussions whatsoever. "But I said, 'No, sorry, that's not going to happen. We have to have references, in general, to whatever is affecting the implementation of the treaty. So, if there's an attack on a nuclear power station, it has to be mentioned.'" The Russians accepted that approach in principle, he recalled, but kept coming to him with requests on many other issues related to the NPT. Zlauvinen and his team shuffled between parties, consulted delegations individually, drafted language, redrafted, negotiated into the night, and slept very little. Toward the end of the third week, Zlauvinen instituted what he called "small groups" to negotiate compromise language where it was still elusive.

As the fourth and final conference week got underway, Zlauvinen knew he had to wrap things up soon. On Wednesday, before presenting his latest draft to all parties in the evening, he used his prerogative as president to soften references to the Ukraine war that could still irk Russia, as well as to conflictual issues important to others. "The Ukrainian delegation went ballistic," he told me, and others were upset about compromise language on this or that aspect, too. But Zlauvinen did what he felt was necessary to steer the delicate diplomatic dance toward consensus. He had reason to feel cautiously optimistic. On Thursday morning, he bumped into a member of the Russian delegation whom he had known for years. The man tapped him on the shoulder and said, "Good work, Gustavo."

Zlauvinen compiled a list of what he guessed might be outstanding irritants for a number of delegations. He then started a process he called "speed dating"—sitting with the head of one delegation at a time to resolve their most important red lines, hoping he could use concessions achieved to get others to drop their own objections. "No one got everything, no one got nothing," he explained to me. He called the Russians for their speed date in the afternoon, expecting little need for haggling, since he assumed he had already taken care of their core demands the day prior. The full Russian delegation showed up for the meeting, which was unusual. "I gave you a lot," Zlauvinen started off. "How do you feel?" To his amazement, the head of the delegation started proposing new edits, though none of them of consequence to the main sensitive issues. He thought Moscow had instructed the diplomats to play hardball. "It's too late for all this," he responded. "I already gave you enough."

By that point, Zlauvinen had a few hours left to finalize the draft document and email it out so all delegations could seek a green light from their capitals overnight, before the final plenary the next day. If he could not produce agreement soon, the conference would end without a consensus document, yet again. He sat down with his team to comb through the language, paragraph by paragraph. They worked late into the night, implementing changes that came from the speed dating, striking out entire sentences here, removing references to Ukraine there, in an effort to make the text acceptable to all.

On Friday morning, delegations had heard back from their governments and were messaging Zlauvinen with their final verdicts. "Paris is okay." "London is okay." "DC is okay." "Brasilia is okay." "Cairo is okay." "Beijing is okay." Excitement took hold among Zlauvinen's team. Could it be true? Could they really have achieved the seemingly impossible—agreement among all parties? Zlauvinen had not, however, heard from the Russians. He messaged them around noon, asking, "Can I take it that you're OK?" Within minutes, he received a negative reply by text. The delegation head followed up with a call to say the draft was unacceptable to Moscow because Russia's requests had not been taken into account.

"It is my understanding that I've given you your red lines," Zlauvinen said.

"No, that's not the case," the Russian retorted. "Moscow is asking for everything." He suggested they meet, yet again, to go over Russia's demands.

"It's too late to reopen the text for negotiation," Zlauvinen insisted. "Please plead with Moscow to take the deal, to accept what it is. Everybody else is onboard. Or at least, do not block consensus, and then disassociate yourself from the text or certain paragraphs." He hung up.

Zlauvinen hustled to get last-minute backing for his appeals to Moscow. He called the office of the UN secretary-general to ask him to weigh in with the Russians. He got on the phone with the Chinese, probing whether Beijing could lean on Moscow. He called other individuals in regular contact with Putin at the time. He also contacted the Americans and said, "We have a problem. I'm trying to resolve it. But you have to assure me that Ukraine is not going to block consensus in the end." The Americans told him he need not worry about Ukraine. Zlauvinen kept postponing the final plenary, by one hour after another.

He was in a state of limbo when his phone finally pinged at 4 p.m. It was the head of the Russian delegation. "Let's meet," the message read.

They convened in a secure room behind the podium of the massive UN General Assembly hall, the Russian bringing his deputy while Zlauvinen corralled a colleague as a witness. "What's going on?" Zlauvinen asked once they closed the metal door meant to prevent eavesdropping. The Russian diplomat seemed nervous. "Moscow has a problem with your text," he said. He handed Zlauvinen a piece of paper listing several demands. Zlauvinen glanced at them and knew straight away they were unacceptable. "But I gave you so much already and I paid a huge political price for that," Zlauvinen protested. "I gave you your red lines." The Russian looked straight at him and replied, "Yes, those were our *red* lines. But these"—he motioned at the paper—"these are our *black* lines."

Zlauvinen explained he could not take the new demands to the other delegations at such a late stage, as that would have meant reopening the entire text for discussion. The Russians then asked him to open the final plenary and inform everyone that, based on his informal consultations, there was no consensus and he as president would therefore withdraw the text. "Tell Moscow that I'm not going to do that," Zlauvinen responded.

It was 7:20 p.m. by the time Zlauvinen called the final plenary to order and posed the all-important question: "May I now ask if the conference is willing to adopt . . . the final document?" Zlauvinen adjusted his glasses and looked up from his papers into the wide hall, his index finger resting on his chin. He knew exactly what was about to happen. "I see that one delegation is asking for the floor," he said. "I give the floor to the representative of the Russian Federation."

Addressing the plenum, the Russian diplomat claimed that many delegations were dissatisfied with the final text. Russia had been willing to work constructively toward common ground until the very end and was still happy to continue such work, he said, but it simply could not support the document in its current form. Russia had blown up the conference. Others had done so before, and Russia's shenanigans in and of themselves would not precipitate a catastrophic collapse of the nuclear nonproliferation regime. Still, the betrayal came at a time of heightened nuclear dangers—a nuclear-armed state, Russia, had just invaded a non-nuclear-armed state, Ukraine—and growing stress on multilateral diplomacy more generally. In the months and years ahead, more states would probably question the purpose of the entire process and the degree to which it was worth committing resources to it.

The Russian delegation in New York had extremely little leeway, Zlauvinen thought. "They were not calling the shots. I knew that I was dealing with Moscow," he said. I asked him if he thought they'd been playing him from the beginning. "I've asked myself this question so many times since the moment this happened." With hindsight, Zlauvinen thought Moscow had hoped all along that others would block consensus. The introduction of "black lines" came as a last resort, once Russian officials back in the capital realized other delegations were prepared to support the document. Moscow did not table those "black lines" earlier because it knew only too well that, had it done so, Zlauvinen would never have made his other concessions to Russia, including considerably diluting the language on Ukraine. "They hoped somebody else was going to do the dirty job, and that they didn't have to kill the baby."

RUSSIA'S OBSTRUCTIONISM AT THE 2022 NPT REVIEW CONFERENCE was not new, but part of a long-standing tradition. Through the

2010s, and especially after the annexation of Crimea, Russia frequently clashed with Western states in various multilateral negotiating bodies. Tensions ran particularly high at the Organization for the Prohibition of Chemical Weapons (OPCW) in The Hague, where countries sparred over Syria's alleged retention and use of chemical weapons, and later over Russia's alleged use of nerve agents in the poisoning of the Skripal family in the UK and of Russian opposition figure Alexey Navalny. Russia claimed Western states were violating OPCW rules by replacing consensus decisions with voting and thereby exploiting the organization to push their anti-Russian agendas.

Writing from Moscow in 2020, Russian journalist Fyodor Lukyanov argued that Russia was becoming increasingly skeptical of international cooperation if it meant "global structures issuing rules." Instead, Moscow would go its own way when required, he warned, joining efforts with like-minded countries. Russia was already doing that on occasion. Starting in 2017, for example, Russia predominantly used the Astana Group, with Iran and Turkey, to discuss the Syrian conflict, rather than turning to the UN.

The invasion of Ukraine further hardened Russia's posture, while leading it to search for new formats and friends. This was partially a function of Russia's anti-Western tilt, and partially the West's own doing. Immediately after the invasion, Western capitals canceled most government-to-government contacts with Russia. Western diplomacy with Russia atrophied to just a few exceptional issues and engagement at the UN. Russia reacted by reorienting its diplomatic machinery. By summer 2022, the ministry of foreign affairs had reassigned 90 percent of its diplomatic staff serving in Western states to its Moscow headquarters or embassies in "friendly countries."

In 2022, Switzerland joined the sanctions campaign against Russia, dampening Moscow's appetite to convene in this traditional venue. Speaking on the sidelines of a meeting on Syria in Geneva in June 2022, special envoy Alexander Lavrentiev suggested the Syrian Constitutional Committee be henceforth moved to a more neutral location. Around the same time, Moscow complained of difficulties in obtaining visas for its diplomats to attend events under UN auspices in New York and floated the hardly viable idea of relocating UN headquarters to another country.

Amid a collapse in direct Russian–Western contacts, several non-Western states made their debuts on the big stage of international diplomacy. Turkey emerged to host initial Russian–Ukrainian peace talks in spring 2022. The Gulf Arab states jumped in, assisting with prisoner exchanges between Russia and Ukraine. In late 2022, Cairo was chosen as the venue to convene US–Russia discussions on nuclear arms control.

In legacy multilateral institutions and negotiating bodies, the consequences of Russian–Western tensions were especially complex. Early into the invasion, a number of European states forbade their diplomats from speaking with their Russian counterparts. Western diplomats would leave the room when the Russians took the floor and tried to exclude Russian officials from events in protest of its aggression against Ukraine. In summer 2023, I traveled to Vienna to observe an NPT meeting and returned a few weeks later for the IAEA General Conference. On the sidelines of both gatherings, I spoke with diplomats from many non-Western countries who said they felt "caught in the middle," "uncomfortable," or "frustrated" amid skyrocketing Russian–Western tensions. Some felt pressure from Western governments to take sides against Russia. One diplomat from an African country summarized the prevailing feeling among small, developing states with a proverb: "When the elephants fight, the grass gets trampled."

The UN First Committee saw an increased tendency toward voting, paragraph by paragraph, on resolutions that used to be passed by consensus in years past. This was partially because Russia tabled new resolutions to compete with Western-backed ones, but also because states exploited the rules of procedure—such as the right to introduce amendments on the floor—more liberally. Russia was especially savvy in playing such games. One diplomat I spoke with mused that the Russians "must be sleeping with the rules of procedure under their pillow."

Russia also stepped up its engagement with non-Western states in multilateral bodies, using every available venue to solidify ties with new partners. It requested observer status at the Group of 77 (G77), a coalition of developing countries at the UN, and reached out to regional organizations like the Agency for the Prohibition of Nuclear Weapons in Latin America and the Caribbean. No longer interested in using legacy fora to advance cooperation with Western countries, Russia focused on trying to corral non-Western states in support of its agenda.

FROM RUSSIA'S PERSPECTIVE, SUCH DIPLOMATIC MANEUVERING was necessary if the country was to prevail against the West. Mikhail Ivanovich Ulyanov has spent his entire career advancing Russia's agenda in these complex multilateral settings, and today serves as ambassador to Russia's permanent mission to international organizations in Vienna. "I have absolutely no interest in bilateral affairs, I find them boring," Ulyanov told me as we sat down on opposite sides of a massive, dark wooden table in the grand protocol hall next to the Russian mission.

At sixty-six, Ulyanov struck me as the quintessential Russian diplomat, with an impressive mustache, stern demeanor, and rare smile. Speaking with him for a good hour and a half, I wanted to understand what had changed for Russia in multilateral diplomacy since the invasion of Ukraine.

"Our approach to multilateral diplomacy did not fundamentally change in 2022," Ulyanov told me. "Multilateralism, as well as multipolarity, remain the foundation of our foreign policy, but it is true that we choose our partners more carefully." To Ulyanov, it became harder to find "common language" with Western states. On top of the stress caused by the war, Ulyanov deplored Western states' excessive focus on what he called "liberal globalist ideas," obsessing over gender-related language even in the context of negotiating technical resolutions on issues like radiological security.

Since February 2022, some diplomats had stopped greeting him in the corridors, but many still did "with a certain sympathy," he said. Those who did were engaging in "a dangerous business," he added mockingly. "The Poles or the Balts, they pay attention which Western countries betray the West's collective position by communicating positively with Russian diplomats." He felt the Western chill toward Russia in other ways. "When the special military operation began," Ulyanov said, using the Kremlin's official euphemism for the war, "some smart heads in Brussels decided that if the Russians uttered the words *Nazism* and *genocide*, then everyone should stand up and leave the hall," he recalled.

Other times, he said, he felt support from some non-Western nations, as during a 2024 meeting of the IAEA board of governors, when someone laid out paper flowers in the colors of the Ukrainian flag on the tables of all those who they believed to be "supporters" of Ukraine. "A number of countries—Singapore, some Latin Americans—raised their hands," Ulyanov recalled, visibly satisfied, "and they said, 'What kind of disgrace is this? We don't need this kind of political signaling, we don't support this.' " To Ulyanov, isolating Russia had never been possible. "Have a look at the map! The collective West can isolate us only in the western direction, and even there not completely. But it is impossible to isolate us to the east and south."

Ulyanov spent a lot of time thinking about messaging. He acknowledged that, "when the special military operation started," Russia's "explanatory" work had been insufficient, but "now we are learning, little by little." He added that Russia's anti-neocolonial narrative was an extremely useful "ploy"—"call it propagandistic, if you wish, but this is actually based on reality, a truth that works well." Ulyanov started using his Twitter account for broader messaging purposes. "Though I would prefer to write on the topics of our international organizations," he explained, "we are now in such times . . . that I have to write something on issues that seem important."

I was already well aware. Ulyanov's Twitter had become known among Russia watchers for channeling the main currencies of

Moscow's wartime discourse. In summer 2022, his account became the source of widespread ridicule when the ambassador got into an argument with a member of the North Atlantic Fella Organization (NAFO), a global internet army employing memes to challenge Russia. Tussling with a NAFO influencer over his post about shelling in Ukraine's Donbas, Ulyanov eventually responded: "You pronounced this nonsense. Not Me." The phrase became a rallying cry for NAFO and won it prominent supporters in Ukraine and beyond. On another occasion, Ulyanov tweeted, "No mercy for the Ukrainian population!" which many interpreted as a call to eliminate Ukrainians. The Austrian foreign ministry summoned him as a result. Ulyanov claimed that his post had been misinterpreted.

What I really wanted to know was the degree of independence Ulyanov felt he had as a diplomat. To what extent did he enjoy latitude to formulate positions, and to what extent was he bound by guidance from Moscow? "This is top secret," he said with a wry smile, leaving me guessing for a second whether he was joking. Then he tried to explain. "Some issues are not worth wasting paper on, they can be solved here," he said. But it's "good practice" to coordinate important matters with the capital. Ambassadors and diplomats posted abroad may not have the "full picture" that can affect Moscow's considerations on a given issue. "If you're not confident that you understand the situation in its entirety, then it might be better to give in, so as not to find yourself in a stupid position," he said. Russian diplomats had always obeyed Kremlin orders, but with the invasion of Ukraine, their margin for agency and flexibility essentially disappeared.

Notwithstanding the friction with Western counterparts, the joint work at international organizations in Vienna continued, resolutions were negotiated, and texts adopted, he said. The famous "Vienna spirit" of cooperation and compromise was not yet fully dead, Ulyanov believed. Evoking Stalin's famous line to the secretary of the Union of Writers in 1946, *drugikh pisateley u menya dlya vas net* ("I don't have any other writers for you"), he grudgingly concluded that Russia did not have any other partners than the ones it had. In the legacy multilateral fora in Vienna, Geneva, and New York, Western states were still a formidable force. That was a reality Russia had to manage.

THE UN SECURITY COUNCIL IN NEW YORK IS THE CROWN JEWEL of international diplomacy. With its fifteen members, it bears primary responsibility for maintaining international peace and security. It can call on states to settle disputes, impose sanctions, and even authorize the use of military force. As a permanent member of the council, Russia holds a veto, just like China, France, the UK, and the US. It is a position of great privilege and immense political power.

As Russia recalibrated its diplomatic statecraft after the invasion, it was initially cautious not to paralyze the council. Russian diplomats descended into shouting matches with Western counterparts over the war in Ukraine but continued to coordinate on other matters. Through 2022, the council imposed a new sanctions regime on Haitian gangs and agreed on a new mandate for the UN to work with the Taliban government to deliver aid to Afghans. Both Russia and Western states seemed willing to use the UN's most powerful body as a space for residual cooperation.

Once the Ukraine war settled into a grinding battle of attrition and the West stepped up its military support for Kyiv, that changed. In June 2023, Moscow's veto on the Security Council forced the withdrawal of UN peacekeepers from Mali, where the Wagner Group had appeared on the scene in 2021. One month later, Russia vetoed the renewal of a Security Council mandate for the UN to deliver aid to rebel-held parts of northwestern Syria from Turkey, bypassing the Assad regime.

By that time, Russia had lost hope that the Ukraine war would end soon. As a result, it became less interested in compromise with Western states and prioritized helping its friends—like Assad and the Malian junta—with its influence on the council. That said, in summer 2023, some issues became ripe for fundamental review on the council, for reasons unrelated to Ukraine. Developments on the ground in

Mali and Syria's Idlib gave Russia an opening to thwart joint action by the council. After October 7, 2023, the Gaza war further escalated tensions on the council, with Russia exploiting grievances over the West's support for Israel.

The Ukraine war fragmented UN diplomacy, but fragmentation preceded February 2022. The war simply became a proximate cause for Russia to blow up something that was already quite fragile, the International Crisis Group's Richard Gowan told me. "It's like you finally turn on the lights in the basement and see that there are rats and mold everywhere."

Lukyanov had made note of Russia's pivot to smaller diplomatic networks and ad hoc alliances years before the full-scale invasion. But even after 2022, he still thought the UN was of enduring value to Russia. "The UN is irreplaceable—whether it works or not, you cannot invent anything to replace it," he said. Uniting all 193 member states, the General Assembly is the UN's main deliberative body. "Its decisions are nonbinding, but everybody watches the votes, watches who supports whom," he said. "It will remain important as a big forum of international monitoring, to measure the atmosphere in the world."

In September 2024, Russian diplomats would catastrophically fail in measuring that atmosphere. That month, world leaders convened in New York for the UN Summit of the Future. Billed as a "once-in-a-generation opportunity," the idea was to forge a new vision for how the UN would deal with current and future global challenges. It was to result in an action-oriented Pact for the Future, to be passed by consensus.

Preparatory work for the summit started in September 2022, with Germany and Namibia named co-facilitators. Meanwhile, a group of detractors formed. Going by the name of the "like-minded group," they were an amorphous assortment of countries, a subset of the G77 led by Pakistan and Egypt, that were uncomfortable with the process. Russia, which disliked the idea of a pact from the get-go, used the like-minded group as a vehicle to advance its own opposition without having to take the lead. According to a diplomat involved, Russia also tried to discredit the co-facilitators, derogatorily referring to the pair as "Germany and its former colony." But the like-minded group and Russia were not fully aligned. While the former wanted references to nuclear disarmament in the pact, such language was a red line for Russia.

Months of arduous negotiations produced many iterations of a draft pact and its subsections, including paragraphs on Security Council reform and a global digital compact. With just a few weeks left until the high-level summit, Russia stepped to the fore in summer 2024. By that time, the like-minded group was dissolving. Apparently, a majority of developing countries saw enough value in the process that they wanted it to succeed after all. Cognizant of that shift, Russian diplomats engaged more actively on the substance of the pact, though not totally unconstructively, according to another diplomat involved.

Then the draft pact was "put under silence," meaning delegations had a chance to object to it (in diplospeak, "to break the silence"). Russia objected to many paragraphs, as did a few other states from the original like-minded group. "Different delegations tried to approach Russia, to engage, to look at language on disarmament, but Russia always said no," the same diplomat told me. "This started to generate a lot of friction, and I would even say bad faith, with some. Because it's one thing to say that you have a red line but may be willing to offer a counterproposal. But if all you're saying is no and no and no, then that's not going to work."

Shortly before the summit, the president of the General Assembly convened a late-night meeting to try to break through the impasse. The small room was packed with the key players: the original like-minded group, the Security Council's permanent members, the G77, some Europeans. The dominant feeling among those convened was that they needed to adopt the pact, and nuclear disarmament had to be in it. At one point, some present were almost shouting at the Russian ambassador, pleading, "You need to let this go! You cannot keep blocking the path! You have to negotiate something!" It was a very tense moment, even by the standards of UN diplomacy. After that meeting, further tweaks were made, in the hope that they would accommodate Russia.

The summit opened on September 22, a Sunday. Russia's deputy foreign minister, Sergey Vershinin, had flown in from Moscow, and when he took the floor, he unleashed on the entire process. Germany and Namibia, the co-facilitators, had included only "provisions that were dictated to them mainly by Western countries" and had ignored Russia's repeated requests for further negotiations, Vershinin claimed. If the planned vote on the pact were not deferred pending further talks, he said, Russia would seek to move an amendment adding language to the effect that the UN "shall not intervene in matters which are essentially within the domestic jurisdiction of any State." The move was designed to dilute the binding nature of the entire pact.

It was the straw that broke the camel's back. The African Union called for a "no-action motion" on Russia's amendment. In the UN's mind-bogglingly complicated rules of procedure, a "no-action motion" can be used when a country, in this case Russia, seeks to adjourn the debate in order to block action on a specific draft resolution or decision. Mexico decided to back the African Union's call. Some 143 states then voted in favor of that motion, while fifteen abstained. In the end, only six countries stood with Russia in opposing it: Belarus, Iran, Nicaragua, North Korea, Sudan, and Syria. The vote was a crushing diplomatic defeat for Russia.

"I must admit that I am still quite confused about why Russia did not quietly withdraw its amendment, rather than face a vote on the issue it was bound to lose," Gowan said. Some diplomats I spoke with thought it was possible the Russian foreign ministry's decision-making gears were stuck, not unlike during the 2022 NPT review conference—that Russian diplomats on the ground in New York understood the unfolding dynamics, but were under strict instructions from Moscow to play hardball—and then it was too late to get updated guidance to avoid a situation in which Russia had to openly block. Others believed Russia genuinely thought its amendment, which framed the pact as a neocolonial Western imposition, would garner greater support.

In the end, the General Assembly adopted the Pact for the Future without a vote, and Russia announced it would dissociate itself from the achievement, the only elegant solution left. Had it insisted that the pact not be adopted at all, it would have risked antagonizing non-Western countries even more.

The Russian diplomatic apparatus was not amused by how things had gone down in New York. Dmitry Polyansky, Russia's deputy permanent representative to the UN, directed his ire at countries in the Global South. "There is nothing to celebrate," he wrote in a social media post soon after the diplomatic showdown. "The UN trampled on its own principles to please a group of delegations from the 'beautiful garden' that usurped negotiations from the outset. And the majority from the 'jungle' like a herd simply didn't have the guts to protest and stand for their rights."

Polyansky's remarks alluded to a diplomatic faux pas by Josep Borrell, the EU's former top diplomat, who had likened Europe to a "garden" and the rest of the world to a "jungle" in a speech in October 2022. Ever since that speech, Russian diplomats had wasted no opportunity to exploit the diplomatic gaffe.

Except, on this occasion, the "jungle" had stood up for itself and spoken in support of the Pact for the Future. The "herd" had supported consensus at the UN, notwithstanding all shortcomings in a document that had been painstakingly negotiated over hundreds, if not thousands, of hours. Trying to enlist the Global South into their efforts to confront the West, Russian diplomats had taken things too far. Trying to convince the "jungle" that it needed protection from the "garden," they had hit their limits at the United Nations. Henceforth, they would have to hustle more actively in other fora to rally the non-Western world behind Moscow's nebulous anti-Western agenda.

CHAPTER 11

Hostess with the Mostest

ON OCTOBER 3, 2024, THE ZARYADYE CONCERT HALL IN CENtral Moscow opened its doors for an unusual spectacle. Russia was hosting the BRICS+ Fashion Summit, one highlight of its ongoing BRICS presidency. Over three days, fashion enthusiasts from all over the world crammed into workshops and master classes to learn about Uzbek fabrics or the barong tagalog, an embroidered long-sleeved shirt for Filipino men. In Zaryadye's Grand Hall, the elite of the Global South's fashion industry got onstage for TED Talks and panel discussions on topics like "fashion exports without borders" and "fashion as cultural diplomacy." Walking through the vast "Heritage" exhibition, with a Moroccan caftan to their left and bridal gowns from Rwanda to their right, visitors could marvel at a concert of colors. Models from Asia and Africa showcased new trends and aesthetics, gracefully gliding down the catwalk.

It was the second such fashion summit hosted by Russia, this one convened under the motto of "decentralization and democratization." Deputy foreign minister Sergey Ryabkov, Russia's BRICS sherpa, had struggled to find the right words when advertising the event a few months prior. "If it will not set global trends, it will at least demonstrate a high degree of compliance . . . with the expectations of the most demanding public," he said in an utterly joyless commentary.

With their drab suits and stern demeanors, Ryabkov and other seasoned Russian diplomats were nothing like the world's fashion moguls, but they knew exactly what they were doing. The BRICS+ Fashion Summit became one of hundreds of events organized by Russia as BRICS chair in 2024 to demonstrate that there was an alternative, even cheerful reality beyond the West. Putin had summarized Russia's agenda for its 2024 BRICS presidency as part of a "painful process" to overthrow the "classic colonialism" of the US-led order. Why not also have a bit of fun and challenge the monopoly of Paris, New York, and Milan as fashion capitals in the process?

The origins of BRICS lie in the economic rise of the non-West and growing anger over what was seen as heedless US foreign policy in the late 1990s and early 2000s. Following a first informal meeting in 2005, Russia assembled the first meeting of BRIC foreign ministers—at that time still without South Africa—on the sidelines of the UN General Assembly in New York in 2006. It was a time when Russia's official rhetoric, reacting to what it called "color revolutions" in Georgia and Ukraine, began to define the country as separate from the West and as an independent pole in international affairs. In 2008, the global financial crisis (and the concomitant discontent with the international economic order) as well as new tensions in Russian–Western relations due to the Russian–Georgian war coincided with the emergence of BRIC on the international arena. In June 2009, the partners convened for an inaugural summit in Russia's Yekaterinburg, before adding South Africa to the grouping a year later.

The West's decoupling from Russia after the 2014 annexation of Crimea greatly elevated BRICS's importance to Russia. Viktoria Panova, a Russian academic and chief strategy planning adviser at Russia's National Committee on BRICS Research at the time, remarked that none of Russia's partners made it feel like it was "an international bête noire or pariah," unlike the West. When Russia presided over BRICS in 2015—by that point kicked out of the G8—Panova took on a leading role in the BRICS Civil Forum, which was set up to create connections between the participating countries' societies and expert communities. This was also a time when Russia took its first steps to reduce its reliance on the US dollar, looking toward BRICS as a vehicle. In 2014, BRICS announced the creation of the New Development Bank, to complement the World Bank and the International Monetary Fund and set up a financial safety net for its members.

Though BRICS became more important to Russia, economically and politically, concrete actions lagged behind grandiose ambitions. Engagement within BRICS remained, in many ways, shallow. Its members had very different priorities, which made it difficult for them to pull in the same direction. By the time the COVID pandemic hit, Viktoria Panova decried the inability of existing international institutions such as the World Health Organization or the G7 to respond effectively, but she also issued a plea and a warning to BRICS. "The BRICS grouping still has the opportunity to offer new solutions to this unprecedented crisis," she wrote, "else it risks becoming another inefficient institution."

The invasion of Ukraine two years later gave Russia reason to root out any remaining inefficiencies. The grouping was to become living proof that Russia could not be isolated, no matter how hard Western capitals tried. If Russia was to lead the "global majority" into a bright and beautiful post-Western future, BRICS was to be Russia's principal vehicle.

Hit hard by Western sanctions, Russia turned to its BRICS partners for economic lifelines. Together, the five behemoths accounted for 40 percent of the world's population and 25 percent of global GDP, a formidable wellspring of potential support. Addressing a virtual BRICS summit hosted by China in June 2022—a time when Western nations were planning the oil price cap to starve Russia's state coffers of revenue—Putin called for solidarity in the face of the West's "ill-considered and selfish actions." The summit was Putin's first major diplomatic outing since he had ordered tanks into Ukraine, and he knew he was among friends. Russia was in the process of redirecting its oil exports to BRICS countries, Putin said, claiming that Russia's trade with them had already jumped 38 percent in the first three months of 2022.

Xi Jinping, who presided over the largest BRICS economy by far, seemed to be of the same mind as Putin, though he spoke a different vernacular. "Human history, like a river, will keep moving forward, with moments of both calm waters and huge waves," he said in a keynote speech. "Despite changes in an evolving global environment," Xi proclaimed solemnly, "our shared desire to meet challenges together through cooperation will remain as strong as ever."

Flanked by several of his ministers, Xi went on to criticize US-led sanctions and "small circles built around hegemony." It was music to Putin's ears. Xi invited the leaders of thirteen other countries—among them Argentina, Egypt, and Indonesia—to join BRICS for a separate gathering on the margins of the summit. Dubbed the High-Level Dialogue on Global Development, the group discussed how it could play a more relevant role in international affairs. Xi also reinvigorated discussions to expand BRICS's membership.

For its own reasons, Russia welcomed China's push to elevate and expand BRICS. Through the summer and fall, Russia hosted several BRICS events, notwithstanding its preoccupation with deteriorating battlefield conditions in Ukraine. In October, Russia organized a BRICS conference on science, technology, and innovation under the auspices of the Russian Academy of Sciences. A month later, over three thousand participants came together in St. Petersburg for the International Municipal BRICS Forum, a large business event. Convening these activities, Russia saw its chance to demonstrate that it was far from isolated internationally.

By early 2023, when South Africa took over the BRICS presidency from China and started preparing for an in-person summit, Russia's diplomatic machinery had truly found its footing in the post-invasion environment and was ready to take its promotion of BRICS to the next level. The new foreign policy concept, released in March, declared it Russia's priority to "eliminate the vestiges of domination by the US and other unfriendly states in global affairs," chiefly by enhancing the capacity and international role of BRICS, the Shanghai Cooperation Organization, and other associations with strong Russian participation. Officials in Moscow came up with all sorts of innovative ideas, suggesting that BRICS create a common "geological platform" to exchange technologies for mining, or a joint BRICS research module on Russia's orbital service station.

Some Russian elites supported the idea of a BRICS common currency. They took their cue from Putin himself, who, a few months into the Ukraine invasion, had called for the creation of an international reserve currency based on a basket of currencies of the BRICS countries. State Duma deputy chairman Alexander Babakov, a nationalist, jumped on the bandwagon to suggest that a new BRICS trade currency could be backed by gold or other rare-earth elements. Russian economist Sergey Glazyev called the emergence of such a new currency "inevitable." Referencing mathematical models, he claimed it would be very stable and much more attractive than the dollar, pound, or euro. All that was needed for the introduction of such a new international currency, Glazyev argued, was political will among the BRICS countries.

Less sure of its feasibility was the ever-practical and sober-minded Nabiullina. "Of course, this idea deserves attention, but I think it will be quite difficult to implement. . . . It requires the consent of many parties," she cautioned a few weeks before South Africa's BRICS summit in Johannesburg. Nabiullina argued that energies were better spent on improving ways to settle trade in national currencies—something she was focused on in an effort to keep the Eurasian roundabout running.

The common currency was not the only endeavor with which Russia faced obstacles. In March 2023, following an investigation of war crimes, crimes against humanity, and genocide, the ICC had issued an arrest warrant for Putin. Since South Africa was a party to the ICC, it was not clear whether Putin could travel to the Johannesburg summit in August—or rather, what would happen if he decided to. The South African government convened a high-level interministerial commission to assess its options. Could Putin come? Could he not? The media even speculated that South Africa might ask another country to host the summit on its behalf, to rid itself of the legal conundrums. The planned visit recalled a scandalous episode from June 2015, when Jacob Zuma hosted Sudanese President Omar al-Bashir, wanted by the ICC. The following year, South Africa's Supreme Court of Appeal ruled that the government's failure to arrest Bashir had been unlawful. After that incident, one senior South African diplomat told me, all domestic legal loopholes were closed, so it was clear Putin would have to be arrested should he decide to come. "Some in the ANC advocated for pulling South Africa out of the ICC," the diplomat said, "but we civil servants never panicked about the issue."

In the end, the Kremlin decided not to put President Ramaphosa in a difficult spot. Putin announced he would not travel to the summit, but would instead join virtually. The Kremlin claimed the ongoing war between Russia and Ukraine did not give Putin the time to participate in person.

When Putin addressed the summit via video link, his voice sounded strangely distorted, almost like Darth Vader. Apparently, there was a technical glitch. This caused widespread ridicule among Western reporters covering the proceedings. But their mockery could not mask the fact that the Johannesburg summit, after two days of consultations, ended with several major outcomes. BRICS declared its intention to reduce its dependence on the US dollar and to increase the pace of de-dollarization in global commerce. More important, six other nations—Argentina, Egypt, Ethiopia, Iran, Saudi Arabia, and the UAE—were invited to join in 2024. Even though Argentina, after electing populist Javier Milei as president, would have a change of heart, it would be a major expansion. Putin had remained confined to his Moscow abode, but Russia scored another win in moving international diplomacy away from Western-dominated legacy institutions.

The August summit was a big deal for Paula Slier, too. Having left

RT in May 2023, she was back in Johannesburg experiencing firsthand the frenzy and media buzz surrounding the event. It inspired her to set up the English-language BRICS Global Television Network, catering to audiences in BRICS countries. Although she wasn't sure the channel would take off—finding sponsors was proving difficult—she thought she was onto a niche idea. As BRICS was becoming more important geopolitically, there would surely be an interest among average people to learn more about life in the partner countries.

Dmitry Trenin, the Russian expert, shared such high hopes for BRICS. In December 2023, as Russia's diplomatic corps was preparing to take over the BRICS chairmanship from South Africa, Trenin and Sergey Karaganov coauthored a treatise about Russia's foreign policy toward the "global majority." They and a few others had emerged after the invasion as Kremlin courtiers of sorts, rationalizing Russia's foreign policy adaptations as masterful strategic moves. In their report, they called BRICS the "vanguard" of the "global majority," a "prototype for an organization of the new world order." Unlike the Cold War-era Non-Aligned Movement, a forum of countries not formally aligned with any major power bloc, the authors concluded, BRICS was not some "ballast" intended to keep "the global boat from turning over." It was fighting for an entirely new order.

In line with that thinking, Russia took the baton from South Africa in January with statements of grand ambition. It would host over two hundred events over the course of the year. To ensure a steady pipeline of fresh ideas and sound advice, the government installed Viktoria Panova as head of a new BRICS Expert Council. The agency Rossotrudnichestvo announced plans to expand its network of Russian Houses in BRICS countries. Russian officials said they wanted BRICS to work on information security, AI, energy, climate, sustainable development, health, and economic cooperation—an incredibly ambitious agenda. Addressing the Federal Assembly in late February, Putin assured his audience that Russia was riding the wave of the future. According to him, BRICS countries would create 37 percent of global GDP in 2028, while GDP from the G7 would fall below 28 percent. "These are the global trends, and there is no escaping them, since they are objective reality," Putin said.

Over the coming months, Russia engaged in a frenzy of activities to capture the hearts and minds of people in partner countries. There was the BRICS International Film Festival in April, the BRICS Theater Schools Festival in June, the BRICS Urban Future Forum, and the BRICS+ Fashion Summit in October. In an attempt to promote "sports multipolarity," Russia hosted BRICS Games for the Future in Kazan, giving its own athletes a chance to compete after they were banned from the Paris Olympics over the war in Ukraine. However, participation and spectator interest were disappointingly limited. At one point, Russian synchronized swimmer Alexandr Maltsev received his gold medal while standing alone on the podium, having been the sole competitor in the freestyle program.

On October 18, two weeks after the fashion summit and a few days before Russia would host the grouping's annual summit, Putin got together with a group of journalists from BRICS countries. It was his chance to review the Russian chairmanship. Putin went to great lengths to emphasize that BRICS was not "anti-Western"—it was simply "non-Western." Countries like Brazil and India were uncomfortable being portrayed as part of an anti-Western club, so making that distinction was important. Putin also claimed that neither Russia nor BRICS was actively trying to change the global order. "It is happening naturally," he said, calling it "an inevitable process."

Putin told a story about BRICS's heralding of a new global order as a process that was preordained, a law of nature. It sat oddly with a Russian chairmanship that, for ten months, had been marked by intense hustling and diplomatic hyperactivity to push BRICS to the forefront of the international agenda. Up to that point, Russia's chairmanship had been a master class in geopolitical Kabuki theater: highly stylized, an enchanting blend of beautiful costumes, exaggerated poses, and dramatic gestures. And the final act was about to begin.

On the morning of October 22, the city of Kazan was as ready as it ever could be to host the grand finale of Russia's BRICS chairmanship. Authorities had spent more than $80 million on city renovation projects in the months prior, while hoteliers outfitted their lodgings with presidential suites. Kazan Federal University relocated students from their dormitories to create additional space for summit participants. Libraries and museums were closed. Authorities partially shut down the internet. On the eve of the summit, policemen from Komi and Chelyabinsk were dispatched to the city to support local forces in ensuring security. Kazan became a city transformed, temporarily colonized by dignitaries from all around the world.

Planes touched down at Kazan International Airport throughout the morning. Around 10 a.m., South African President Cyril Ramaphosa arrived, greeted by young Russian women dressed in national costumes. They offered him the traditional karavai bread, which is often served at weddings, and chak-chak, a terribly sweet fried-dough dish popular in Tatarstan and Central Asia. Ramaphosa took a small bite of chak-chak, then quickly put the rest back down. "Thank you! Wow!" he politely exclaimed. "And you ladies look lovely." China's Xi Jinping arrived by special plane, escorted by a Russian fighter jet. Guards of honor lined up on both sides of the red carpet to salute him. Then flew in Narendra Modi of India, greeted by Tatarstan's head, Rustam Minnikhanov, with what must have been one of the longest handshakes in recorded history.

Over the coming three days, Putin basked in the attention of world leaders. He held sixteen bilateral meetings, including with the heads of China, India, South Africa, Egypt, Turkey, Iran, and Ethiopia. When he met Venezuela's Nicolás Maduro, he brought along Igor Sechin to talk oil. On the second day, UN Secretary-General António Guterres arrived, despite strong criticism from Ukraine—a major diplomatic coup for Moscow.

Ukraine had other reasons to feel unnerved. Meetings on the

sidelines of the summit saw discussions of a Brazilian–Chinese initiative for peace in Ukraine. Putin's aide Yuri Ushakov praised the ideas presented as "useful." But the peace missions or plans put forward by Russia's BRICS partners—by Brazil and China, but also by South Africa with its African Peace Initiative a year prior—effectively served as a stimulus to the Russian war effort. They were easy to propose and, while paying lip service to Ukrainian sovereignty and territorial integrity, offered no viable path for Kyiv. Meanwhile, predictably tepid responses from Ukraine and the West to these plans fueled narratives of Western intransigence, a key Russian talking point, as if the West that, in their telling, caused the war in the first place were also the ones prolonging it.

The atmosphere in Kazan was cheerful, as leaders toe-tapped to a concert of Russian music. Even the mood between historical rivals China and India was more upbeat than usual. On the night before the summit, the two countries had reached an agreement on patrolling arrangements along the Line of Actual Control on their border, a site of regular friction. Reporting from Kazan, the newspaper *Kommersant* cheered that "BRICS is bringing China and India closer together."

Xi received special attention, as befitted Putin's plans for deeper connections between China and Russia. In Alabuga, a two-and-a-half-hour drive west from Kazan, Russian workers were frantically constructing a new logistics hub worth just under $700 million that was designed to facilitate cargo transportation between China and Russia. Once completed, the hub—sprawling across 160 acres, about the size of Disneyland—would handle 100,000 containers a year, according to a promotional video. Meeting Xi at the summit, Putin updated him on the progress at the hub, which was to be named after former Chinese leader Deng Xiaoping. In this Kabuki act, Russia was performing the *saikeirei*—the deepest bow in Japanese etiquette, which is reserved for showing utmost respect—before its senior partner, China.

Speaking at an event on the sidelines of the summit, Margarita Simonyan echoed such sycophancy. She conjured parallels in Russia's and China's past suffering at the hands of the West, before elaborating on their common vision for the future. "We're tired of the hypocrisy and the dictates of the collective West, led by the United States," she said. "We're tired of their attempts to make us someone else, to carve pieces off us—whether it's Taiwan from China, or various parts from us. Thank you for being tired along with us. We'll get to relax together when truth prevails and the unipolar world, which is already drawing its last breaths, finally ends."

Small details here and there, however, suggested the hosts found it difficult to fully shed historical ballast. Though Moscow was hard at work to de-dollarize BRICS trade, the summit's official website still advised participants to come with cash in US dollars or euros. Saudi Arabia, historically a close US ally that had been invited to join BRICS at the Johannesburg summit, continued to sit on the fence all year. Russia treated the Saudis as if they were in the grouping, a South African diplomat told me, and "sometimes we asked, 'Why are they even in the room?'" In the end, all the courting was to no avail. Riyadh sent its foreign minister, rather than the crown prince, to Kazan. On the second day of the summit, Ushakov admitted begrudgingly that the Saudis had not embraced full BRICS membership after all. Kazakhstan's President Tokayev and Armenia's Prime Minister Pashinyan showed up in Kazan, but made clear their countries would not apply for BRICS membership, either. Kazakhstan gave "priority to the UN as the universal organization with no alternative," Tokayev's spokesperson explained.

Still, the summit became the largest geopolitical event hosted by Russia since the invasion of Ukraine, with every continent except North America represented. The final communiqué touched on a wide range of topics, from the wars in Ukraine and Gaza to the need for new financial mechanisms. Unlike the Johannesburg summit, which had ushered in a sensational outcome with the group's first expansion, the Kazan declaration showcased more incremental progress. Whatever noise there had been on a BRICS currency in 2023, by the time of the Kazan summit, the conversation had firmly shifted to the issue of cross-border payment systems, and that was just fine by Nabiullina.

When Putin, presented with a fake BRICS banknote in Kazan, handed it to Nabiullina with a smile, she reportedly was not amused.

In Kazan, BRICS also created a new "partner country" category for an initial thirteen states that would not become full BRICS members but would engage closely with the club and benefit from some of its initiatives. Among those offered this status were Algeria, Kazakhstan, Nigeria, and even NATO ally Turkey.

A senior Indian diplomat I met in New Delhi gave Russia "full marks" for the Kazan summit, and applauded Russia's chairmanship in general. Still, he indicated that India and Russia held slightly different perspectives on BRICS's utility. Where India saw it as a "platform," Russia saw it as a "political vehicle" to "break out of isolation," he said. The two countries did not always see eye to eye. The diplomat raised the issue of Russia lobbying to include ideas on new financial mechanisms in a joint BRICS report. India pushed back. "We have very different financial systems, we don't talk about de-dollarization, most of our trade is in US dollars," he said.

Russia had put on a great Kabuki performance, and its visitors rhapsodized about the splendid scenery and beautiful props. And yet, some wondered how much Russia's BRICS hype could really deliver for them. Such doubts, it turned out, made their rounds inside Russia, too.

Five months after the summit in Kazan, Viktoria Panova stood on the terrace of the swanky Taj Palace Hotel, looking out over its sumptuous gardens. A tall woman with long, dyed-blond hair draped over an elegant, printed dress, she had flown to New Delhi for the Raisina Dialogue, an annual international conference, and appeared slightly fatigued from the countless interviews and meetings she was conducting on the event's sidelines. Having acted as Russia's spokeswoman of sorts on all BRICS-related matters for well over a decade, she was in high demand.

Russia had handed the rotating BRICS presidency to Brazil four months prior. Now, reflecting on the Russian chairmanship, Panova saw one of the country's main roles as bridging the divide between those who had been longtime members of BRICS and the newer arrivals. "For us original BRICS members, what we do is all natural," Panova told me. When the new countries joined in early 2024, Panova explained, some did so "not fully understanding what BRICS is. They expected it to be another donor grouping," she said. Russia's key tasks as chair were therefore what Panova called "explanation" and "integration."

She conceded that some of the newcomers had been "terrified" by the high number of events Russia put on during the year of its chairmanship. Some counterparts had asked Panova, "Where do you find the people for all this?" But, for the most part, Panova thought Russia had managed well. Those who expected greater progress on cross-border trade and financial arrangements were charlatans, she thought, her harsh commentary reminding me of the unsentimental Nabiullina. "The professionals always understood how many technicalities there are to consider, and how expensive they are," she said.

A few weeks before I met her in New Delhi, Ryabkov had awarded Panova a badge for her contributions to Russia's chairmanship. "BRICS is a posh thing," she told me. "Whenever you have the presidency, the popularity of BRICS rises, and media interest with it."

Now, as Brazil was ramping up its own presidency, with an agenda focused on AI and climate, Panova and her colleagues looked back with satisfaction to what they had achieved in 2024. Of the thirteen countries invited to become BRICS partners in Kazan, nine were onboard, and more started toying with the idea of deepening their ties with the club. Most important, the Kazan summit had dispelled any remaining myths that Russia could be isolated internationally.

At the same time, it seemed to dawn on Russia's most ardent supporters of BRICS that the grouping had its limitations. "I'm no longer that big of a fan of the idea of BRICS as a parallel structure," Trenin admitted to me. He had realized that "getting BRICS to agree on things is not easy," he said, given continued dependence among

Russia's partners on the West for trade. Panova was less forthcoming in her introspection but seemed similarly preoccupied by the need for BRICS to produce tangible results. "It is time to pause," she told me, as her aide gestured politely that they needed to rush to another meeting and account for the New Delhi rush-hour traffic. "We need to make sure that the orchestra plays well."

Three months later, as Brazil finalized preparations for its BRICS summit in Rio in early July, there were signs of fatigue. Xi said he would skip the event for the first time in twelve years. The Kremlin announced Putin would attend the summit virtually—just as he had in 2023—given the outstanding ICC arrest warrant against him. And in the Middle East, spiraling tensions threatened to create a dangerous distraction to an effective summit outcome that would require BRICS's diverse members—including Iran and Gulf Arab countries—to land on the same page.

BRICS had served a war-waging Russia well. The audience watched Russia stage its chairmanship with delight, captivated by the complex and colorful choreography. But when the curtain fell, the crowd wondered about the spectacle's lasting impact. There was no doubt that Russia would continue to benefit economically from closer ties with BRICS partners, especially as a capricious President Trump would call the club "anti-American" and antagonize its members, one after the other. Yet, a vehicle for Russia to mold to its liking and to lead the "global majority" into a glorious post-Western future, BRICS was not—and probably never would be.

Part VI

DEFEATING THE WEST

CHAPTER 12

There Must Be Fear

RUSSIAN DEFENSE MINISTER SERGEY SHOIGU ARRIVED IN THE Arctic village of Belushya Guba at the crack of dawn. A mild breeze caressed the wooden St. Nicholas Church, which stood surrounded by dreary apartment blocks housing military personnel. Four years earlier, this small settlement had become a worldwide sensation when dozens of polar bears roamed the area during wintertime, scavenging through dumpsters and even entering people's homes. This time, in August 2023, the TV cameras were back to accompany Shoigu on an unusual mission.

From Belushya, he would fly up to the Matochkin Strait, the narrow waters that separate the northern and southern islands of the Arctic archipelago known as Novaya Zemlya. As Shoigu boarded a yellow-and-blue helicopter, he was joined by Alexey Likhachev, the head of Russia's state nuclear company, Rosatom. Inside the tiny compartment, the two men huddled over paperwork, large headphones protecting their ears from the deafening roar of the rotor blades.

Shoigu was dressed in military camouflage, Likhachev in a dark coat and baseball cap.

As they headed north, Shoigu enjoyed the scenery through the small windows. Otherworldly light blue engulfed the sky. Dots of land emerged from the calm waters. Shoigu peeked out at what was known as the Central Training Ground, where the Soviet Union once conducted more than 130 nuclear-weapons tests. During the Cold War, the Soviets also carried out hundreds of tests in the empire's outer reaches, including Kazakhstan, but it was here, in Novaya Zemlya, that scientists detonated the infamous thermonuclear Tsar Bomba, the largest nuclear weapon ever tested, in 1961.

The last time nuclear explosions took place at Novaya Zemlya was on October 24, 1990. After the end of the Cold War, Russia and the other P5 states—permanent members of the UN Security Council and nuclear-weapons possessors, namely China, France, the UK, and the US—announced moratoria against nuclear testing. But after the invasion of Ukraine, Putin signaled that that moratorium need not apply forever. Addressing the Federal Assembly in February 2023, he accused "some politicians in Washington" of considering a return to nuclear testing and asked Russia to be vigilant. "The defense ministry and Rosatom must make everything ready for Russia to conduct nuclear tests. We will not be the first to proceed with these tests, but if the United States goes ahead with them, we will as well," he warned. Six months later, Shoigu's highly publicized visit to Novaya Zemlya intended to show that Putin meant business.

This was only one among a string of measures Russia undertook to raise the nuclear temperature vis-à-vis the West. In an effort to deter NATO's direct entry into the conflict and to halt—or at least slow—Western weapons deliveries to Ukraine, prominent Russian voices rattled the nuclear saber, repeatedly insinuating that the war could escalate into a global nuclear conflagration. Russia took other steps up the nuclear escalation ladder, preparing nuclear deployments to its neighboring ally Belarus and changing the country's nuclear doctrine. Putin also turned his back on nuclear arms control, announcing in the

February address that Russia was suspending its participation in the New START agreement with the United States. Westerners "are not idiots," Putin riled. "They are not stupid after all. They want to inflict a strategic defeat on us and also to get to our nuclear sites." He would make sure that Russia would not be fooled.

Russia's reckless actions injected uncertainty, fear, and, at times, hysteria into a complex nuclear environment that Moscow and Washington had jointly managed for decades.

As their geopolitical rivalry heated up during the early Cold War, the Soviet Union and the United States, building up their respective nuclear arsenals, established a relationship of deterrence via "mutually assured destruction." The thinking was that since each superpower had enough nuclear weaponry to destroy the other, neither side would be reckless enough to attempt a first strike, and the logic of deterrence would prevail. While Moscow and Washington agreed that the further spread of nuclear weapons should be limited—jointly leading the negotiations on the NPT—they also signed various agreements over the decades to manage their nuclear arms race and limit the risk that misunderstandings could spiral into nuclear war. The 1962 Cuban Missile Crisis, when Cold War tensions nearly spilled over into a nuclear conflict, gave impetus to such efforts.

Once the Cold War ended, Russia and the US drastically reduced their nuclear stockpiles but remained locked in a deterrence relationship that required continued management. Russia's outlook on deterrence evolved significantly through the post–Cold War decades. Catching up with American thinking, Russian strategists started toying with ideas about limited nuclear war and "escalation ladders," a concept first championed by American physicist Herman Kahn that describes escalation between adversaries, beginning with crisis and ending at strategic nuclear war. A debate within the Russian strategic community produced the idea that threats of nuclear-weapons use could be suitable not just to deter all-out nuclear war, but also to curb aggression against Russia with conventional weapons. Limited nuclear use could even help de-escalate or terminate certain types of war on terms acceptable to Moscow. Ideas for deterring (preventing the enemy from doing something) or compelling (coercing the enemy into doing something) became ever more elaborate. As political scientist Dmitry Adamsky has written, with time, deterrence "à la russe" became a holistic construct.

While Russia's strategists thought hard about the versatile utility of the country's nuclear arsenal, its diplomats remained eager to build on the Cold War's legacy of arms control and nonproliferation. Early in Putin's first presidency, Russia and the US signed the Strategic Offensive Reductions Treaty, also known as the Moscow Treaty, agreeing to significantly cut the number of deployed strategic nuclear warheads within ten years. When worries about Iran's nuclear program burst into the open in the mid-2000s, Russia cooperated with Western states at the IAEA and on the UN Security Council to help mediate the dispute. Barack Obama and Dmitry Medvedev signed the New START, another strategic nuclear arms reduction agreement, during the height of the "reset" in 2010.

After the annexation of Crimea, dark clouds assembled over the arms control horizon. The US charged that Russia was testing and deploying a cruise missile prohibited by the INF Treaty and eventually withdrew from it in August 2019. A year later, the Trump administration pulled out of the multiparty Open Skies Treaty, again alleging Russian abuse and noncompliance. Trump walked away from the Iran nuclear deal, known as the Joint Comprehensive Plan of Action (JCPOA), in May 2018, launching a "maximum pressure" campaign of sanctions against Tehran that unnerved Moscow. The US also became increasingly concerned about China building up its nuclear arsenal.

With just days left before the New START expired, Biden and Putin agreed in early 2021 to extend the treaty for another five years. Meeting in Geneva a few months later, they also relaunched a Strategic Stability Dialogue, previously convened during the first Trump administration, to talk about the future of arms control. But these steps could not mask the fundamental reality that the nuclear order—a mosaic of treaties, organizations, informal practices, and regional agreements—was under great stress on the eve of the Ukraine invasion.

Turning a cold shoulder to nuclear arms control and nonproliferation after February 2022, Russia made sure things would go from bad to worse.

To be fair, the West had set a precedent by abandoning the idea that cooperation on critically important dossiers—which included all things nuclear—should be walled off, or "compartmentalized," from broader tensions. In the months following Russia's annexation of Crimea, NATO suspended all practical cooperation with Russia, arguing there could be "no business as usual." The Obama administration stopped working with Russia on space exploration, missile defense, Afghanistan, and other pressing problems. Western states viewed the suspension of routine business with Russia both as punishment and as leverage to elicit a change in Russian behavior. But Russia was unmoved.

After February 2022, Russia began to mirror that practice, though not immediately. Russian officials initially seemed eager to separate the implementation of New START—which entailed mutual onsite inspections of nuclear and military facilities on both countries' territories, suspended since the pandemic—from the war in Ukraine. The Biden administration, meanwhile, stopped the Strategic Stability Dialogue with Russia because of the invasion. By August, when diplomats were assembled in New York for the NPT review conference, Moscow announced that New START inspections still could not resume on Russian territory, claiming that travel restrictions imposed by the Biden administration hindered Russian inspectors from entering the US.

Sergey Ryabkov may well have been unnerved by that decision, but he was just the messenger. Besides taking a keen interest in BRICS, the deputy foreign minister was also among the Russian diplomats most knowledgeable about nuclear issues. Before the invasion, Ryabkov led Russia's delegations to countless meetings with American counterparts, including in the Strategic Stability Dialogue.

On November 28, 2022, he and his team were sitting in Moscow on packed suitcases, ready to fly to Cairo for meetings with US officials in the Bilateral Consultative Commission, to discuss how activities under New START could finally be revived. But at the last minute, the Kremlin instructed Ryabkov to stay put. When he went before the press to explain the "indefinite postponement" of the Cairo meeting, he said that there could be no more "business as usual" with the United States on nuclear arms control. Ryabkov hinted that the decision had been taken above his pay grade. "It was made at the political level," he said.

The cancellation sent a strong signal that, as far as the Kremlin was concerned, the Russia–US standoff over Ukraine precluded any further routine business on nuclear arms control. Any Russian "positive signals or concessions" related to New START, Moscow added soon afterward, would be "unjustified, untimely, and inappropriate until Washington reviews its hostile policy toward Russia."

In his address to the Russian Federal Assembly in February 2023, Putin escalated the issue even further, announcing that Moscow would suspend altogether its implementation of New START—a step that partially ended its exchange of notifications on important data like the number and location of missiles that could carry nuclear warheads, compounding the problem of frozen onsite inspections. As Putin upped the ante, he was eager to offset the impression that Russia was breaking the rules. Citing various international and Russian domestic laws, the government provided a web of intricate legal justifications to make the case that Russia had every right to disrupt the treaty. Whether in seeking to derail UN summits or destroying the nuclear arms control architecture, Russia always claimed to be following proper procedure. If Russia was to appeal to the rest of the world in its effort to outlast the West, it had to show it wasn't just some nation gone rogue.

The Biden administration tried to get Putin back to the table, but without compromising on Ukraine. In early June 2023, Biden's national security adviser, Jake Sullivan, expressed the US's "willingness to engage in bilateral arms control discussions . . . without preconditions" in a landmark speech before the Arms Control Association in Washington. The olive branch was met with different responses from different parts of the Russian government. Dmitry Peskov called the US invitation "important and positive," while the foreign ministry was more lukewarm.

Taking the stage at the St. Petersburg International Economic Forum on June 16, Putin indulged in nuclear machismo that left little doubt as to his feelings. "We have more nuclear weapons than NATO; that's why they keep proposing reductions. Screw that," he said. Over the course of 2023 and 2024, Russia's position would not fundamentally change. Without ever shutting the door entirely to the idea of future nuclear arms control talks, the Kremlin insisted such talks would only become possible once the US changed its "hostile" attitude toward Russia. It was diplospeak for "stop supporting Ukraine."

Russia's lukewarm attitude to engagement extended to the area of nonproliferation, too. Before the invasion, efforts were underway in Vienna to restore the Iran nuclear deal (JCPOA), from which Trump had withdrawn in May 2018—and Russian diplomats, especially Ambassador Mikhail Ulyanov, played an important role mediating between the different parties. By some estimates, they averted a collapse of the talks at least a half dozen times in 2021. On occasion, Russian diplomats also criticized Iran over its breaches with the nuclear accord and over its stalling tactics.

That all changed with the invasion of Ukraine. Two weeks into war, Lavrov warned that Western sanctions imposed against Russia had become a stumbling block in restoring the nuclear deal, unless Russian national interests were taken into account. He demanded written US guarantees that Russia's trade and cooperation with Iran would not be hindered in any way by such sanctions. The Russians eventually walked back those demands, but the damage was done. Russia's machinations had disrupted the diplomatic momentum toward reaching a final agreement, which had been within reach.

Ulyanov fueled the impression that Russia was no longer interested in insulating the nuclear talks from its tensions with the West. In May, he tweeted that, if circumstances were different, Russia could provide its "good offices" to Iran and the West to finalize an agreement, "but not now." When we spoke, Ulyanov confirmed that an agreement on restoring the deal was 98 percent done at the end of February 2022, with "literally just a few lines left to finalize," but asserted that others were to blame for the failure to get it across the finish line. Iran used every opportunity for further "fine-tuning," in line with its longstanding diplomatic practice, he said, while the Europeans essentially "disappeared" from Vienna. He claimed that this may have been due to "their reluctance to conclude the negotiations on a positive note with Russia's participation."

Yet, all this was happening while Russia was turning to Iran for the Shahed drones. Growing more dependent on Tehran, Moscow apparently became less willing to nudge, let alone criticize, the Iranians over the nuclear deal. Skyrocketing tensions over Ukraine also reduced Moscow's appetite to invest significant diplomatic capital to cooperate with Western partners on a problem that was of great importance to them. It's even possible that Moscow regarded the protracted uncertainty over the fate of the JCPOA as useful. Such uncertainty left Iran sitting at the "nuclear threshold," a condition in which a country is assumed to be able to arm itself with nuclear weapons in a short period of time. Iran's nuclear threshold status generated quandary and tensions in the Middle East, a convenient distraction from Ukraine—at least while no one took military action to deal with the problem. Russia's new equivocation over the fate of the deal was not the only, let alone the decisive, factor that derailed the talks, but it did not help—and a window of opportunity to seal a deal closed after summer 2022.

There were signs that Russia's attitude toward nonproliferation was perhaps changing more fundamentally. A growing chorus of

Russian voices, channeling the main currencies of political discourse in wartime Moscow, expressed such sentiments. The idea that nuclear "multipolarity"—the emergence of more nuclear-armed states—might suit Moscow by creating problems for Washington began to percolate in the Russian strategic community. Even among less hawkish constituencies, there was a feeling that the global nonproliferation machinery had lost its previous value for Moscow. When Washington thought about nonproliferation, it mostly targeted the nuclear activities or ambitions of states like Iran, North Korea, or Syria. "Why engage in any discussions whatsoever concerning the countries that have become more and more important as partners in forming a new multipolar world?" Sergey Semenov of the PIR Center, a Moscow-based think tank, asked. In April 2024, Russia ended its support for the UN Panel of Experts for North Korea, which was monitoring the country's compliance with UN sanctions.

Russian diplomats rationalized these decisions, rejecting accusations that Russia was opening the floodgates to nuclear proliferation. "Russia definitely doesn't need any additional nuclear countries," Ulyanov told me. Commenting on those compatriots who advocated for nuclear multipolarity, Ulyanov quipped that Russia was a "free country," in which analysts had the "right to talk purga," which literally means "blizzard" but is used colloquially to mean "nonsense."

Sergey Karaganov was one of those engaged most actively in talking purga. He had "a calm attitude toward both the emergence of new nuclear powers and the strengthening of old ones," Karaganov wrote in summer 2024—because for Russia to prevail against the West, "there must be fear."

Dmitry Trenin remembered the moment he first felt that Russia needed to bring back the fear. It was September 2022, and Ukraine's forces, enabled by Western weaponry, were beginning their surprising Kharkiv offensive, steamrolling across hundreds of square miles to retake territory occupied by Russia. Trenin went on a weekly TV program hosted by Lukyanov and bemoaned that Russia had not been able to deter the West. A version of his remarks was later published with the title "Bring Back The Fear!" In it, Trenin argued that Russia needed to re-instill America's fear of nuclear war, even of a nuclear strike against the US homeland—otherwise, Biden was not going to stop supporting Ukraine. "The only thing that can stop the United States . . . is fear—its own fear of the next step. That's it, there's nothing else," he said.

After the piece was published, Lukyanov received a few calls from Westerners on both sides of the Atlantic, enquiring about Trenin's mental health.

Born in the early days of the Cold War in downtown Moscow, an area home to many embassies and the Soviet foreign ministry, Trenin grew up fascinated with Russia's prerevolutionary history and with foreign lands. He graduated from the military institute in Moscow and, after a short stint in Iraq, served as a liaison officer in the Soviet external relations branch in East Germany. When the Cold War ended, he quit the military and served on the Russian delegation at the Geneva talks on nuclear and space weapons, before receiving an invitation to join the NATO Defense College as a research fellow. Later, Trenin, who has impeccable English, led the Carnegie Moscow Center for well over a decade. I first met him there in 2015.

After the invasion of Ukraine, Trenin informed his American colleagues he would stick with his country, come what may. His pivot—from directing a Western think tank to providing the intellectual underpinnings for Russia's nuclear scares—horrified his former Western interlocutors. Many cut all contact with him, appalled by what they viewed as an analyst-turned-propagandist engaged in fearmongering. When we spoke in spring 2025, Trenin defended his positions as logical. "Like many others, I was looking for ways for the Russian leadership to come up with a more credible policy, because . . . otherwise the West, emboldened by our inaction, would eventually have put us into a situation in which the only possible choice was between basic surrender and another death of Russia—the third death of Russia in one hundred years," he told me. For him, Russia had temporarily "ceased to exist" in 1917, and then again in 1991. Trenin was referring to the February Revolution of 1917, which forced the abdication of Czar Nicholas II and ushered in a period of intense turmoil, and the collapse of the USSR in 1991.

Trenin's televised outburst in September 2022 was the product of pent-up frustration. Through the spring and summer of 2022, Russian elites and officials had issued warnings—sometimes veiled, sometimes rather blatant—that the West, in supporting Ukraine, was risking nuclear war. Particularly active was Dmitry Medvedev, deputy secretary of Russia's Security Council and former president. Medvedev had undergone quite the political transformation since his time in the Kremlin. When he became Russia's president back in 2008, he had promised modernization and liberalization, and visited Silicon Valley. After February 2022, Medvedev emerged as the most enthusiastic scaremonger attacking the West. "I'm often asked why my Telegram posts are so harsh," he wrote at one point. "Well, I'll answer: I hate them. They are bastards and degenerates. They want us, Russia, to die. And while I'm still alive, I will do everything to make them disappear." He did not specify whether the "they" in question referred to Ukrainians, the West, or both. Medvedev's regular diatribes often included nuclear intimidation. In one instance, he warned that, should Washington continue with its "destructive aims," the world could face a dystopian crisis that would end in a "big nuclear explosion." He regularly repeated such threats, especially during Ukraine's Kharkiv offensive in September.

Trenin increasingly thought such rhetoric insufficient to the task. In a November 2022 essay, he called Russian deterrence "inadequate" and argued that Russia's "information campaign," intended to scare the West, had clearly not produced the desired results. "Where there is no fear, there is no security," he repeated in January 2023, and asked, "Is (Russia's) current nuclear strategy a paper tiger or a death sentence for all of humanity? I have no answer to this question." But the prodigiously productive Trenin and others were working to find it.

By summer 2023, the casual nuclear talk in Moscow had transcended the strategic community to reach mainstream media coverage and public discourse in a veritable nuclear fever. Nobel Peace Prize winner Dmitry Muratov likened Russian domestic television coverage of nuclear-weapons use to "dog food commercials." In June, Karaganov entered the fray with an article entitled "A Difficult but Necessary Decision," which triggered a debate that would further push the boundaries of the acceptable in Russia's discussions on nuclear deterrence and cause a big outcry in Western capitals. Karaganov argued that, should the US and Europe fail to stop supporting Ukraine, Moscow would have to resort to preemptive nuclear strikes against Western countries, hinting specifically at Poland and the Baltic states. He conceded that the employment of "God's weapon" would bring "grave spiritual losses" for his country and that Russia's non-Western friends might be appalled at first. But, since "winners are not judged," Russia would ultimately be forgiven for having broken the eight-decade-old nuclear taboo. Importantly, Russia could engage in such strikes without risking a US nuclear response, since Washington was not going to get into nuclear war with Russia over Europe. Karaganov's article landed like a bombshell.

Some in the Russian strategic community felt he was going too far. They urged Russia's retention of a high bar for nuclear use. A group of scholars at Moscow's Institute of World Economy and International Relations, led by Alexey Arbatov, a highly respected thinker and former nuclear arms control negotiator, penned a piece in *Kommersant* questioning the suitability of limited nuclear use for preventing further escalation. Arbatov also challenged Karaganov's reckless optimism that nuclear strikes on Europe would not trigger a US nuclear response, mockingly calling on him to "share his secret with the General Staff, which has been trying to solve this problem for many decades." Karaganov himself rounded off the debate he had triggered by publishing a second, more strident piece, in which he offered two dozen recommendations for moving up the nuclear escalation ladder.

For Western observers reading Karaganov's shocking appeal

from afar, the fact he had dared write such things was a scandal. But not for Trenin, who wrote his own contribution to the debate. Though he stopped short of calling for nuclear strikes against Europe, Trenin urged the Russian leadership to put the "nuclear bullet" into the "revolver drum," wanting to see nuclear signaling in action, not just rhetoric. "I'm basically with Sergey Karaganov on many points," Trenin told me. "He has a different temperament than I do, he's more prone to provoking, to hit where it hurts. By nature, I'm not that way," he said. "Karaganov's ideas of bombing European cities may sound outrageous, but if we're serious about deterrence, about what it means, about why we need to deter, then in my world, it's alright. You need to be clear about the worst potential consequences of reckless policies. And I found the West's policies, primarily those of the US, to be incredibly provocative and incredibly dangerous from the start."

To give an example, Trenin recalled an incident from April 2022, when Ukrainian anti-ship missile strikes sank the *Moskva*, the flagship of Russia's Black Sea fleet. "I'm happy that I'm not in a position to have to make decisions," Trenin said about the episode, "but in my world, it called for a similar attack on some Western cruiser, or at least a frigate, given that a NATO country provided critical intelligence support for the Ukrainian strike. . . . Nothing of that kind should go unpunished. You may decide not to hit back, but then you're inviting another strike. Basically, your peacefulness, your restraint, adds oil to the fire." Returning to Karaganov's arguments, he concluded, "In other words, I see the threat of nuclear strikes against cities, in particular, as being very useful to uphold deterrence."

When we spoke, Trenin appeared to have made peace with the fact that many of his former Western colleagues had come to regard him as a source of venom and vitriol. He said he simply articulated what was in Russia's best interest.

What Trenin truly believed is, of course, impossible to know. With the invasion, Russia descended further into autocracy, by some accounts even into totalitarianism. In such systems, expertise has its own logic. Complying with unwritten rules and informal practices, experts and advisers create and constitute knowledge regimes that produce ideas reflecting the leadership's preferences, rather than openly critiquing them, and rarely do they speak truth to power. In fall 2021, a few months before the invasion, Trenin had published an essay in which he cautioned against the idea that Russia gobble up Ukraine. When I asked Trenin what had changed for him since and whether he was wrong at the time, he conceded that, right up until February 24, 2022, he had considered a full-scale invasion impossible. "My thesis in late 2021 was that we shouldn't be concerned with adding Ukraine to the territory that we control, that . . . not all of Ukraine was a brotherly nation, . . . that we should not be afraid of NATO, . . . but that we would be so much more likely to be undermined from within," he told me. But then, he said, "that's all overtaken by events."

Like Trenin, many Russian experts would end up justifying a war that they had either advised against or deemed implausible until the day it happened. Still, the majority of voices within Russia's strategic community, as well as the military elites, did not embrace calls for preemptive nuclear use or the extreme types of "active" deterrence advocated by Trenin and Karaganov. At a minimum, the fact that both men could say and write what they did indicated a tacit approval, a laissez-faire attitude by the Kremlin. At worst, it channeled a rethink among its upper echelons. "It's not a game of numbers," Trenin told me when I asked whether he thought his views had become shared more widely in Moscow. "On these issues, there's only one opinion that matters, and that's Putin's," he said. "But I think we moved the needle a bit."

WHAT PUTIN REALLY THINKS OF NUCLEAR WEAPONS REMAINS a subject of intense speculation. On the one hand, Putin appears to have always viewed these weapons as instruments of deterrence that could never actually be used. On one occasion, he said it was "impossible" to consider nuclear weapons "as a factor in any potential aggression, because it . . . would probably mean the end of our civilization." On the other hand, he repeatedly pointed out that it was the US that first used nuclear weapons in Hiroshima and Nagasaki. That hint appeared ominous insofar as Putin seemed convinced that Russia had the right to emulate any and all aspects of US conduct. If the US could deploy nuclear weapons on the territories of European allies, then Russia could do the same in Belarus. If the US could withdraw from nuclear agreements, so could Russia. Similarly worrying were the messianic overtones when Putin, in 2018, argued that Russia would be forced to defend itself using all available means if its very existence was at stake. "Why would we want a world without Russia?" he asked at the time. In another statement, Putin asserted that Russians "will go to heaven" in the event of nuclear war. The ominous subtext here was that Russians, in Putin's telling, were fulfilling a higher, even spiritual purpose in defending their country's interests—and willing to end human civilization in the process, if need be.

While Putin's threshold for using nuclear weapons remained unclear, he seemed happy for the strategic community to continue to debate how to enhance the country's coercive credibility. In summer 2024, Trenin and Arbatov engaged in another repartee, in which Arbatov criticized the "offensive" nuclear deterrence advocated by the Karaganov–Trenin camp. The course of the war in Ukraine, Trenin pushed back, had exposed the Americans' faith in their "own omnipotence" and the Europeans' "strategic parasitism," forcing Russia to resort to "active nuclear deterrence." Though shocking, the chatter never took Russia truly outside the bounds of established thinking. As Russian military experts Michael Kofman and Anya Fink have shown, Russian strategic deterrence has long foreseen the heavy use of nuclear signaling, partially to create the impression that the country is far looser with its thinking on nuclear use than is actually the case. After February 2022, such signaling just became louder and shriller and was suddenly everywhere.

To give greater heft to such fearmongering, the Russian government moved from words to more actions, desperate to find antidotes to the diminishing returns of its saber-rattling. It proceeded with the deployment of short-range nuclear weapons to Belarus. In November 2023, three months after Shoigu's visit to Novaya Zemlya, Putin signed a law on Russia's de-ratification of the Comprehensive Nuclear-Test-Ban Treaty (CTBT). By ending explosive nuclear-weapons testing, the CTBT's conclusion in 1996 had marked a key nonproliferation breakthrough, though several states including China and the US never ratified the treaty. Moscow justified its de-ratification by citing a need to maintain parity in obligations with the US. Though Russian officials stressed that Moscow would continue to adhere to its nuclear testing moratorium, provided that the US did the same, the move was seen as another effort to raise the nuclear temperature.

Around the same time, the idea of overhauling the country's nuclear doctrine seems to have been planted. Russia's doctrine, a 2020 document known as "Basic Principles of State Policy of the Russian Federation on Nuclear Deterrence," laid out the conditions under which the country might resort to using nuclear weapons. When Karaganov asked Putin at the annual Valdai conference in October 2023 whether the doctrine required updating, the president responded that he saw no need, though he "respected" the perspectives of "patriotic experts" like Karaganov. But by spring 2024, Russian diplomats hinted that they were working on an update after all. In June, Putin took the stage at the St. Petersburg International Economic Forum and called the country's nuclear doctrine a "living document" to which changes could not be ruled out.

Putin's remarks were the signal Russia's hawks had been waiting for. Karaganov said he had submitted his recommendations, while Trenin spoke with *Kommersant* to lay out his advice: A new doctrine should explicitly state Russia's readiness to use nuclear weapons first, and proclaim that Russia might consider nuclear use against nonnuclear NATO members. In late September, the process was concluded and Putin emerged before the press to announce amendments to Russia's nuclear doctrine. In essence, the new document sought to create the impression of a lowered threshold for nuclear use, but did not actually represent a fundamental change in Russia's nuclear strategy.

Was Russia's climb up the escalation ladder effective? Russia's threats proved a useful psychological ploy in its effort to outlast the West, keeping Western audiences, both the wider public and decision-makers, on edge. They seem to have delayed or slowed the West's release of certain weapons for Ukraine, including ATACMS missiles and German Leopard tanks. In spring 2024, US news anchor Jim Sciutto revealed that, around the time of Ukraine's 2022 Kharkiv offensive, the Biden administration had been intensely worried that Russia might actually use a tactical nuclear weapon in Ukraine. When Western capitals pondered, in fall 2024, whether to allow Ukraine to use their weapons to strike behind Russian borders, Russian nuclear threats again figured prominently in the debate. All that said, Russia's ascent up the escalation ladder did not deter the West from supporting Ukraine in myriad ways. It is impossible to ascertain what Western governments would or would not have done, had Russia not so openly rattled the nuclear saber.

What is certain is that Russia's fearmongering caused frictions within the Western camp. German Chancellor Olaf Scholz's fears of Russian retaliation seemed to underpin his reluctance to send Taurus missiles to Ukraine in 2024. His restraint found support among segments of German society but earned him widespread criticism elsewhere in Europe. Officials in the Baltic states and Eastern Europe, all advocates of more forward-leaning support for Ukraine, warned of falling into a trap of "self-deterrence," of succumbing to "nuclear blackmail," of becoming too afraid of Russia.

Trenin thought that he, Karaganov, and other like-minded voices helped make Russia's deterrence more effective over time. Asked for evidence, Trenin pointed to the fact that Putin, having announced doctrinal changes in September 2024, waited to formalize them until mid-November—when Russia was ready to test a new intermediate-range ballistic missile called Oreshnik. The timing, Trenin told me, suggested an understanding in the Kremlin that words needed to be backed by action. "I haven't been to Washington for a long time," Trenin conceded when I asked him whether he thought the new doctrine had

had an effect on the West, "but Donald Trump's one consistent theme has been that Joe Biden brought the United States to the brink of a nuclear war with Russia. You may think it's just rhetoric; I tend to think otherwise. . . . So, I think it did cool a few heads in Washington."

In walking away from nuclear arms control, in chilling its cooperation on nonproliferation, and in putting a premium on nuclear threats, Moscow elevated the salience of nuclear weapons and became the midwife of a more dangerous nuclear environment. Just as infiltrating the West with its propaganda was integral to outlasting the West, so was intimidating it. Yet, in its effort to scare, Russia only had so many cards to play—and the nuclear threat was the most potent source of intimidation. Its effectiveness may have worn off with time, but there were always enough average people and politicians susceptible to it.

Russia was not the only architect of new nuclear dangers, which also arose from growing US–China tensions and from a wave of technological breakthroughs, including in the realm of AI. But the cumulative impact of Russia's actions after February 2022 was especially detrimental to the health of the nuclear order.

Trenin would surely disagree with that conclusion. In December 2024, he released a book, coauthored with Karaganov and retired Russian admiral Sergey Avakyants, entitled *From Deterrence to Intimidation.* In it, the authors called for Russia to develop a new, non-Western theory of deterrence, together with intellectual and political elites in countries of the "global majority." They warned that, even if the war in Ukraine were to end, Russia's confrontation with the West would continue for at least a generation. Russia had no choice but to "bring back the fear into the collective West's decision-making," to disabuse anyone of the illusion that the country could be defeated on the battlefield. Ultimately, they argued, bringing back the fear would allow Russia to reclaim the great power status it had enjoyed, once upon a time.

CHAPTER 13

Of Saboteurs and Spies

MORNINGS WERE ALWAYS THE HARDEST FOR ALSU KURMAsheva. She had no watch, so she trained herself to wake up naturally just before 6 a.m., when breakfast started. Those few minutes were her cherished moments of quiet and solitude. To mentally prepare herself for the hardships of the day ahead, she would gently release her eyes into the dark and warm before opening them fully to the prison world surrounding her.

Kurmasheva made use of the daily allowance to stroll in the prison courtyard, even when the temperatures sank to minus-22 degrees Fahrenheit. Sometimes, she went for jogs, doing forty laps in the twenty-five square meters that were available to her. When the yard was blanketed with snow, she asked for a shovel, eager to keep moving. Some of her fellow prisoners, one of them an architect, crafted spellbinding sculptures out of the snow.

Eventually, Kurmasheva got permission to access the prison library, and friends and relatives sent books, too. She read *Mothers and Daughters* by Yelena Bonner, the Soviet dissident and wife of Nobel

Prize-winning physicist Andrey Sakharov. The memoir describes Bonner's coming of age in the Soviet system. It inspired Kurmasheva, who is of Muslim Tatar descent, to write a series of letters to her own teenage daughters during Ramadan. She penned one letter each day, sharing what was on her mind, but she never posted them, reluctant to bother her lawyer with additional requests. On the last day of Ramadan, she sat in her cell, ending her final letter by channeling her innermost desire: "Right now, as I write these words, I pray that we will read these letters together next Ramadan."

Kurmasheva's voice cracked, her eyes welling as she shared the anecdote with me when we met in Prague in January 2025. Kurmasheva, a dual US–Russian citizen and journalist with Radio Free Europe/Radio Liberty (RFE/RL), was charged and detained as a "foreign agent" in her hometown of Kazan in October 2023. The authorities accused her of having illegally collected information about the Russian military.

With that, she became one of several Western journalists and citizens seized by the Kremlin as bargaining chips in its coercive diplomacy with the West after the invasion of Ukraine. Born in Petropavlovsk in northern Kazakhstan, where her Tatar family had been sent by Stalin's orders, Kurmasheva moved to Kazan as a child in the mid-1980s. Her school offered advanced English, a class that opened her eyes to the outside world—to politics, to America, to different cultures—during the twilight years of the Soviet Union. Though she initially wanted to work for the UN, in 1998 she received an invitation from RFE/RL in Prague to try out as a radio moderator. She accepted and has been at the outlet ever since.

Kurmasheva specialized in broadcasts about issues related to Tatar culture. She saw her work as educational, a source to help Tatars—a society she considers herself to be a part of—"make informed decisions about their lives," she told me. She also covered the stories of victims of domestic violence in Russia, trying to shine light on a taboo issue. Eventually, RFE/RL's online Tatar language instruction via a YouTube channel counted more than thirty thousand subscribers. It became a thorn in the side of the Kremlin, which saw such activities as threatening its control over the Tatarstan region. Once they arrested her, her captors asked Kurmasheva over and over about the operations of RFE/RL, which the Kremlin had designated "an undesirable organization." She didn't have much to say. "My work was always open," she told me. "They were asking questions to which the answers could be found on the internet."

For much of the post–Cold War period, the kind of realpolitik hostage-taking that swept up Kurmasheva seemed like a thing of the past. At the start of his first term, in 2000, Putin had even personally pardoned US businessman Edmond Pope, who was being held at Moscow's infamous Lefortovo prison on a spying conviction he vigorously denied. But as Russia's foreign policy became more aggressive, that changed.

In 2020, Paul Whelan, an ex-US Marine from Michigan, was given a sixteen-year jail sentence on charges of espionage, which he denied. Marc Fogel, an American teacher in Russia, was arrested in 2021 for allegedly carrying medically prescribed marijuana and sentenced to fourteen years on drug smuggling charges that the US described as "unjust." US basketball star Brittney Griner was detained at a Moscow airport just one week before the Ukraine invasion, after authorities found cannabis oil in her luggage. She was exchanged for Russian arms dealer Viktor Bout in late 2022.

Then, authorities came for the foreign journalists. In March 2023, Russia's Federal Security Service detained *Wall Street Journal* correspondent Evan Gershkovich while he was on a reporting trip in Yekaterinburg. Gershkovich became the first foreign correspondent to be charged with espionage in Russia since the collapse of the Soviet Union. Seven months later, Kurmasheva, too, disappeared into a Russian prison cell. Gershkovich and Kurmasheva denied the allegations against them. With the arrests, Putin sent a twin message. The first was to Western journalists: You are no longer safe, reporting from Russia. The second was to Western capitals: Russia will not give in.

When we spoke in Prague a few months after her release from prison, Kurmasheva, wearing a cozy wool sweater, still exuded the passions of that twentysomething aspiring journalist. "Let's start with the arrest," I suggested.

In May 2023, Kurmasheva traveled to Russia to visit her ailing mother. Ten days later, just before she was to board a plane to Sochi, from where she would fly out of the country, authorities at the Kazan airport confiscated her passport and stopped her from leaving. She returned to her mother's house. "I was in fear day and night," Kurmasheva told me, reflecting on the summer months that followed, "because all those cases against journalists were political cases, and their number was on the rise." Four months later, she was ordered to pay a fine of ten thousand rubles (approximately one hundred US dollars) for having failed to register her US citizenship—which she obtained via a program for employees of US-sponsored media abroad. It was the smallest possible fine for this kind of offense, and she worried that it probably wasn't the end of the story.

On October 18, a Wednesday, Kurmasheva was at her mother's home cooking lunch, a traditional *plov* with beef, rice, raisins, dried apricots, and spices. Suddenly, six or seven men in black masks stormed into the building. Kurmasheva refused to let them into the apartment, frantically calling her lawyer. Once the men threatened to cut through the door, she relented. She barely had time to put on proper clothes before they handcuffed her and dragged her to the police station. During the hours of interrogations that followed, she was presented with the foreign agent charges. "It wasn't much of an interrogation," Kurmasheva recalled. "They had their worldview. The things we journalists are proud of doing, they reversed it as a crime."

After that initial interrogation, Kurmasheva was sent to a temporary detention center for five days. "I felt like in a coma," she recalled. "I couldn't breathe, I couldn't eat." It was only when she was transferred to a SIZO—a pretrial detention center—and the cell door shut firmly behind her, that her fear disappeared. It yielded to an intense survival instinct.

In December, authorities opened another case against Kurmasheva, this one under the law against "fakes" about the Russian Army that had been adopted in March 2022 to crack down on antiwar protests. The charges were introduced over a 2022 book, *Saying No to War*, coedited by Kurmasheva, which featured the stories of forty Russians opposed to the invasion of Ukraine. "Some of the story tellers want to do right by their grandchildren, others have relatives in Ukraine, and still others have no connection with Ukraine, but they are protesting all the same," Kurmasheva and her coeditors wrote in the book's foreword. "All of this comes for one purpose, and that is to stop the criminal war and steer the country from a path, where the final station is the abyss." Kurmasheva sought to give a voice to those the Kremlin would prefer to make voiceless, and she was punished for it. Christmas was coming up, and the realization that Kurmasheva would spend it separated from her family began to sink in.

The prison facilities at the SIZO were dismal. She was confined to a small cell that she shared with one or two other inmates. A hole in the floor served as the toilet. She used a *kipyatilnik*, a Soviet-designed immersion heater, to warm up the ice-cold water to brush her teeth. A vegetarian, Kurmasheva started eating the canned meat and fish her family sent to make sure she got some protein. When I asked what she craved most during her time in prison, Kurmasheva said, "A clean glass of clean water."

Kurmasheva took the interrogations seriously at first. "I thoroughly prepared myself," she recalled. "I tried to explain my worldview, what journalism means. And after each interrogation, I would come back to the cell feeling physically sick, second-guessing whether I said the right thing, whether I should have put something differently." She soon realized that her efforts were for nothing. "They didn't want me to confess anything and they were asking questions to which the answers could be found on the internet—information about Radio Free Europe, about my book."

During that period, Kurmasheva read Gulag literature from the prison library, one book after another. *Life Is an Unpaired Boot* by Tamara Petkevich, who in 1943 was sentenced to seven years in Soviet forced labor camps, left a particular impression on her. The memoir reminded Kurmasheva of her own experience.

Yet, in other ways, Kurmasheva's and Gershkovich's prison ordeals stood in stark contrast to Soviet times. As historian Mark Kramer observes, during the Cold War, Moscow and Washington tended to arrest spies but rarely took political prisoners. In recent years, and especially after 2022, Kramer says, Russia has evolved into an abductor state, seizing and imprisoning Western citizens—accredited journalists or researchers engaged in activities that had generally been tolerated in the past—as hostages, to be traded for Russian criminals, spies, and assassins.

The Kremlin seemed smug in response to questions or criticism over the arrests. When journalists challenged Kremlin spokesman Peskov over Gershkovich's detention in spring 2023, he answered confidently. "We're not talking about suspicions," he said. "He was caught red-handed." In December 2023, *The New York Times*'s Valerie Hopkins asked Putin about Gershkovich and Whelan during the Kremlin's staged end-of-year press conference: "What will it take to bring them home?"

Putin, who did not usually comment on such detentions, seemed confused as to who Gershkovich was—possibly because the interpreter had translated Hopkins's remarks imprecisely—then said, "It's not that we have refused to send them back—we have not—but we want to come to terms [with the American side] and we want these agreements to be *mutually acceptable*."

Three and a half months later, during a pretrial hearing in early April 2024, Kurmasheva stood in a glass cage in a Kazan courtroom. Her face motionless as the TV cameras broadcasting the proceedings zoomed in on her, she listened to the judge extend her detention for yet another two months. "Those pretrial hearings were very hard for me, because I knew that my family was watching," Kurmasheva recalled. "So, I tried to look cheerful, because I didn't see the point of me crying there or falling apart. But, of course, it's not how I felt inside," she said.

"After every hearing, I would go back to my cell feeling absolutely sick, and I would just stay in bed for one or two days."

Then came Kurmasheva's trial. Shortly beforehand, she had learned that Gershkovich would be tried on the same day, and it had given her huge amounts of hope, because she was aware the campaign for her release was connected to his. She focused her entire inner life on the idea that a prisoner exchange might be in the works.

On July 19, in a farcical procedure held behind closed doors, a Kazan court found Kurmasheva guilty of spreading false information about the Russian Army and sentenced her to six and a half years in prison. Some five hundred miles east, a Yekaterinburg court convicted Gershkovich of espionage and sentenced him to sixteen years behind bars.

It was a hot day in Kazan, and as Kurmasheva was led from the courtroom to a transition cell before returning to prison, she collapsed. She asked for tea and a moment to lie down on the floor. "No ambulance," she said to the guard. "I will be okay." She took a couple of deep breaths. It had all been too much. She hadn't told anyone in her cell that it was the day of her trial, but when she returned later that evening, her emotions were hard to hide. "What's happening? What did they do to you?" the other women asked.

The verdict was followed by what felt like Kurmasheva's longest week in prison yet. After seven days, she was taken out of her cell and told she was being transferred to Moscow. One of the other women in her cell, a Ukrainian, realized what was about to happen. As they said goodbye, she whispered into Kurmasheva's ear, "See you there. Wait for me." Once in Moscow, Kurmasheva spent four days in Lefortovo.

From there, everything happened quickly. On August 1, she was put on a bus with other prisoners. Gershkovich took a seat behind her. They greeted each other, and Kurmasheva gave Gershkovich her favorite book, Milan Kundera's *The Unbearable Lightness of Being*, which she had read through her trial days, trying to block out the ramblings of the prosecutor and the judge. They boarded an Aeroflot plane to Ankara. From there, they took a special aircraft back to the United States.

In the early hours of August 2, before sunrise, the plane touched down at Joint Base Andrews in Maryland. Joe Biden and Kamala Harris, as well as relatives and friends, were waiting on the tarmac, spotlights shooting through the pitch darkness. Whelan, the longest-held US prisoner, stepped off the plane first. Then came Gershkovich, lifting his mother up in the air in their precious moment of reunion. Finally, a frail-looking Kurmasheva emerged, wearing gray pants, a blue sweater, and sneakers, waving shyly as she stepped onto American soil after 288 days in Russian detention. As she exchanged a few words with the president and vice president, her daughters could barely contain their emotions. When Kurmasheva sprinted over, embracing them at long last, they burst into tears.

Overall, twenty-four people were involved in the prisoner exchange between Russia and several Western countries that came as the result of mind-bogglingly complicated diplomatic choreography. Besides Whelan, Gershkovich, and Kurmasheva, Russia also freed Russian dissident Vladimir Kara-Murza, opposition politician Ilya Yashin, human rights activist Oleg Orlov, German nationals Kevin Lik and Rico Krieger (who was detained in Belarus) and a few others. Rather than just getting out three American citizens, the Biden White House had successfully negotiated for the release of prominent Russian opposition figures, human rights defenders, and anti-war activists.

Back in Russia, Putin had gotten his "mutually acceptable" deal. Waiting at Moscow's Vnukovo Airport, he rolled out the red carpet for a coterie of hackers, money launderers, murderers, and spies who were released from Western countries as part of the exchange. The most infamous among them was Vadim Krasikov, who had been serving a life sentence in Germany for the 2019 murder of an exiled Chechen in Berlin's Tierpark. Russian agents Artem Dultsev and Anna Dultseva, released from Slovenia, arrived at Vnukovo with their young children, who only learned on the plane from Ankara that they were Russian nationals. All were individuals convicted in Western countries of charges like murder, spying, or cybercrime.

Though the prisoner exchange was an act of pragmatism on Putin's part, it served another purpose for the Russian president: restoring confidence among his agents, including those doing the Kremlin's bidding in Western countries, that they could count on him should they be caught. Giving the returnees a hero's welcome, the Kremlin telegraphed that it would stand by those faithfully serving on dangerous missions abroad. Releasing Kurmasheva and the other prisoners, Putin was not sending a conciliatory message to the West. Rather, he made clear that Russia was only getting ready for the next round of confrontation.

EUROPE BECAME THE STAGING GROUND FOR THAT NEXT ROUND. As Russia's war against Ukraine dragged on, Moscow complemented its effort to stoke the fear of nuclear war with a wider campaign of hybrid warfare against the West. US and allied intelligence agencies tracked an increasing number of covert operations, which they attributed to agents, arsonists, and assassins hired by the Kremlin. Investigative journalists followed their trails to actors or agencies usually associated with Russia's military intelligence agency, the GRU. While Russia's campaign spanned the globe—with Mexico, for instance, emerging as a playground for Russian spies due to its proximity to the US—Europe was the priority.

The hybrid campaign was versatile, with its fronts encompassing everything from military installations, weapons factories, and critical underwater infrastructure—all vulnerable to sabotage—via the information space vulnerable to Russian disinformation, to European borders vulnerable to sudden migrant flows. With time, attacks on these disparate fronts became increasingly brazen.

In April 2024, Bavarian police arrested two German-Russian nationals accused of scouting US military facilities on German soil and planning attacks with explosives. The same month, Baltic governments charged that Russia had stepped up its GPS jamming in the region, raising the risk of an air disaster. Authorities registered arsons or attempted arsons targeting a wide range of sites, including a warehouse in England, a paint factory in Poland, an Ikea store in Lithuania, and a factory near Berlin. All were blamed on individuals with links to Russia. Besides unleashing its saboteurs and spies, Moscow also stepped up disinformation campaigns in Europe to plant fake news and pro-Russian narratives, especially ahead of elections.

Things heated up in the summer of 2024. For the first time in a decade, US military bases across Europe were placed on a heightened state of alert—Force Protection Condition "Charlie"—given intelligence that Russian-backed actors were planning sabotage attacks. Bombs, presumed to have been placed by Russian agents, ignited DHL logistics hubs in Leipzig, Germany, and Birmingham, England. Ahead of the Paris Olympics, arson attacks targeted the French railway system, and a forty-year-old Russian was arrested over a suspected plot targeting the Games.

Such so-called "hybrid" actions against Western states came with several benefits for Russia. They were inexpensive. They were not the same as a direct military attack, yet they still served to test NATO's resolve and exhaust its populations, presumably to erode its unity from within. Some Europeans increasingly worried that hybrid actions could mark the opening salvo to a future Russian war with the alliance, designed to poke defenses and infrastructure for weaknesses. Perhaps most important, they were usually deniable and hard to pin on Russia. Proving a link between local recruits and the Russian state could be notoriously difficult, so governments were cautious—at least initially—about explicitly blaming Moscow.

Russia generally denied responsibility for these incidents, but it insinuated on occasion that it would find appropriate ways to respond to what it called Western "warfare"—Western aid for Ukraine and sanctions against Russia. Early into the invasion, for example, Putin lambasted sanctions as equivalent to the West declaring war on Russia.

Peskov characterized the sanctions as "banditry" and vowed that Moscow would respond. In April 2024, *The Washington Post* revealed a secret addendum to Russia's 2023 foreign policy concept that called for an "offensive information campaign" and other measures spanning "the military-political, economic and trade and informational psychological spheres" against "unfriendly countries." Russia should find these countries' "vulnerable points" with the aim of developing steps to weaken them, said the document, provided to the newspaper by a European intelligence service.

Russia's post-2022 sabotage operations mimicked the Soviet Union's doctrine and modus operandi in important ways, but there was, as Cold War historian Sergey Radchenko put it to *The Economist*, a crucial difference. "Whereas previously, special operations supported foreign policy, today special operations *are* foreign policy," Radchenko said. To him, the Soviet Union's Cold War thinking had given way to a new foreign policy nihilism in Russia. "It is as if the Russians no longer feel they have a stake in preserving anything of the postwar international order," he said.

Several analyses conducted after the invasion pointed to a clear escalation in hybrid operations. According to a research team at Leiden University in the Netherlands, Russian operations in Europe surged from six in 2022, to thirteen in 2023, to forty-four in 2024. A separate dataset, compiled by the Center for Strategic and International Studies in Washington and based on slightly different metrics, counted three attacks in 2022, twelve in 2023, and thirty-four in 2024.

The uptick in attacks was clear, but the Kremlin seemed unrepentant. Antti Helanterä, Finland's ambassador to Russia from September 2020 until August 2024, recalled challenging one of Russia's leading security experts over the sabotage spree. "Why are you doing this? Your measures keep Western societies mobilized against Russia—it is counterproductive!" Russia's actions were merely a response to the West's economic sanctions, which Moscow regarded as its own form of hybrid warfare, the expert replied.

HELANTERÄ WAS RIGHT TO BE CONCERNED. FINLAND BECAME a priority front for Russian hybrid warfare after it joined NATO in April 2023. Though that decision ended a decades-long tradition of military non-alignment, Finland had long harbored suspicions of its neighbor.

When the Soviets attacked Finland in 1939, the country had 3.5 million inhabitants, fewer than the city of St. Petersburg. Assuming the position of commander in chief at the age of seventy-two, Finnish General Gustaf Mannerheim famously told the defense forces: "You know me and I know you. . . . This war is nothing other than the . . . final act of our War of Independence. We are fighting for our homes, our faith, and our country." Average people resisted Soviet tanks with Molotov cocktails. Finland paid an extreme price: During the "Winter War," it lost approximately 96,000 citizens and up to 12 percent of its territory to the Soviet Union. But, together with Norway, it would remain the only country sharing a direct border with the USSR to remain free from Soviet dominion. The lesson that resilience pays off was seared into the minds of generations of Finns.

After the war, and even following the collapse of the USSR, the two countries maintained strict procedures to manage their shared eight-hundred-mile-long border. But as relations deteriorated following Finland's accession to NATO—with mutual expulsions of diplomats and Russia closing the Finnish General Consulate in St. Petersburg—Finnish border guards noticed unusual movement on the Russian side. Despite cold temperatures, troves of people were making their way toward the crossings—on bicycles, no less. In November and December of 2023, more than a thousand asylum seekers rode or walked across the border, many of them Iraqi or Syrian. The Finnish government reacted by closing all land border crossings with Russia.

"The border issue compounded everything," Helanterä told me one month after his return from Moscow. When migrants started coming across the border, he asked for a meeting at the Russian foreign ministry to express Finland's concerns and request an explanation. "We are only acting in accordance with Russian law," was the faux-naïf response he received. "But your law hasn't changed," Helanterä protested. His counterparts' vague replies left him with the impression that "this was Russia's way to demonstrate that there were not going to be any more favors and that this was how the relationship would look like henceforth."

The 2023 crossings were not totally without precedent. In 2015, at the height of the European migrant crisis, Russia had brought busloads of asylum seekers to Finnish border posts in Lapland and sold them cars or bicycles at extortionate prices. Finland regarded the short-lived episode as a Russian breach of confidence and initiated a fundamental overhaul of its intelligence legislation. The spat was only resolved once Finland threatened to cancel then President Sauli Niinistö's visit to Moscow.

After the crisis subsided, the border remained peaceful and incidents rare. Russian border guards would stop those wanting to cross into Finland to check whether they held valid Schengen visas.

In fall 2023, they stopped that practice, Colonel Marko Turunen recalled. Today the deputy head of Finland's border and coast guard division, when Turunen was stationed with the North Karelia border guard he saw evidence of truck drivers on the Russian side handing bikes to migrants. The Kremlin knew that sending migrants across the border was more than a symbolic stab, given how explosive and politically divisive an issue the 2015 migrant crisis had become in several European countries. When the Finnish side sent inquiries, the blasé response it received was "If people want to cross, well, we cannot stop them." An investigation by the independent news site *Fontanka* revealed that migrants were taken to the Finnish border in vehicles with Russian license plates, but couldn't prove that the Russian state had orchestrated the crisis.

As we sat in his Helsinki office, Turunen seemed slightly nostalgic, flipping through a presentation with photographs of past meetings and joint patrols with Russian guards. The pictures showed mostly men, Finns and Russians, standing in the woods in snow gear, smiling. "The Russian border guards are true professionals," Turunen said, and I sensed his desire to differentiate between his Russian counterparts on the ground and those giving orders from Moscow. Before 2023, he said, there would be ten to twelve such meetings per year to discuss mundane border business. With the border closed, that joint activity atrophied. Since Russia had not closed its side of the border, he said, Finland needed to maintain constant surveillance.

Ongoing surveillance was just one measure the Finns took to secure their border against a menacing Russia. They were building a fence along parts of it, too. In summer 2024, a few weeks before my visit to Helsinki, Finland's parliament passed a controversial law, the Border Security Act, that allowed the border guards to refuse entry to asylum seekers. On July 16, President Alexander Stubb signed the time-limited legislation.

Stubb believed there could be no complacency in the face of threats from Russia. "Total defense starts from societal resilience," he told the audience at the Helsinki Security Forum. Finland has obligatory military service for male citizens and a national emergency supply agency tasked with ensuring society could function even under exceptional circumstances, he added. The mindset that Finland needed to be prepared for war, at all times and at all levels of society, resonated more deeply after Russia's invasion of Ukraine, but had existed since the Winter War.

During World War II, people hid weapons for resistance, "in case the Soviets come," Kari Pietiläinen, the training director of Finland's National Defense Training Association, known as the MPK, told me. The MPK was founded after the dissolution of the USSR with a mandate to improve and support the readiness of the regular defense forces, offer military training for reservists, and hone the safety, security, and preparedness skills of average people. After Russia invaded Ukraine, enrollment in the MPK's courses increased fivefold, Pietiläinen said. Meeting such high demand required lots of "train the trainers" efforts together with the Finnish Defense Forces.

In light of Russia's sabotage spree across Europe, the MPK also continued to enhance its focus on cybersecurity, building on its long-standing partnership with the Virginia National Guard to simulate attacks on Finnish water and energy infrastructure and develop responses. Listening to Pietiläinen, I had a flashback to my visit to VOMA in Yerevan just two months prior. Russia's invasion of Ukraine had jolted both average Armenians and Finns into preparing for a future war, yet for starkly different reasons: the Armenians because they felt abandoned by Russia; the Finns because they worried Russia might be coming for them next.

I only fully realized what societal resilience meant in Finland after passing through an airlock door and descending many flights of metal stairs into the Hakaniemi civil defense shelter. Built seventy feet down into solid bedrock, the shelter can fit up to six thousand people. Still catching my breath and mentally adjusting to being so deep underground, I walked past recreational sport courts, a children's playground, and a big food court. "In peacetime, the spaces here are rented out to private businesses for their routine operations," the staff running the facility told me. "That's doubly convenient. If something breaks, it will be reported and repaired. And it normalizes people's experience going into a shelter."

The shelter can go into complete lockup mode and withstand the impact of a tactical nuclear weapon. Were an emergency to arise, the shelter would have seventy-two hours to get ready once the interior ministry gave the order. A crew of three hundred, including firefighters, medical staff, and childcare specialists, would be required to run the place. A core crew of one hundred would come from the City of Helsinki, and an additional two hundred would be recruited from the shelter population, some of them likely having been trained at one point by the MPK. I passed a section of bunk beds where those sheltering would sleep in shifts.

When Russia invaded Ukraine, Finland, with its population of 5.6 million, already had 50,500 civil defense shelters with space for a total of 4.8 million people. After February 2022, shelter legislation was updated to mandate eight square feet of shelter space for each Finn, the equivalent of a big bath towel. "I sleep my nights very well, considering the state of societal resilience," Stubb said at the time of my September visit. "Few countries are as prepared as we are for a tight situation." That was true. Other European countries remained woefully unequipped for civil defense, with limited bunkers, dismantled siren systems, and a lack of basic emergency training for citizens.

And yet Finland needed to stay vigilant. Over the summer, mysterious intruders had broken into Finnish water towers and treatment plants, possibly to scout them for future attacks. In September, the Finnish defense ministry announced the establishment of a NATO army command in the southeastern town of Mikkeli, less than 125 miles from its eastern border with Russia, to "send a message" to Moscow. In November, the interior ministry launched a new website to further step up household emergency preparedness across society.

Christmas was approaching. Through December, Finns gathered at *pikkujoulu* ("little Christmas") parties and enjoyed mulled wine and spicy Bundt cake at the country's many pristine Christmas markets. The winter season, with its scarcity of daylight hours, makes Scandinavians especially eager to seek out sources of comfort and coziness. Danes or Norwegians call this practice "hygge," but the Finns use the concept of *kalsarikännit*, which literally means "drinking at home, alone, in your underwear."

Out on the stormy sea, a far distance from Helsinki's cozy living rooms, Finnish border guards were having the opposite of a *kalsarikännit* time. Around Christmas, the *Eagle S* tanker entered Finnish waters. In the early hours of Boxing Day, Finnish special forces rappelled from a helicopter to seize control of the vessel. The day before, a submarine cable carrying electricity between Finland and Estonia called the Estlink 2 had been cut, and investigators found a seabed trail around the site. The destruction seemed to be the result of a brazen act of sabotage. And the *Eagle S* was the prime suspect.

THE *EAGLE S*'S DETENTION IN DECEMBER 2024 CAPPED A STRING of incidents in European waters involving critical undersea infrastructure (CUI), such as internet or electricity cables and gas pipelines. In spring 2023, four Russian vessels sailed through Ireland's exclusive economic zone, rousing suspicion they could be mapping or interfering with subsea cables that transfer data between Ireland and the US. In October that year, the Balticconnector gas pipeline between Finland and Estonia was damaged. Finnish police investigated whether a Chinese vessel had dragged its anchor along the seabed, causing the rupture. In November 2024, two underwater internet cables in the Baltic Sea were cut, the first connecting Lithuania to Sweden, the second Germany to Finland. Again, a Chinese-registered ship, having picked up cargo in Russia, was spotted near the sites of both outages, but European lawmakers and intelligence officials also hinted at possible Russian involvement. There were other murky cases in Norwegian waters. The underwater world, it seemed, was becoming the latest front in Russian hybrid warfare.

Internet cables are the lifelines of the European economy. Of the approximately 250 active cables that ensure the EU is connected to the global internet, two-thirds are underwater. But when it comes to damage to such critical underwater infrastructure, proving the culprit and proof of intent is notoriously difficult. In some of these instances, Russian trawlers were sailing near a damaged cable at the time of the incident. But that does not prove deliberate sabotage.

What is clear is that Russia was becoming more active in the Baltic Sea. In 2023, Russia's navy ramped up its mapping of CUI in the region, according to NATO. Russian naval or spy ships hovered near cables. There were other unfriendly incidents. On one occasion, a Russian ship fired signaling ammunition at a German military helicopter on a reconnaissance mission. When journalists broke the news in summer 2023 that Western countries may have been complicit in blowing up the Nord Stream gas pipelines—four leaks were detected in late September 2022—former Russian President Dmitry Medvedev warned this gave Russia a "free hand" to destroy the undersea communications cables of its enemies.

The *Eagle S* incident compounded the West's headaches by raising a new, uncomfortable prospect: Russia might be benefiting doubly from its shadow fleet, using the vessels not just to export oil but also for acts of sabotage. "I think at some point Russia realized, 'Oh, we have all these vessels that we're using; we might as well use a few of them to cause a little extra harm,'" Swedish security expert Elisabeth Braw told *The New York Times* after the *Eagle S*'s detention.

Russia has thought about—and developed the capabilities for—holding CUI at risk ever since Soviet times. The Russian Navy and a special organization called the Main Directorate of Deep-Sea Research (also known as GUGI) have long maintained a fleet of ships and special submarines that can be used for espionage and other covert operations. Deep-diving submarines can sever or tap cables at depth. Surface vessels don't pose the same level of threat, but it is also harder to attribute any malign activity to them, since they're nominally just research vessels.

Eager to get to the bottom of this threat to critical undersea infrastructure and what the West was doing about it, I arrived in the UK on a rainy morning in November 2024. When my car pulled up at NATO's Allied Maritime Command in Northwood, Captain Pål Bratbak awaited me at an entrance gate surrounded by barbed-wire fencing. Bratbak, a Norwegian, oversaw a new center focusing on underwater assets amid Russian sabotage concerns. It went by the long and complicated name of NATO Maritime Centre for the Security of Critical Undersea Infrastructure.

When I visited the center, it had only begun to find its footing. Bratbak wore a dark blue uniform with the Norwegian flag patched onto his upper arm and a three-day stubble that made him look like a true sailor. He had started out as a Norwegian coast guard officer in the 1990s, carrying out search and rescue missions and protecting fishing. "If you like sailing and your family accepts you being away for three weeks at a time, it's a fantastic job," he reminisced. "And we had really good relations with the Russian fishing authorities." After obtaining a master's degree and further qualifications, Bratbak became a staff officer in the navy, then the commander of the coast guard. In those years, he was part of the Norwegian military sailing team, a pastime that on occasion involved drinking with Russian sailors. When NATO decided to create the new center in Northwood, they asked Bratbak to lead it.

"Cables have existed since the nineteenth century, but until the Nord Stream explosion, there was no real doctrine for how to protect critical undersea infrastructure," he explained. It's not always straightforward to determine what infrastructure is most threatened, and how bad the threat is, he added. Pipelines deep undersea may be less protected from explosions, but at the same time, they are more robust than cables. And the criticality of a cable or pipeline can change over time. If one supply line fails, another can suddenly become vital for a certain country. For instance, only two cables transport electricity from the Norwegian mainland to the Svalbard archipelago. If one were to stop working, that would pose a serious issue.

When CUI is damaged, it can often be the result of an accident, aging, or natural operation causes, Bratbak explained. According to the International Cable Protection Committee, a trade group, up to 80 percent of cable-damage incidents globally are caused by accidents linked to commercial fishing and ship anchors. "When fishing vessels trawl," Bratbak said, his posture straightening as he got excited at the opportunity to explain the nuts and bolts of fishing, "they lower their nets to the bottom of the sea, where they will float." The trawl doors are made of metal or steel, which can damage cables, he said.

"How do you know whether something was an accident or deliberate sabotage?" I asked. Bratbak acknowledged that was difficult to answer. "If the water depth is shallow, you can dive there and have a look," he said.

The new center was a networking and knowledge sharing center of sorts, and together with colleagues at NATO headquarters was building a CUI network to share information and best practices with NATO countries and industry. Its military engineers were assessing which infrastructure was critical at a national level and which might be "mission vital" in the event of war. The center was using all sorts of sensors—satellites, hydrophones, unmanned underwater vehicles, and radars—to collect data and run exercises, which Bratbak called "tactical actions."

"Since protecting or defending CUI is so difficult, we say we're trying to enhance security," he said. "We may say that we *defend* once the politics catches up." Defending against, or even just mitigating, the effects of sabotage was still extremely difficult. Bratbak gave me an example. "You could use tailored sensor packages on cables or pipelines, to reduce the notice-to-effect time," he said. Damage to the Balticconnector pipeline, for instance, was only spotted after ten hours—valuable time that was lost to engineers trying to contain the harm. Bratbak said the center's ultimate goal was to "deny the deniability" of sabotage, to the extent possible. "You need really solid evidence, irrefutable evidence, to convince the public that something was sabotage, so that there is no doubt left in anyone's mind," he said.

When I asked what had changed since the invasion of Ukraine, Bratbak cautiously weighed his answer. "I cannot confirm or deny that Russian attacks against CUI increased," he said. "I can say that Russia has mapped our CUI for a long time. And it is easy and cheap to attack, and incredibly expensive and hard to detect."

With its kaleidoscope of hostile actions—rattling the nuclear saber, arresting American journalists like Alsu Kurmasheva, sending migrants across the Finnish border, and dispatching agents to sabotage critical infrastructure in Europe—the Kremlin had kept the Europeans on edge. It was Russia's way of signaling that there was a price to be paid for supporting Ukraine. It was also a way of probing the societal resilience and political unity of individual European countries, and European solidarity as a whole.

At the start of 2025, further CUI incidents were sporadically reported in the press. In January, an undersea cable between Latvia and Sweden was severed, prompting Swedish authorities to board a suspected Bulgarian-owned vessel that had been sailing from Russia. A few weeks later, Finland released the *Eagle S* into international waters but continued its investigation into the Christmas Day incident. Meanwhile, a *Wall Street Journal* investigation into a shadowy unit based at GRU headquarters, the SSD, concluded that its covert activities had peaked in summer 2024 and somewhat subsided since—possibly to create diplomatic space for Moscow. But halfway across the world, a new administration had just entered the White House. The world would soon look very different, and Russia would open new fronts in its campaign to outlast the West.

CHAPTER 14

Disruptor in Chief

VOLODYMYR ZELENSKY ARRIVED IN WASHINGTON ON FEBRUARY 28, 2025, three years into Russia's invasion, to secure continued US support for his beleaguered nation. Donald Trump was back in the White House, having won both the popular and electoral vote on a campaign that promised to keep immigrants out of America, and America out of major wars. Zelensky was hoping to finalize a rare-minerals deal, a move proposed by the US to pay it back for its investment in the war.

The conversation began cordially enough, with Zelensky, in his usual military-style attire, seated next to Trump, whose aides, including Vice President JD Vance, occupied a sofa nearby. Trump noted the work ahead, and blamed his predecessor, Joe Biden, for failing to speak with Putin to end the war. Nearly forty minutes in, things began to unravel, as Vance defended US efforts to reach out to Russia. "The path to peace and the path to prosperity is maybe engaging in diplomacy," Vance said, channeling the administration's view that the war had gone on for too long, that there were limits to what the United

States could do to support Ukraine, and that Washington should act as an honest broker, favoring neither Russia nor Ukraine.

Zelensky had had enough and interrupted the vice president to lay out Putin's yearslong campaign against Ukraine. The moment opened the floodgates for a tense argument. "It's disrespectful for you to come into the Oval Office and try to litigate this in front of the American media," Vance blurted out. "Offer some words of appreciation for the United States of America and the president who's trying to save your country." Hunched over in his chair, Trump occasionally interjected to remind the Ukrainian leader that his country was in "big trouble" and "not winning."

Asked what would happen if the Russians broke the ceasefire Trump was calling for, the US president retorted in his usual style. "What if anything? What if a bomb drops on your head right now?" he said. "They broke it with Biden because Biden, they didn't respect him. They didn't respect Obama. They respect me."

A reporter with Real America's Voice, a right-wing outlet, asked Zelensky why he hadn't put on a suit and whether he even owned one. Shrinking in her chair and putting her head in her hands, Ukrainian Ambassador Oksana Markarova channeled the discomfort I felt watching the episode.

The televised acrimony left those in the room—and around the world—stunned. Trump and Vance's insistence that Zelensky should be more thankful led pundits to quip that American foreign policy had become the "politics of gratitude," with "be thankful" the new Trump doctrine. Some observers speculated that US leaders had ambushed Zelensky and had planned to humiliate him all along, while others saw a poorly advised Zelensky as at least partially responsible for an avoidable shouting match. Zelensky later told *Time* magazine he had come to the Oval Office that day with gifts, a plan, and only the best of intentions.

Whether it was a setup or a mishap, the reception in Moscow was one of delight. Dmitry Medvedev wrote that "the insolent pig finally got a proper slap down in the Oval Office," while Margarita Simonyan marveled that "the Oval Office has seen a lot, but never this." "The new administration is rapidly changing all foreign policy configurations," a more well-mannered statement from the Kremlin read. "This largely aligns with our vision."

To Europeans, that apparent alignment in vision was deeply unsettling but not necessarily surprising. On his first trip abroad as vice president, Vance declared a culture war on Europe at the Munich Security Conference. He accused the Europeans of threatening democracy and free speech, singling out Germany's actions against the rising far-right Alternative für Deutschland party. "In Washington, there is a new sheriff in town," he warned. I watched as the Europeans in the audience sat with their arms crossed, gobsmacked, frozen in a silence that was only interrupted by the occasional gasp.

Kaja Kallas, the EU's top diplomat, suggested that the US administration was trying to "pick a fight" with Europe, while German Chancellor Olaf Scholz went onstage to reject any such "interference" in German politics. In the corridors and coffee-break rooms at the Bayerischer Hof hotel, the mood among Europeans oscillated between puzzlement and indignation. Even though Vance moderated his tone in subsequent weeks, his speech had made a mark. The problem wasn't just that America wanted the Europeans to pay more for their own defense and that of Ukraine. The rift went deeper.

Three years into the invasion, the second Trump administration emerged on the international scene as disruptor in chief, berating Ukraine and suggesting that America and Europe might no longer be playing on the same team. Ukraine's security and survival, it seemed, were hanging by a thread and it would henceforth be largely up to Europe to throw Kyiv lifelines. Trump's Ukraine policy was shaping up to be a boon to Russia. Yet, as would soon become clear, the US president would affect Russia's campaign to outlast the West in ways that were much more sweeping—and occasionally surprising.

TRUMP HAD LONG MADE HIS PERSONAL AFFINITY FOR PUTIN, and his aversion to supporting Ukraine through an open-ended war with Russia, well known.

Despite his repeated praise for the Russian president—Trump had called him "so nice" and a "strong leader" on the campaign trail and once elected—hopes for a honeymoon in US–Russia relations did not materialize in Trump's first term. US investigations into Russia's alleged interference in the 2016 election put any engagement with Moscow under intense scrutiny from the get-go. When the White House declined a one-on-one meeting between Putin and Trump in May 2017, Russian expectations for a sea change in relations dissipated. "We don't see any positive moves in any direction," Fyodor Lukyanov said at the time, "and I don't think there are any expectations in Russia anymore regarding any kind of deal."

In 2018, the US joined Europe in imposing new sanctions against Russia after accusing the Kremlin of the attempted murder of former spy Sergei Skripal and his daughter with a nerve agent. A year later, the US withdrew from the INF Treaty over accusations that a new Russian missile system violated it. The US expelled Russian diplomats, closed Russian consulates, and delivered antitank Javelin missiles to Ukraine. Ordering cruise missile strikes against Syria in 2017 and 2018 and withdrawing from the JCPOA in May 2018, the Trump administration also remained at odds with Russia in the Middle East.

Still, Trump spoke highly of Putin, and often. Standing next to the Russian president at a joint press conference in Helsinki in July 2018, Trump sided with Putin over his own intelligence agencies when replying to a reporter's questions about alleged interference in the 2016 election. "I have great confidence in my intelligence people but I will tell you that President Putin was extremely strong and powerful in his denial today," he said.

While much of the Republican Party continued to harbor a deep suspicion of and aversion toward Russia, Trump had for decades cultivated an interest in doing real estate deals, both in Russia and with Russian elites. Meanwhile, in a backlash against "woke" culture and progressive politics, a broader set of political and cultural ideas was bubbling up on the American right that suggested an affinity for Russia, at least on the rhetorical level. These ideas put forth a very different vision of the post–Cold War world, and America's role in it, from the grand strategies embraced by presidents Bush, Clinton, and Obama. The cultural pillar, originally espoused by a small cadre of conservative elites, channeled a disdain for secularism, multiculturalism, and "woke" attitudes. During Trump's first term, these political-cultural ideas gained traction in the Republican Party, forming an intellectual architecture that married isolationism, nationalism, and traditionalism—guideposts for American foreign policy that pleased Russia. But what was conceptualized as a foreign policy of greater restraint was marked by a degree of chaos in the delivery—and not always to Russia's liking.

When Trump returned to the White House in January 2025, it soon became clear he had not shed his admiration-cum-awe for Putin. During his time out of office, he had called Putin a "genius" and "savvy" for invading Ukraine in February 2022. Meeting the British prime minister in the Oval Office one day before the showdown with Zelensky, he praised Putin as trustworthy when it came to a possible deal on Ukraine. "I think he'll keep his word," Trump said. "I've known him for a long time now, and I think he will."

Russia did its best to pander to Trump's susceptibility to flattery. In a March 2025 interview with Tucker Carlson, Trump's special envoy Steve Witkoff said Putin had commissioned a "beautiful portrait" of Trump from a leading Russian artist as a gift for the US president, and that he had gone to his local church and prayed for Trump following an assassination attempt at a rally in Butler, Pennsylvania, in July 2024.

By the time of Witkoff's interview, the US had begun to engage Russia in direct diplomacy, both to assess whether a ceasefire in Ukraine was possible and to normalize the bilateral relationship.

Delegations met on several occasions, in Riyadh and Istanbul, and Trump and Putin dispatched their personal envoys for visits. Trump repeatedly telegraphed impatience for a deal with Moscow and for ending what he called "Biden's war." Apparently quite afraid of nuclear escalation and averse to major wars, he appeared genuinely puzzled by the idea that the US remained mired in a conflict with Russia over Ukraine. It made no sense to Trump. If Putin could choose between fighting on at great cost and making some concessions as part of a settlement—getting sanctions relief and business deals with US companies in return—surely he would go for the latter, Trump's advisers surmised. Yet Trump seemed fundamentally uninterested in the details of the underlying security problems in Europe, let alone the unglamorous and painstaking work required to solve them.

Moscow embraced the opportunity to reset its relations with Washington, calculating that there was far more to gain than to lose. Cultivating ties and presenting itself as the reasonable party would bring Russia closer to achieving its aims in Ukraine, whether through continued war or through diplomacy. Engagement with Washington would also allow Russia to further overcome its international pariah status and peel the US off Europe, thereby deepening the transatlantic rift. At the same time, the Kremlin remained careful.

Russian elites knew Trump could be fickle and, in any event, would not sit in the White House forever. Their continued belief in a "deep state" in Washington, pathologically hostile to Russia, mandated caution. Remembering the disappointments of Trump's first administration, they knew not to expect too much. Steeled by years of confrontation, which had only firmed up Russia's geopolitical *stoykost*—the ability to absorb blows without giving in—the Kremlin would not be amenable to quick fixes, let alone concessions, especially not on Ukraine.

It initially seemed that the return of an anti-globalist, anti-interventionist, and anti-liberal American foreign policy would offer Russia considerable breathing space in its campaign to outlast the West.

To Moscow's delight, the US administration quickly embraced the Kremlin's version of the origins of the Ukraine war, with Trump himself claiming in mid-February that Ukraine had been the aggressor. A few weeks later, Secretary of State Marco Rubio appeared live on television and called the war in Ukraine a "proxy war" between the US and Russia that needed to come to an end. "We can and want to agree with it, and we agree with it. That's the way it is," Peskov said in reaction.

The Kremlin welcomed other initiatives taken by the Trump White House. During his first months in office, Trump targeted free speech on campuses, ended policies protecting LGBTQ+ rights, dismantled USAID, and telegraphed an appetite for gobbling up Canada, Greenland, the Panama Canal, and Gaza. The State Department closed its Counter Foreign Information Manipulation and Interference Hub, an office that tracked and countered global disinformation, including from Russia. Trump moved to gut Voice of America and Radio Free Europe/Radio Liberty, where Alsu Kurmasheva had returned to work after her release from Russian prison. Pavel Butorin, Kurmasheva's husband and director of Radio Free Europe, said Trump's funding cuts were "a shock" that must leave Russian officials in Moscow "popping the champagne." "Russian propaganda turned out to be true," a Russian official said, applauding the closure of USAID, long criticized by Russia as an instrument of US meddling in other countries' internal affairs.

As seen from Moscow, the Trump White House brought US foreign policy into closer alignment with its own illiberal and conservative messaging. And the collapse of USAID programs in Africa threatened to diminish key elements of America's presence on the continent. Russia (as well as China, Turkey, and others) stood ready to exploit the void, building on recent efforts of its Russian Houses, propagandists, and Africa Corps. Following Trump's announcement to close USAID, the Russian House in Bangui posted pictures of its director handing over boxes of medicine for tuberculosis and HIV to officials. In *The New York Review of Books*, essayist Joshua Craze warned anti-imperialists cheering the end of US interference that "USAID's decline might not mean a less imperialistic world but rather one with more varied imperialisms."

Granting a ninety-minute interview to three conservative American video bloggers in mid-March, Lavrov praised the Trump administration for reversing the Democrats' "departure from Christian values." Soon after, the State Department disseminated calls for "civilizational allies" in Europe based on "common culture, faith, familial ties," and "cultural heritage."

For decades, Russia had viewed the "collective West" as its main Other, its principal frame of reference, its adversary in chief. America's and Europe's unwavering self-identification as part of one West, based on shared values and a belief in the post–World War II liberal international order, sustained Russia's mental map. Suddenly, America's global conduct seemed to shake that geopolitical coordinate system. Even more radically, Vance and other MAGA acolytes seemed to embrace Putin's Russia as very much *part* of the West (a white, Christian, traditional West) while questioning some Europeans' sense of belonging to that West.

As welcome as these pivots seemed at first sight, MAGA was stealing Russia's limelight in the global culture wars by announcing itself as an ally of anti-woke movements around the world. For years, Russia cultivated a loyal followership among conservative, Christian, and alt-right constituencies around the globe. But wherever the US goes, it leads, and Russia, used to being a beacon for these groups, suddenly had to contend with stiff competition. When Trump offered to resettle white Afrikaners from South Africa in the United States, for instance, he was intruding on territory that, until recently, was the preserve of Kremlin propagandists. If it turned out that the United States was no longer the liberal imperialist power spreading its tentacles everywhere, or a bastion for "woke" ideas, then Russia would have to think of new narratives—even if it might not have to abandon wholesale the rhetorical binary of Russia versus the West. In spring 2025, Kremlin media was already toning down its criticism of the US, focusing its ire on Europe instead.

On the diplomatic and economic fronts, the balance sheet for Russia was similarly mixed. On the one hand, a handful of individuals in the Trump administration, led by Steve Witkoff, engaged Russia in diplomacy over the war in Ukraine. On the other, administration officials said they would not lift sanctions on Moscow until the war in Ukraine was over. Trump even threatened the Kremlin with additional sanctions and tariffs should Russia drag its feet in negotiating with Ukraine.

Despite the at times tough rhetoric, there were indications the US was willing to go softer on Russia. In early March 2025, the US rejected a Canadian proposal, circulated ahead of a G7 meeting, to establish a task force that would tackle Russia's "shadow fleet" of oil tankers. The Trump administration also stopped engaging in working groups set up with European allies to crack down on Russia's Eurasian roundabout trade and efforts at evading sanctions. Sensing the changing geopolitical winds, Putin ordered his cabinet to prepare for the return of Western companies to Russia.

Yet, Russian voices counseled against being too optimistic. Russian sanctions expert Ivan Timofeev cautioned that the unwinding of sanctions would take a long time and that the process would likely be uneven and could be reversed by a new administration. Timofeev's warnings of an erratic US approach to global commerce were prescient. In early April, Trump declared a "Liberation Day," instituting massive tariffs on almost all countries around the globe, with some exceptions—like Russia and North Korea. Dmitry Medvedev, invoking an old Chinese proverb, rejoiced that Russia would "sit by the river, waiting for the body of the enemy to float by. The decaying corpse of the EU economy."

But, facing its own economic slowdown, Russia had little reason to gloat over Trump's tariff spree. Nabiullina warned that, should the tariff war escalate, the result could be a slowdown in global trade and a global economic recession, resulting in a drop in demand for Russian oil and gas exports. A collapse in earnings from oil exports could force the Kremlin to increase borrowing, cut nonmilitary spending, or draw down its remaining reserves. There were some potential upsides for Russia, too. Trump's unpredictable economic policymaking would likely damage the US dollar's status as a haven for global capital, fund managers warned, advancing Russia's strategic goal that others join it in de-dollarizing. And over the medium term, Russia might find opportunities to substitute the US in the Chinese market. However, these were medium- to long-term prospects, and Russia's ability to capitalize on them were contingent on many "ifs."

IN MAY 2025, I CHECKED IN WITH TAMAR JAKELI TO SEE HOW the Trump's administration's foreign policy disruptions were affecting organizations like Tbilisi Pride. Jakeli had just left Georgia, after spending months protesting alongside thousands of Georgians who had taken to Rustaveli Avenue almost daily to resist the GD government and its repressive agenda. Jakeli felt at direct risk, as GD was about to enact a new law that threatened directors or board members of noncompliant civil society organizations with huge fines or even up to five years' imprisonment. Jakeli's colleagues had already packed up the office on Giorgi Akhvlediani Street, lowered the rainbow flag on its balcony, moved all activities online, and were about to hand Jakeli's resignation letter to the public registry. "I feel guilty that I'm not there," she told me, "but it's better to lie low for a while. This is a lifelong struggle."

Jakeli was convinced the Trump administration only worsened the hostile climate faced by Tbilisi Pride and like-minded organizations. The GD-aligned channel TV Imedi was using Trump's language to justify the party's crackdown on queer rights, she said. But whether Bidzina Ivanishvili could reset Georgia–US relations on the basis of shared conservative values remained to be seen, she cautioned, given momentum in the US Congress to keep up the pressure on GD. Still, she felt certain that liberal values and human rights would play a diminished role in US foreign policy toward the region. Reflecting on what she called a "realist" and "anti-values" turn in geopolitics, she said the new zeitgeist made it harder for groups like Tbilisi Pride to position themselves. "Before Trump," she said, "there was an alignment between our political argument in favor of Georgia's Euro-Atlantic integration, away from Russia, and a values-based argument." Now that alignment was falling apart.

What gave her hope amid what she called an overall depressing trajectory was that Georgians still seemed willing to protect liberal values. A defiant spirit marked a 2025 open-air music festival at Lisi Wonderland, the site of the Tbilisi Pride raid in summer 2023, she told me. And though Tbilisi Pride had officially closed its book club, participants continued to meet informally in parks and cafés. "GD cannot move Georgia toward a fully consolidated authoritarianism, like in Belarus," Jakeli told me. The Georgian people would not allow it.

Across the border, in Armenia, Trump's transactional style similarly affected calculations. The Russian peacekeeping presence in Nagorno-Karabakh had given the Kremlin huge leverage over both Armenia and Azerbaijan; with that presence gone for good, Russia's clout would be a shadow of its former self. Still, given the unfinished business in the peace process with Azerbaijan, the Pashinyan government figured it needed to navigate cautiously. Prime Minister Pashinyan announced he would attend the May 9 Victory Day parade in Moscow, after boycotting it in 2024. "Pashinyan is maneuvering between all sides, trying to maintain some balance," Azat Adamyan told me, "and it is unclear where he will eventually turn."

In Kazakhstan, liberal elites watched the topsy-turviness in US rhetoric and action with apprehensions, too. Should Trump allow Putin to come out on top in Ukraine, and potentially even lift sanctions, the result would be an "increased authoritarianism in a region that Putin considers Russia's uncontested sphere of influence," Dimash Alzhanov, the Kazakh political activist, said in an interview with independent outlet *Respublika*. Should that happen, Kazakhstan would remain formally independent, but Russia would bind the country even closer and step up its meddling in Kazakh culture, the economy, and politics, he warned.

And so, for countries in Central Asia and the South Caucasus, the remaking of US statecraft, with its blurring of business and geopolitics, had mixed implications. On the one hand, Trump's outreach to Russia made it easier for them to simultaneously engage Washington and Moscow, increasing their opportunities for geopolitical maneuvering. But in prioritizing economic deal-making, the Trump administration also telegraphed a disinterest in censoring domestic repression in these countries, effectively giving their leaderships greater leeway to emulate Russian practices.

In more far-flung theaters, it seemed less certain that Moscow could capitalize on shifts in American foreign policy. Though Trump signaled he might finally withdraw US forces from northeast Syria and lifted the US's Assad-era sanctions, such recalibrations would hardly allow Moscow to restore the degree of influence it had enjoyed before Assad's fall. Trump retained close support for Israel, courted Gulf capitals, and engaged Iran in talks on its nuclear program while simultaneously threatening to go to war with it should diplomacy fail. As of spring 2025, the second Trump administration's emergent Middle East policy seemed a mixed blessing for Russia.

Navigating a complex global environment, Moscow showed no desire to distance itself from Beijing, Pyongyang, and Tehran—something the Trump administration, in resetting relations with Russia, was hoping to achieve. On the three-year anniversary of the invasion, Putin called Xi and promised that the development of relations with Beijing would neither "be affected by transient events" nor "disrupted by external factors." The following week, Putin dispatched officials to Tehran and Beijing and made time in his own busy schedule to receive a delegation from North Korea's Workers' Party. Having invested considerably in defense ties with all three partners, Putin was in no mood to drastically decouple. Russia would probably prove willing to somewhat limit cooperation, perhaps avoiding the most sensitive areas, as a gesture of goodwill to the Trump White House. But the underlying trajectory would remain one of growing cooperation within this anti-Western coterie.

Meanwhile, there were reasons to believe that Trump's penchant for bullying other nations into surrendering to his demands might make it easier for Russia to corral a bigger circle of partners into efforts to circumvent the West. Within days of assuming office, Trump threatened BRICS with "100 percent tariffs" should they "want to play games with the dollar." Though Trump's tariff spree proved fickle, it seemed the precedent would only drive BRICS to further reduce their dependencies on the US. Xi made clear that China welcomed new partners with open arms. "Certain countries, through exclusionary blocs and tariff barriers, engage in politicization and weaponization of trade issues. China's door will only open wider," he said in a speech in Beijing.

While it was threatening BRICS, the US seemed prepared to weaken or dismantle legacy multilateral institutions faster than anyone had anticipated. Trump's ninety-day suspension of all foreign assistance within days of his inauguration forced UN agencies like the UN High Commissioner for Refugees to cut back operations. The White House's announcement days later that the US was putting its support to all international organizations under review sent shockwaves through Geneva, Vienna, and New York. Though multilateral institutions did not fall directly into the remit of the Department of Government Efficiency, they faced similar ideological pressures, with US officials sending them questionnaires to verify their alignment with "America First." For Russia, which had spent years pursuing anti-Western agendas in multilateral fora while remaining fundamentally interested in a functioning United Nations, US efforts must have seemed like a double-edged sword.

An unexpected showdown at the UN Security Council and in the UN General Assembly, however, gave Russia reason to score an early victory. Around the three-year anniversary of the invasion, the Trump administration sided with Russia in votes on the Ukraine war in both bodies. Joining Russia in the General Assembly vote, the US delegation found itself in the company of states like Belarus, North Korea, Nicaragua, the Sahelian juntas, and the CAR. Going forward, it seemed, European policymakers would need to navigate a UN system in which the US was a potential adversary.

But the Europeans had even bigger problems. After Vance's Munich speech and initial US–Russia talks in Riyadh, a Russian tabloid gloated that "for so long, Europe had gone around all puffed up, thinking of itself as the civilized world and as a Garden of Eden. It failed to notice it had lost its trousers . . . now its old comrade across the Atlantic has pointed that out." The desire to meddle more in Europe, potentially even transform it, that had emanated from Vance's speech was one problem to grapple with. Yet more urgent was the challenge posed by American flip-floppery on Ukraine, as well as the question of the United States' continued security commitments to NATO allies in Europe, both conventionally and with nuclear weapons.

Fearful that the United States might one day withdraw its forward-deployed nuclear weapons from Europe, officials descended into a frenzied discussion on whether and how Europe could deter Russia on its own. Some called for a European bomb, others for arrangements to extend the French or British nuclear umbrellas. Distrustful of their European allies' willingness to come to their rescue, some central European elites telegraphed a desire for greater self-reliance. Polish voices suggested the country should acquire its own nuclear capabilities. Squeezed between a menacing Russia and a seemingly unreliable America, Europe was in for a major stress test that brought with it the specter of fragmentation.

Smelling an opportunity, some in Russia argued that now was the time to play hardball with Europe. An FSB-affiliated think tank produced a document arguing that Russia should stoke tensions between the Trump administration and its allies, with a view to strengthening its hand in negotiations on Ukraine. Two months later, Russia's Foreign Intelligence Service issued a press release warning that "Eurofascism" had returned and again become "the common enemy of Moscow and Washington." Others in Moscow argued it was unwise to further stoke anti-Russian sentiments in Europe, and that allocating excessive resources to countering Europe came at the expense of other priorities.

But in many ways, Russia's decision to wage war against Ukraine had consolidated rather than fragmented Europe—and Trump's constant disruptions would only reinforce that trend. Finland and Sweden had already joined NATO. Now, Germany and France teamed up to call for a united Europe. Five years after Brexit, the United Kingdom was inching back closer to the EU. London also joined Paris and other capitals in a "Coalition of the Willing" to think through the modalities for security guarantees for Ukraine. Signs of consolidation extended beyond Europe. In elections in Canada and Australia, centrist forces managed to rally major support while right-wing parties that had borrowed from the MAGA playbook were punished. And major industrialized democracies—France, the United Kingdom, Canada, and Japan—bolstered cooperation with each other and without the United States. Middle powers, it seemed, were forming new alliances in the shadow of the great powers gone rogue.

WHEN WE SPOKE IN LATE SPRING 2025, RUSSIAN JOURNALIST Fyodor Lukyanov characterized Trump's second arrival on the world stage as a mixed blessing for Russia. "Is Russia good or bad? Trump doesn't care," Lukyanov told me. "Trump simply believes that Russia should not be an obstacle to implementing his broader agenda, which has little to do with Russia." It was an idea channeled by Lavrov in an interview a couple of months earlier. "The United States still has the same goal," which is "to be number one country in the world," Lavrov told *Krasnaya Zvezda*. "Trump's goal is MAGA Make America Great Again—all the same."

The US president's prioritization of results over ideals, and his abandonment of the idea that America should support liberal democracies and transform the world in its image, were welcome shifts from Russia's perspective. But the Trumpian worldview, Lukyanov thought, also tended to trivialize the Russia problem. Russia, to Trump, was important only "as a means to achieve particular goals," rather than as a "main frame of reference," he said. While craving the laurels of premier peacemaker, Trump showed no appetite for the hard and unglamorous work on the details of settling Russia's problems with

Europe. He liked to think he could settle complex conflicts in a day. Whereas generations of Western diplomats had considered the post-Soviet challenges of Eastern Europe a hard nut to crack, Trump seemed to envision an easy fix.

That's where Lukyanov thought America might eventually stumble. "The more the Americans deal with Russia, the more clearly they will see how difficult it is, because there are really big issues to solve, it's not just bloody Ukrainians against bloody Russians." That the US and Russia could move toward a normal relationship was therefore highly contingent. "It depends on a lot of ifs," Lukyanov said.

As Russia embarked on its fourth year of the invasion, Trump's foreign policy disruption forced average people and politicians around the globe to ponder the "ifs," and to plan for contingencies, even the far-fetched ones. Those sitting in the Kremlin were no exception to that rule. Of one thing, however, Putin could be certain: The world was changing, and irreversibly so. The "West"—no longer fully real, but not yet entirely imagined, either—would remain a formidable force for Russia to reckon with. But the cracks were showing. A new, messy (dis-)order was crystallizing, one in which relationships would be complex and protean and in which the rules were in flux. It would be a hospitable milieu for a relentlessly adaptive Russia.

CONCLUSION

We Shall Outlast Them

THE RUSSIAN CAPITAL SEEMED FROZEN IN TIME. IN JUST A FEW days, Muscovites would mark the May 9 holiday with the annual Victory Parade on Red Square. This year, 2025, they were celebrating the eighty-year anniversary of the defeat of Nazi Germany, and the Kremlin had planned especially spectacular festivities. A nightly rehearsal offered a glimpse into the event, with scores of tanks and artillery rolling past the Kremlin's wall, the lights of the grand palace twinkling magically on the Moscow River.

Hints of disquiet mixed with the anticipation. In the days leading up to the parade, Ukraine attacked the city with drones, causing flight suspensions at several Moscow airports that left thousands of passengers delayed or diverted. Even though Putin had announced a ceasefire in Ukraine from May 8 through May 10, the Kremlin feared Ukraine might try to strike the Russian capital on the day of the parade. Mayor Sergey Sobyanin could not take any chances. He introduced heavy-handed security measures, blocking car and pedestrian traffic, closing businesses, and even curtailing internet access.

Ever since World War II, Russian children had grown up with the phrase *spasibo za mirnoe nebo nad golovoy* ("thank you for the peaceful sky above our heads"), a sentiment exchanged on May 9 to express gratitude for the peace that the USSR's perseverance in the war had brought to the country. Eighty years on, Ukraine's drones, launched in self-defense against a menacing Russia, posed a new deadly threat from above. By Russia's own doing, its skies were no longer peaceful.

To distract Russians from the drone attacks and get them into the mood for the holiday, state television aired a carefully choreographed film about Putin's quarter century as paramount leader. From his private kitchen in the Kremlin, it showed Putin talking with Russian journalist Pavel Zarubin. "I continue to breathe the very same air as millions of Russian citizens," Putin said. "God willing that it continues as long as possible." When asked whether the war in Ukraine could have escalated into a nuclear conflagration, Putin said that even though the West had tried to "provoke" Russia into making mistakes, there had been "no need to use those weapons" and he hoped that would remain the case in the future. "We have enough strength and means to bring what was started in 2022 to a logical conclusion with the outcome Russia requires," he said.

As May 9 drew closer, the media speculated as to which foreign dignitaries would show in Moscow. Xi Jinping, Nicolás Maduro, Lula da Silva of Brazil, and twenty-six other foreign leaders had accepted the invitation. Given escalating tensions over Kashmir, Narendra Modi couldn't make it, but India and South Africa, another BRICS partner, would still send senior officials. Former leaders now living in Russia were not invited, Peskov said, cryptically confirming that Putin had no intention to rehabilitate the tarred-and-feathered Bashar al-Assad. Netanyahu had no plans to attend, but he called in advance to congratulate Putin. Claims by Zvezda, the Russian defense ministry's TV channel, that Marco Rubio might make an appearance added further intrigue to endless gossip about the guest list.

The EU hoped to stand united in its boycott of the festivities, but there were outliers, including a few members of the European

Parliament. Robert Fico, the Slovak prime minister, was going to go, saying with irritation that Kaja Kallas, the EU's top diplomat, could not tell him what he could or couldn't do. Baiba Braža, Latvia's foreign minister, thought it all regrettable. "Countries make their own choices whether to attend the Butcher in the Kremlin's fake propaganda events," she said. "We would prefer that our allies and partners do not show that type of respect for Russian propaganda." Poland's prime minister concurred, saying that those attending Russia's parade "bring shame" on themselves. In a show of deep displeasure with the event, Estonia, Latvia, Lithuania, and Poland denied Fico's plane the use of their airspace en route to Moscow. Serbia's president, Aleksandar Vučić, faced the same restrictions. His plane was even forced to stop in Baku as he awaited permission to land in Moscow amid airport closures caused by Ukrainian drone attacks.

Margarita Simonyan could hardly catch her breath, so busy was her schedule in the leadup to May 9. RT hosted the Cuban president for an exclusive interview on the eve of the parade, in which he railed against the West's "systemic campaign to write the real victors of World War II out of history." "We are in a cultural and ideological battle," he warned RT's audience. Simonyan proceeded to record her own holiday greetings for Russian soldiers at the Ukrainian front. Then she hurried to a press conference. Xi had flown to Moscow for a full four days and was about to address journalists alongside Putin. He joined the Russian leader in pledging to counter US efforts at "dual containment" of Russia and China. Russia and China should be "friends of steel," he said. Simonyan got her own moment of glory at the press conference, signing a memorandum of cooperation with Shen Haixiong, head of the China Media Group.

Finally, the big day arrived. It was a chilly but sunny morning on Red Square when the air swelled with the grand sounds of "Get up, immense nation, get up for a mortal fight," the lyrics of a famous WWII-era song called "Sacred War." On the central stand, Putin took a seat near the heads of over twenty countries. Right next to him was Xi, a few chairs further down Kazakhstan's Tokayev. Armenia's Pashinyan had come, too. Given Russia's successes in Ukraine, Trump's election, and GD's consolidation of power in neighboring Georgia, it was better to talk to the Russians, he figured. A bit less central sat Lula, Egypt's Abdel Fattah el-Sisi, and Burkina Faso's Ibrahim Traoré, whom the Kremlin had flown in on a Russian plane. On the neighboring tribunes, World War II veterans weighed down with medals were joined by grizzled Russian soldiers on leave from the front. Even North Korean generals, adorned with medals, were in attendance.

The parade was a microcosm of the new world in which Russia needed to survive and thrive—a world in which Atlanticism was put to the test; a world in which Europe struggled to show real leadership; and, most important, a kaleidoscopic geopolitical landscape in which most countries around the globe chose neither this nor that camp, but decided how to position themselves based solely on their own interests in a never-ending process of reevaluation, a great global hedge. It was a world in which the cards were constantly being reshuffled.

Addressing the crowd in Moscow, Putin linked the country's past victories to its current mission. "Our fathers . . . bequeathed to us to firmly defend our national interests, our thousand-year-old history, culture and traditional values," he said. While avoiding direct condemnations of the United States, unlike in previous years, he elevated China's role in defeating Nazism. "We'll always remember that opening the second front brought victory closer," he said, in reference to the Second Sino-Japanese War. "Our duty is to defend the honor of the Red Army . . . and the heroism of fighters of different ethnic backgrounds who will forever remain *Russian* soldiers in world history," Putin said. His usurpation of the Soviet Union's victory as a Russian victory recalled similar Russian efforts to eclipse the role that other Soviet republics, especially Ukraine, had played in supporting the anti-apartheid struggle in South Africa.

Once Putin finished, Russian soldiers and cadets marched across Red Square's cobblestones, joined by visiting detachments from thirteen allied nations. More than 180 pieces of military hardware followed, including some of Russia's latest artillery systems and armored vehicles. For the first time, the parade showcased the Iranian-origin Shahed drones, which were mounted on a column of trucks. "How terrible, imagine how the Ukrainians must feel, watching this deadly technology that threatens their lives each day," said a commentator on TV Dozhd, an independent Russian channel based outside the country.

"Obtaining the technology for the Shahed drones from Iran was Russia's most consequential achievement," Ukraine's former foreign minister Dmytro Kuleba told me when we spoke around the May 9 parade. "Also, striking a deal with China that allowed Russia to ramp up its defense-industrial complex. These two things were truly, truly detrimental for us Ukrainians." Kuleba went on to admit that while Russia's global moves had, by and large, not surprised him, he had not expected North Korea's willingness to send troops to support Russia. "Finding an ally ready to die next to you—in return for something meaningful, of course, but still entirely for your goals—it is quite remarkable," he said.

Russia had relatively little to offer the rest of the world, Kuleba added. It sells fossil fuels. It exports security or insecurity—depending on how you look at it—to places like Africa. The only area in which Russia was truly equal to the US was perhaps in the number of nuclear warheads. "It's very sad," Kuleba told me, "because by all accounts, the West is much stronger than Russia. But Russia is stronger than the West on one account, and it turns out that that is the most consequential one: Russia believes in itself."

Kuleba argued that a self-confident Russia was very consistent in pursuing the one goal that truly mattered to it: subjugating Ukraine and compromising European unity. If and when Russia needed to prioritize, the fate of the Karabakh Armenians or of Syria's Assad were simply less important. "What's their endgame in all this?" I asked. "Their real dream is for the United States to treat Russia as an equal," Kuleba responded. "They are obsessed with this idea. Yeltsin was severely traumatized by this [the West not respecting Russia], and Putin inherited this trauma from him. They have come so close to China now . . . but old dreams die hard."

THE MAY 9 PARADE MAY HAVE HELPED PUTIN DISTRACT HIS people from war fatigue, court his international partners, and put on a grand spectacle. But the triumph was brief, and new challenges emerged in the months that followed.

The first test came with war in the Middle East. In the early hours of June 13, Israel launched Operation Rising Lion, carrying out waves of air strikes targeting Iran's military sites, nuclear facilities, and energy infrastructure, in what it said was an effort to stop the country from developing nuclear weapons. Iran responded with waves of attacks on Israel. A week into the escalation, which became known as the "Twelve-Day War," Trump joined in, ordering the US Air Force to drop massive "bunker buster" bombs on three of Iran's nuclear sites.

While Iran was suffering its biggest blow in decades, Russia was not prepared to do much of anything about it. Rather than lending any meaningful assistance to Iran, Putin offered Trump his services as mediator between the conflicting sides, an overture the US president rebuffed.

The episode provided a window into the nature of Russia's global alliances. Russia backed partners in anticipation of concrete gains and at calculable risk to the Kremlin. It nudged closer to Iran when it became lucrative, given Russia's need for Shahed drones after the invasion. Russia also backed the Sahelian juntas, deploying Africa Corps after the Wagner Group's demise, because doing so promised to advance Russia's anti-Western agenda in Africa at little risk to the Kremlin. But Putin would not stick out his neck for his partners if saving them meant hurting Russia's interests. China, too, stood aside during the Twelve-Day War, raising serious questions over the extent to which partners in the purported "axis of upheaval" were willing to support each other in times of trouble.

The episode also served as an example of Russia's return to "compartmentalization" in its relations with the United States. Having stonewalled all cooperation on geopolitical dossiers with the Biden administration, the Kremlin pivoted to offer Trump support with Iran. Soon enough, Russia would revive the nuclear arms control agenda, offering the US an informal one-year extension of the New START limits, and it also refrained from vetoing a single UN Security Council resolution through all of 2025. This diplomatic volte-face went to show just to what extent Russia's desire to subjugate Ukraine dictated the rest of its foreign policy. Putin shunned cooperation with Biden in an effort to force him to abandon Ukraine. Shifting to the playbook of obsequiousness, he then tried to resume cooperation with Trump, only this time to lure him into taking Russia's side against Ukraine. Whether in wielding pressure or praise, Russia's end goal remained the same: isolating Ukraine from its most formidable partner, the United States.

Finally, the Middle Eastern events of June 2025 suggested that Russia had at least some reason to worry about Trump's mercurial temperament, even propensity for using force, which sat oddly with his anti-interventionist and anti-globalist impulses. When Trump telegraphed an appetite for gobbling up Canada, Greenland, and the Panama Canal early into his second term, Putin might have watched gleefully from the sidelines. After all, "the strong do what they can and the weak suffer what they must" is a rule to Russia's liking. If Trump endorsed the concept of America, Russia, and China carving the world into spheres of influence, then Russia's old dream would finally come true.

But Russia, it seemed, had a problem. Its retreats in the Middle East and the South Caucasus suggested that Russia had limited wherewithal to throw itself around in a Trumpian-Thucydidean world, especially while it remained bogged down in its forever war in Ukraine. Meanwhile, through the summer, Trump showed signs of growing impatience with Putin, criticizing his relentless bombing campaign in Ukraine, issuing ultimatums, and even ratcheting up tariffs on India over its purchases of Russian oil. Obsessed with claiming the laurels of peacemaker, Trump hosted a peace summit with the leaders of Armenia and Azerbaijan to great fanfare, sidelining Russia, the traditional regional hegemon. To make matters worse, for all his scolding of Europe since assuming office, Trump did not reduce the US military presence on the continent. And for all his flip-flopping over US support for Ukraine, he had not handed the country to Russia, and surely was not about to.

Or . . . was he? A few weeks after the Twelve-Day War, the inattentive yet impatient Trump stunned the Western world when he offered Putin a face-to-face meeting—without Zelensky and the Europeans—in the hope of reaching an immediate ceasefire in Ukraine. The summit would be held in Alaska, on US territory. It was the perfect gift for the Kremlin.

On August 15, Putin's presidential plane touched down at Elmendorf Air Force Base. The images of US soldiers kneeling at the end of the staircase wheeled out for Putin to step down from the aircraft went around the world. Putin strolled down a red carpet on the tarmac, met with Trump's applause. The two men walked around, laughing, before Trump invited Putin to take a private ride with him in his armored presidential limousine. "Western media are on the verge of completely losing it," Russia's foreign ministry spokeswoman Maria Zakharova marveled, "They spent three years telling everyone Russia was isolated, and today they saw the beautiful red carpet laid out for the Russian president in the US."

It was quite the display of camaraderie. Ukraine's supporters panicked that Trump was about to finish what he had started in his tense White House contretemps with Zelensky six months earlier: He would sell out Ukraine, and he would make a deal with Putin.

In the end, the summit turned out to be one big nothingburger. Putin and Trump spent less time together than originally scheduled. Lunch was canceled. They even scrapped plans to hold a news conference and instead just delivered short back-to-back statements, without answering any questions from the many reporters who had flocked to Alaska from all around the world. Both men spoke positively about the meeting afterward; Trump called it a "ten"; Putin praised Trump as "very frank and informative." But in the weeks and months that followed, there was no breakthrough, and Russia continued to pound Ukrainian cities with record-breaking waves of Shahed drones.

Putin had maneuvered the Alaska spectacle skillfully, seeing value in staying in Trump's good graces, but he had no intention to fundamentally revise Russia's aims. Putin wanted to keep Ukraine out of NATO (and NATO troops out of Ukraine), to limit the size of its military, to install a government pliant to Russia; in essence, he wanted Ukraine's capitulation. These demands, never mind Russia's broader asks related to NATO's presence in Europe, were not about to be granted at a rushed summit, and Putin knew that. But he believed time was on Russia's side, and by stringing Trump along, he had just bought a little extra time on top.

Still, a full Russian victory in Ukraine remained elusive, and Russia's efforts to outlast the West a never-ending work in progress. The EU implemented a lower oil price cap at $47.60 per barrel and eventually agreed to indefinitely freeze Russia's central bank assets. After hitting Russian oil refineries relentlessly, causing long lines and empty pumps at Russia's gas stations and bringing the pain of war closer to average Russians, Ukrainian drones started taking aim at Russia's shadow fleet, too. Having brokered a precarious ceasefire in Gaza, Trump refocused his attention on Europe. When his plan to hold another summit with Putin in Hungary unraveled, Trump imposed sanctions on Sechin's Rosneft and Russian oil major Lukoil. In response, India's Reliance Industries announced it would stop importing Russian crude into the Jamnagar refinery.

Faced with these pressures, Russia continued its own game of adaptation. "None of us can fully foresee the future," Putin told Lukyanov at the annual Valdai meeting in October 2025. "However, that does not absolve us of the responsibility to be prepared for it . . . we must be ready for anything." And Russia showed that it was ready. Within the space of eight days, Putin flaunted two Russian doomsday weapons, the nuclear-armed Poseidon underwater drone and the Burevestnik cruise missile, resuming its nuclear saber-rattling after a protracted break. Having terrorized Ukraine with nearly fifty thousand drones in 2025 alone, Russia continued its grinding advance onto Pokrovsk, a key stronghold in the country's east. And in early December, Putin visited India—Sechin and Simonyan in tow—to attend the festive opening of RT India and offer the country "uninterrupted" oil supplies, notwithstanding the US sanctions against Rosneft.

Such was the state of the world when the year moved to a close, amid relentless Russian airstrikes on Ukraine's power grid intended to freeze Ukrainians into submission. Europe had barely woken from its winter slumber when Trump took his campaign of shock and awe to another level. In early January, he toppled Venezuelan strongman and Russia's partner Nicolás Maduro in a special military operation that Putin could only dream of. Much like during Assad's ouster and the "Twelve-Day War," Russia was looking rather helpless. To add insult to injury, Trump launched a new international conflict-settlement body, the "Board of Peace," crowning himself chairman in perpetuity. Rather than granting Russia the kind of special status it enjoys on the UN Security Council, Trump offered Putin the privilege of being his subordinate. Confronted with such displays of US chutzpah, Russian observers enjoyed a brief moment of relish when Trump upped his designs on Greenland, threatening to plunge the transatlantic relationship into an unprecedented crisis. But faced with pushback from within his own party, nervous financial markets, and the Europeans switching from flattery to firmness, Trump walked back his threats to take the island by force.

Then, Trump initiated his biggest gamble yet. In late February, the United States attacked Iran for a second time. Trump's promulgation of "Operation Epic Fury" as a shorthand for war bore an uncanny resemblance to Putin's launch of a "special military operation" against Ukraine four years prior. In a reversal of fortunes, what initially looked like another display of US military might amid Russian impotence turned into a bonanza for the Kremlin. Days into the war, Iran's closure of the Strait of Hormuz sent shock waves through global energy markets, prompting the US to ease its oil sanctions on Russia and the EU to delay the adoption of its twentieth sanctions package. Writing from Moscow, Trenin and Lukyanov lamented Trump's foreign policy adventurism as fundamentally unwelcome to Russia: It proved that the US still wanted to dominate the rest of the world. It also proved that the US—Trump's displays of bonhomie toward Putin aside—could never be trusted and that Russia had to outlast the West in Ukraine at all cost. Still, Russia would not waste a good opportunity to benefit from the unintended fallout of Trump's ventures—and proceeded to rake in billions in extra oil revenue.

Since February 2022, Russia had secured lifelines to keep its economy afloat and to feed its war machine. Its anti-Western propaganda had won disciples around the globe. Its nuclear weapons still induced fear. The loss or weakening of its Syrian, Iranian, and Venezuelan allies would not materially affect Russia's campaign in Ukraine. China was unlikely to abandon Russia, and North Korea had emerged as a wellspring of fighting men and munitions. Russia, in other words, had *stoykost*. The United States was the confused hegemon. Non-Western powers, unwilling to break with Russia, were inexorably rising. And Europe, in Putin's telling, was decadent and divided, and would eventually falter in its support for Ukraine—if only Russia held out long enough.

How can one make sense of Russia's global adaptation after the full-scale invasion of Ukraine? It was a dizzying amalgamation of disparate efforts to stay afloat, even to get ahead. It was both strategic in its intent to outlast the West and highly opportunistic in its execution. There was the comedy of Russia's BRICS chairmanship extravaganza and of its antics at the UN; there was the melodrama of Russia's outrageous nuclear threats; there was the theater of the absurd, when Russia claimed its soldiers were dying in Ukraine so that Africa could be free; and there was the drama of Prigozhin's failed mutiny, which ushered in the creation of Africa Corps.

The question for Russia is whether Putin has also condemned the country to the fate of tragedy.

Russia's global game appears economically sustainable for Russia, which is not (yet) outspending itself—though its finances are under growing strain and the structural imbalances in its economy, the result of its militarization, are increasingly showing. But if Russia's endless capacity for adaptation gives it agility, it also bespeaks a certain nihilism, which is most pronounced in Russia's almost obsessive anti-Westernism. Anti-Westernism will always be in vogue, it will always find enthusiastic disciples across the globe, but it also makes for a lot of strange, disparate bedfellows.

In many ways, Russia's foreign policy has become dangerously shortsighted, for instance in sacrificing influence in other regions for the sake of Putin's obsession with Ukraine. And Russia's war has produced a host of unintended and undesirable consequences for Russia—pushing Finland and Sweden to join NATO, and Russia's Eurasian neighbors to diversify their ties. It has also strengthened Ukrainian national unity and identity and put the country on the map. Claiming to be waging war in pursuit of greater security, Russia in many ways has made itself less secure.

These shortcomings do not make Russia's global projection of power inconsequential—far from it. Russia's combative statecraft has fueled forces of consolidation, but more often of fragmentation, across the globe. It has pushed countries close to Russia—Armenia, Georgia, and Kazakhstan—into their own forms of hedging and adaptation. Russia's actions in many ways have united Europe. But they have also fragmented energy markets and international finance and fueled polarization within societies. Russia's retreats fractured the regional orders in the Middle East and the South Caucasus, leaving a vacuum for others to fill. Most critically, Russia eroded the norms, rules, and institutions that have long underpinned the liberal international order, amplifying the stresses that order experienced from within.

Its chief antagonist, the West, has been more than a bit player in this story. In responding to Russia's actions, looking for ways to outsmart or punish the Kremlin; in making itself repeatedly guilty of double standards and hypocrisy; and in failing to understand and address the sources of Russia's enduring appeal around the globe, the West has been its own source of fragmentation.

History counsels humility in prediction, but it seems that no matter which way its war against Ukraine ends, Russia's engagement with the world will not return to what it was before February 2022. If and when the guns fall silent, Russia will remain a dangerous, highly militarized nation, stewing in revanchism toward Europe. Russian intellectuals may claim that this war did the country good. That a complete break with a West that showed insufficient respect for Russia after the end of the Cold War was long overdue. That Russia's true friends are in the east and south.

Narratives that justify, even glorify, war are as old as war itself. But it seems that Putin's resolve to chase the chimera of Ukraine's subjugation can only do Russia harm in the long run. It may not usher in the protagonist's sudden downfall, common in Greek tragedy. And it will not produce cathartic feelings of pity among the audience, either. The denouement may well be prolonged, perhaps with sudden convulsions, perhaps altogether drama-less, a quiet degradation. But tragic it will be, because it will leave Russia in a worse place.

More than one million Russian troops have been killed or wounded in Ukraine. The war has disfigured the Russian economy and pushed the country from a tacit dictatorship into the direction of a full-blown one. Russia is succumbing to China's embrace. Culturally and geographically part of Europe, Russia has become totally estranged from Europe. Where it has lost clout, both close to home and farther afield, it will struggle to recover it. Most important of all, Ukrainians and many other people across the vast Eurasian landmass will fear and distrust Russia for years, if not generations, to come.

Putin may well outlast the West. But he has gambled Russia's future.

ACKNOWLEDGMENTS

Writing this book was a complex endeavor, given the global scope of the story. I am deeply grateful to the many people, in many countries, who helped along the way.

Without my fantastic editor, Caroline Adams at W. W. Norton, this book wouldn't have made its journey from inception to print. Caroline embraced the idea for *We Shall Outlast Them* enthusiastically and made me believe that I could pull this off. Working with the entire team at Norton has been a pleasure. I am lucky to have a wonderful agent, Don Fehr at Trident Media Group, who took me on and then moved swiftly to find a home for this book. The Kathryn Wasserman Davis Collaborative in Conflict Transformation at Middlebury College gave me a generous grant that helped finance some of the reporting trips. Finally, I am immensely grateful to Miriam Elder for a first edit of the manuscript. Miriam's good judgment made every sentence better, and she taught me a thing (or two) about writing in the process.

I am indebted to the individuals whose stories I tell on these pages, and to countless others who shared their expertise in conversations with me and enriched my analysis. Some of them, especially diplomats, preferred speaking not-for-attribution so that they could be candid. I have not been able to return to Russia since I left on February 23, 2022, the day before the full-scale invasion of Ukraine. I am grateful to my Russian contacts who still correspond with me or share their views when we meet in third countries. I understand that some—though not all—are troubled by the path their country has taken, and I thank them for the courage to speak with me, especially since engagement with Western scholars can be perilous for them.

My early thinking about the book was sharpened by conversations with Andrew Monaghan, Joby Warrick, and Meghan Hauser. Friends and colleagues whose work I greatly admire read parts of the manuscript, providing valuable feedback. Special thanks to Michael Kimmage—first reader of the entire text, my coauthor on the pages of *Foreign Affairs*, mentor, and friend. I am also grateful to Michael Kofman, Alexandra Prokopenko, William Potter, Tigran Grigoryan, Olesya Vartanyan, Temur Umarov, Alex Yusupov, Milan Czerny, Jade McGlynn, Hilary Lynd, Nicole Grajewski, Ingrid Kirsten, Micah Reddy, and Joel Linnainmäki for reading different chapters. Neil MacFarlane, who supervised my doctoral thesis on Russian foreign policy at Oxford University many years ago, read the chapters on the South Caucasus and thus continued to enrich my work with his wit and deep expertise.

Fieldwork for this book was occasionally challenging, since it thrust me into environments in which I had not previously worked. Friends and colleagues offered helpful introductions that made my trips to India, Israel, Kazakhstan, South Africa, the South Caucasus, and various other destinations worth my while. Thank you, in no particular order, to: Olga Oliker, Shant Khatcherian, Steven Erlanger, Eden Kristal, Jeremy Issacharoff, Chen Zak Kane, Dena Sholk, Manik Jolly, Anton Troianovski, Nicholas Bauer, Gregor Jäcke, Hendrik Sittig, Paolo Sorbello, Daniel Rakov, Robyn Dixon, Lesley Wroughton, Irina Filatova, Minna Ålander, Eka Metreveli, Tina Dolbaia, Emma Louise Powell, Sanjay Singh, Vasabjit Banerjee, Manpreet Sethi, Indrani Bagchi, Thorsten Benner, Ofer Zalzberg, Temur Umarov, Alex Yusupov, Emily Holland, Richard Gowan, and Zarina Akhmatova. Erin Bates was a lifesaver for my research in South Africa. I owe a debt of gratitude to Henri Thulliez, who arranged for me to meet with Ephrem Yalike-Ngonzo. I am grateful to Benjamin Hilgenstock and Isaac Levi for the valuable correspondence on the shadow fleet, and to Omar Tabuni for providing documents on Mohammed Enbis's case. Thank you to other colleagues who helped with tips or introductions—you know who you are.

Perhaps the greatest pleasure of working on this book has been the companionship and support of talented individuals who also work on Russia. Alexander Gabuev provided a sounding board for many of the ideas presented—and took me out for the occasional dinner while I was in the midst of writing. One of the few silver linings of this terrible war has been the influx into Berlin of fellow Russia watchers, both journalists and experts, from Moscow. Conversations with Anatoly Kurmanaev, Valerie Hopkins, Paul Sonne, Max Seddon, Polina Ivanova, Anastasiya Stognei, Mary Ilyushina, Joshua Yaffa, Maxim Samorukov, and Alexandra Prokopenko are always enriching; so is reading their work.

My deep gratitude goes to John Bell, Julie Newton, and Anna Vassilieva. They have been mentors and friends over many years, accompanied my career since my student days, and opened many doors. I would not be where I am today without them. William Potter, my boss at the James Martin Center for Nonproliferation Studies (CNS), has tendered much encouragement for this book, and I cannot thank him enough for the support over the years. I am also grateful to my other colleagues at CNS and its European branch, the Vienna Center for Disarmament and Non-Proliferation. They taught me everything I know about nuclear issues, arms control, and nonproliferation. I have worked especially closely with Chen Zak Kane, Jim Lamson, and Sarah Bidgood, and could not wish for more supportive colleagues. Thanks also to Max Bergmann, Maria Snegovaya, and the rest of the Europe, Russia, and Eurasia Program at the Center for Strategic and International Studies. Coming onboard as a nonresident associate has been a true pleasure, and I have deeply appreciated the exposure it has given me in Washington, DC. I am also grateful to the (opinion) editors at the *Financial Times* (Alice Fishburn, Sasha Polakow-Suransky, and Jonathan Derbyshire), *The New York Times* (Tim Schneider and Louise Loftus), and *Foreign Affairs* (Justin Vogt and Dan Kurtz-Phelan) for giving me the opportunity to write for them and share my analysis with a wide readership.

Working and writing for an American think tank out of Berlin can be challenging and, above all, lonely. Colleagues at the Carnegie

Russia Eurasia Center, Stiftung Wissenschaft und Politik, the European Council on Foreign Relations, the Global Public Policy Institute, Körber Stiftung, the Konrad Adenauer Stiftung, the Friedrich Ebert Stiftung, the Berlin office of the Munich Security Conference, and the German Council on Foreign Relations have welcomed and integrated me into the Berlin policy-watcher community, for which I'm grateful. I always enjoy conversations with Sabine Fischer, Margarete Klein, Janis Kluge, Leslie Schübel, Sarah Pagung, Oliver Meier, Jana Puglierin, and many others.

It's hard to imagine my life in Berlin without my dear friends Katherine Wilkins, Valerie Hopkins, Timofey Neshitov, Anchalee Rüland, Szabina Altsach, Jan-Jonathan Bock, and Johannes Meier. Valerie and Timofey's little daughter Zoe was born just as I started working on the manuscript. Spending time with Zoe in the evenings, after long days of writing in solitude, gave me so much joy. Other friends brought their kindness and support to the task of me getting this book across the finish line from afar, especially Leila Ullrich, Alexandra Zeitz, Brett Rosenberg, Emma Lecavalier, Johanna Lehne, Steffi (Bryson) Swartz, and Angelica Allen. Thank you, Joachim Carr, for sharpening my eyes for the shades of gray between all the black and white in this world.

Above all, I want to thank my entire family for all their support over the many years of my Russia-focused journey, especially my parents, who have followed this book's evolution with curiosity and good wishes, and my sisters, Kathrin and Sophie, who are my soulmates and greatest fans.

NOTES

INTRODUCTION

7 **most astute observers of Russia:** For comprehensive accounts of that period in Russian foreign policy and in US–Russia relations—the 2000s and 2010s—see, for instance: Angela Stent, *The Limits of Partnership* (Princeton University Press, 2015); Kathryn Stoner, *Russia Resurrected: Its Power and Purpose in a New Global Order* (Oxford University Press, 2020); Jeffrey Mankoff, *Russian Foreign Policy: The Return of Great Power Politics* (Rowman & Littlefield, 2011).

8 **cultural/ideological obsession with the victim:** See, for instance: Vladimir Putin, "On the Historical Unity of Russians and Ukrainians," July 12, 2021.

8 **story that reached its erstwhile apex:** This book does not chronicle the invasion, nor does it go deeply into Putin's reasons for launching the war. For accounts addressing these issues, see, for instance: Michael Kimmage, *Collisions* (Oxford University Press, 2024); Matthew Owens, *Overreach: The Inside Story of Putin and Russia's War Against Ukraine* (Mudlark, 2022); Serhii Plokhy, The Russo-*Ukrainian War: The Return of History* (W. W. Norton, 2023).

8 **Putting Western states:** For a historical perspective on this theme, in his seminal account *To Run the World*, Sergey Radchenko shows how delusions of grandeur and desire for recognition propelled Moscow on a quest for global power during the Cold War: Sergey Radchenko, *To Run the World: The Kremlin's Cold War Bid for Global Power* (Cambridge University Press, 2024).

11 **In a May 2023 speech, Fiona Hill:** Fiona Hill, "Ukraine in the New World Disorder: The Rest's Rebellion Against the United States," Lennart Meri Lecture, Lennart Meri Conference 2023, Tallinn, Estonia, May 13, 2023.

11 **Not everything that Russia did was new:** For a comprehensive take on Russia's growing focus on non-Western countries in the years leading up to the Ukraine invasion, see, for instance: Angela Stent, *Putin's World: Russia Against the West and with the Rest* (Twelve, 2019).

CHAPTER 1

18 **Russia's oil and gas revenues:** For a comprehensive account of the evolution of the Russian oil industry through the 1990s and 2000s, see: Thane Gustafson, *Wheel of Fortune: The Battle for Oil and Power in Russia* (Harvard University Press, 2012).

19 **Sergey Vakulenko . . . was one of them:** Sergey Vakulenko, "How Russia Could Thwart an Oil Price Cap," *Carnegie Politika*, July 5, 2022; Sergey Vakulenko, "The Flaw in the Plan to Cap Russian Oil Prices," *Carnegie Politika*, September 8, 2022.

20 **turned to bogus insurance outfits:** Elisabeth Braw, "We Started Checking Russian Shadow Vessel Insurance. Now What?" *Politico*, April 17, 2025.

20 **The shadow fleet . . . had grown to around 153:** Denis Kasyanchuk, "Does the Price Cap on Russian Oil Actually Work?" *Bell*, October 28, 2023.

20 **Rosneft relied on a subset of the shadow fleet:** Joe Wallace, Anna Hirtenstein, and Coastas Paris, "The Secret Oil-Trading Ring That Funds Russia's War," *Wall Street Journal*, February 19, 2024.

20 **the "Rosneft shadow fleet":** David Ignatius, "A Wary White House Views Russia Oil Sanctions Through Lens of Inflation," *Washington Post*, June 18, 2024.

21 **He then served in the army:** "Sechin, Igor," Lentapedia (lenta.ru/lib), accessed June 29, 2025.

21 **In his biography of Putin:** Philip Short, *Putin* (Vintage, 2022), 162.

22 **70 percent of its seaborne oil:** Benjamin Hilgenstock, Anatoliy Kravtsev, Yuliia Pavytska, and Anna Vlaysuk, "Creating 'Shadow-Free' Zones," KSE Institute, October 2024.

24 **164 were shadow tankers:** Data provided to the author by the Centre for Research on Energy and Clean Air.

25 **accounting for 34 percent of all Russian crude:** Data provided to the author by the KSE Institute, an analytical center at the Kyiv School of Economics.

29 **Had the price cap been applied properly:** Vaibhav Raghunandan, Petras Katinas, Isaac Levi, and Luke Wickenden, "Three Years of Invasion: EU Imports of Russian Fossil Fuels in Third Year of Invasion Surpass Financial Aid Sent to Ukraine," Centre for Research on Energy and Clean Air, February 2025.

30 **In 2024 alone, Russia had earned:** Benjamin Hilgenstock and Yuliia Pavytska, "KSE Institute Russia Chartbook: The Russian Economy at the Start of 2025," KSE Institute, January 2025.

30 **the EU paid more for these imports:** Raghunandan et al., "Three Years of Invasion."

CHAPTER 2

32 **Russia's decade of humiliation:** For accounts of Russia's difficult economic transition during the 1990s, see: Anders Åslund, *Russia's Capitalist Revolution: Why Market Reform Succeeded and Democracy Failed* (Peterson Institute for International Economics, 2007); Clifford G. Gaddy and Barry W. Ickes, *Russia's Virtual Economy* (Brookings Institution Press, 2002).

33 **the Laleli market became especially famous:** For an overview of the Laleli trade, see: M. Eder, A. Yakovlev, and A. Çarkoglu, "Suitcase Trade Between Turkey and Russia: Microeconomics and Institutional Structure," Working paper WP4/2003/07, Moscow: State University—Higher School of Economics,

2003; Deniz Yükseker, "Shuttling Goods, Weaving Consumer Tastes: Informal Trade Between Turkey and Russia," *International Journal of Urban and Regional Research* 31, no. 1 (March 2007): 60–72.

35 **An individual shuttle trader:** "Russkii bazar v Turtsii: kak rabotayut novye 'sanktsionnye chelnoki'" ["The Russian Bazaar in Turkey: How the New 'Sanctions Shuttle Traders' Operate"], REN TV, August 1, 2022.

36 **became major transshipment hubs:** Georgi Kantchev, Paul Hannon, and Laurence Norman, "How Sanctioned Western Goods Are Still Flowing into Russia," *Wall Street Journal*, May 14, 2023.

36 **Russia could import almost any product:** "A Loophole in the Sanctions," *Verstka*, August 9, 2023.

37 **As *The Economist* coolly noted:** "Rogue Russia Threatens the World, Not Just Ukraine," *Economist*, March 14, 2024.

38 **One case uncovered by researchers:** Maria Zholobova, Benjamin Bidder, Vyacheslav Abramov, and Ilya Lozovsky, "Kazakhstan Has Become a Pathway for the Supply of Russia's War Machine. Here's How It Works," Organized Crime and Corruption Reporting Project, May 19, 2023.

40 **settling trade in nondollar currencies:** For a detailed discussion, see: Daniel McDowell, *Bucking the Buck: US Financial Sanctions and the International Backlash Against the Dollar* (Oxford University Press, 2023).

40 **they laid a foundation for de-dollarizing:** Gal Luft and Anne Korin, *De-Dollarization: The Revolt Against the Dollar and the Rise of a New Financial World Order* (Independently published, 2019).

40 **turned to the clandestine, barter-like exchanges:** Alexandra Prokopenko, "How the Latest Sanctions Will Impact Russia—and the World," *Carnegie Politika*, June 20, 2024.

40 **de-dollarization was . . . turning into yuanization:** Alexandra Prokopenko, "How Sanctions Have Changed Russian Economic Policy," *Carnegie Politika*, May 9, 2023.

41 **deepening vassalage to China was the price:** Alexander Gabuev, "With Putin in Charge, Russia's Vassalage to China Will Only Deepen," *Carnegie Politika*, September 8, 2025.

42 **according to several groundbreaking investigations:** "Alabuga: Iranian Drones Under Franchise," *Protokol*, July 3, 2023; "Alabuga. Proizvodstvo smerti rukami studentov" ["Alabuga: Production of Death by Students"], *Protokol*, July 24, 2023; Spencer Faragasso and David Albright, "Youth Exploited for Military Drone Production at the Alabuga Special Economic Zone," Institute for Science and International Security, July 1, 2024.

43 **Russian payments for Iranian drone technology:** Omar Al-Ghusbi and Conrad Rousseau, "Airborne Axis: Inside the Deal That Brought Iranian Drone Technology to Russia," C4ADS, May 2025.

43 **Alabuga Start's flagship educational program:** Faragasso and Albright, "Youth Exploited for Military Drone Production."

43 **some of the African women:** Emma Burrows and Lori Hinnant, "Africans

Recruited to Work in Russia Say They Were Duped into Building Drones for Use in Ukraine," Associated Press, October 10, 2024.

44 **Interpol in Botswana began investigating:** As of December 2025, the investigation appeared to be ongoing. Alabuga Start declined to comment when contacted by news agencies about the accusations.

44 **Since the 1990s, Russia has provided:** Russia (and before it the Soviet Union) and Iran have a complex historical relationship that was riven by mutual mistrust. For accounts of that history, see: Louise Fawcett, *Iran and the Cold War: The Azerbaijan Crisis of 1946* (Middle East Library, 1992); Clément Therme, *Les Relations entre Téhéran et Moscou depuis 1979* (The Graduate Institute, Geneva, 2012). For an account of more recent Russian-Iranian relations, see: Nicole Grajewski, *Russia and Iran: Partners in Defiance from Syria to Ukraine* (C. Hurst, 2025).

46 **"when the sky collapsed":** Siobhán O'Grady and Serhii Korolchuk, "What the North Koreans Took into Battle Against Ukraine," *Washington Post*, January 19, 2025.

CHAPTER 3

51 **Russian propaganda has consistently portrayed Ukraine:** Jade McGlynn, *Russia's War* (Polity Press, 2023).

52 **It became the discursive foundation:** For work on the conceptual and discursive underpinnings of Russian foreign policy historically, see: Andrei Tsygankov, "Irreplaceable Russia: Fortresses and Bridges of the 'Russian Idea,'" *Russia in Global Affairs* 21, no. 4 (October–December 2023): 66–76. Andrei Tsygankov, *Russia's Foreign Policy: Change and Continuity in National Identity*, 4th ed. (Rowman & Littlefield, 2016).

53 **article that portrayed Nicholas II:** Pyotr Multatuli, "Antikolonial'nyj kharakter pomoshhi imperatora Nikolaya II Abissinii, Siamu i gosudarstvam Yuzhnoi Afriki v bor'be za ikh nezavisimost'" ["The Anti-Colonial Nature of Emperor Nicholas II's Assistance to Abyssinia, Siam, and the States of South Africa in the Struggle for Their Independence"], Mezhdunarodnaya Zhizn, 2023.

53 **position infused by anti-imperialist tropes:** African National Congress, "Resolutions: International Relations," 55th National Conference, Gauteng, December 16–20, 2022. See also: Priyal Singh, "Wheels Come Off South Africa's Hollow Version of Non-Alignment," Institute for Security Studies, May 22, 2023.

54 **"hoping to put Russia in its place":** African National Congress, "Resolutions: International Relations," 55th National Conference, paragraph 22.

55 **was pardoned while on death row:** For a fuller account of Robert McBride's life, see: Bryan Rostron, *Robert McBride: The Struggle Continues* (Tafelberg, 2019).

56 **"There was a great spirit":** Ronnie Kasrils, *Armed and Dangerous: From Undercover Struggle to Freedom* (Jacana, 1993), 61. For other accounts by ANC veterans who chronicle their time spent in the USSR, see: Ronnie Kasrils and Fidelis

Hove, *Comrade and Commander: The Life and Times of Joe Modise* (Jacana, 2024); Khulu Mbatha, *Scattered: A Personal Story of the 1976 Generation* (KMM Review Publishing, 2022).

56 **Filatova calls this imprint:** Irina Filatova and Apollon Davidson, *The Hidden Thread: Russia and South Africa in the Soviet Era* (Jonathan Ball, 2013). Besides Filatova, another scholar who has chronicled ANC–Soviet relations extensively is Russian academic Vladimir Shubin. See: Vladimir Shubin, *ANC: A View from Moscow* (Jacana, 2008); Vladimir Shubin, *The Hot "Cold War": The USSR in Southern Africa* (Pluto Press, 2008).

56 **When his mother passed:** Bheki Langa recounts the episode in his short memoir: Bheki Langa, *Tales of the Grindstone* (Econoculture, 2024), 60.

57 **one that echoed the ANC's contention:** African National Congress, "6th National Policy Conference Report," Gauteng, July 28–31, 2022, 76.

58 **the ANC's manifestos still commit:** African National Congress, "6th National Policy Conference Report," Gauteng, July 28–31, 2022, 69.

63 **president with extremely close Kremlin ties:** David Pilling and Rob Rose, "South Africa Opposition Group Claims Russia Is Funding Jacob Zuma's Party," *Financial Times*, June 7, 2024. In late 2025, media reports alleged that Zuma's daughter, Duduzile Zuma-Sambudla, had recruited South Africans to fight on behalf of Russia against Ukraine.

64 **criticized the constitution as "neoliberal":** Lindiwe Sisulu, "Hi Mzansi, Have We Seen Justice?" IOL.za, January 7, 2022.

64 **When I met Gumede in Johannesburg:** William Gumede wrote a seminal account of the history of the ANC: William Mervin Gumede, *Thabo Mbeki and the Battle for the Soul of the ANC* (Zebra Press, 2007).

65 **"imperialism is only imperialism if Americans do it":** Hilary Lynd, "The Politics of Imperial Gratitude," *Africa Is a Country*, March 14, 2022.

66 **period of sharp estrangement:** For analysis on a cooling in ANC–Soviet relations during the perestroika era in the late 1980s, see: Irina Filatova, "Soviet Public Engagements with the ANC: Disillusionment and Pressures," in Helder Adegar Fonseca, Chris Saunders, and Lena Dallywater, eds., *Communist Actors in African Decolonial Transitions: Comparative Perspectives* (De Gruyter Brill, 2025).

CHAPTER 4

69 **start with a minuscule budget:** Mona Elswah and Philip N. Howard, "'Anything That Causes Chaos': The Organizational Behavior of Russia Today (RT)," *Journal of Communication* 70, no. 5 (October 2020): 623–45.

70 **preceded by provocative Russian actions:** Independent International Fact-Finding Mission on the Conflict in Georgia, "Report," vol. 1 (Max Planck Institute, September 2009).

70 **The 2008 war was Russia Today's "crucible":** Julia Ioffe, "What Is Russia Today?" *Columbia Journalism Review*, September 28, 2010.

71 **Simonyan commissioned a TV viewership survey:** "RT Claims 70m Weekly Viewers," *Advanced Television*, March 10, 2016.

71 **RT's Facebook pages were especially successful:** Stephen Hutchings et al., *Russia, Disinformation, and the Liberal Order: RT as Populist Pariah* (Cornell University Press, 2024).

71 **Another data-driven study showed:** Rhys Crilley, Marie Gillespie, Bertie Vidgen, and Alistair Willis, "Understanding RT's Audiences: Exposure Not Endorsement for Twitter Followers of Russian State-Sponsored Media," *International Journal of Press/Politics* 27, no. 1 (January 2022): 220–42.

78 **Bloggers based in the St. Petersburg headquarters:** Shaun Walker, "The Russian Troll Factory at the Heart of the Meddling Allegations," *Guardian*, April 2, 2015.

78 **the Dossier Center found that the troll factories:** "Kibervoyska Prigozhina: Kak ustroena IT-infrastruktura 'Vagnera,' 'Fabriki trolley' i 'Konkorda'" ["Prigozhin's Cyber Troops: How the IT Infrastructure of 'Wagner,' 'Troll Factory,' and 'Concord' Is Organized"], Dossier Center, March 18, 2023.

78 **pro-Russian "buzzers" emerged:** Herman Wasserman and Murmur, "How Russia Uses 'Hybrid Warfare' to Amplify Its Narratives in the South African Discourse," *Daily Maverick*, November 22, 2024.

81 **The militia stood accused:** "Ali Darassa," UN Security Council (narrative summary of reasons for the listing for individuals and entities included in the sanctions list), December 21, 2021.

82 **views on Wagner were far from monolithic:** John Lechner, "Are Russian Mercenaries Bad for the Central African Republic?" *Responsible Statecraft*, April 11, 2023.

83 **which first broke the story:** Léa Peruchon, "In the Central African Republic, a Former Propagandist Lifts the Veil on the Inner Workings of Russian Disinformation," *Forbidden Stories*, November 21, 2024.

84 **media machine across several African countries:** Léa Peruchon, "Propaganda Machine: Russia's Information Offensive in the Sahel," *Forbidden Stories*, November 21, 2024.

85 **Jade McGlynn defines "memory diplomacy":** Jade McGlynn, *Memory Makers: The Politics of the Past in Putin's Russia* (Bloomsbury, 2023).

CHAPTER 5

91 **Russia's strategic tilt toward Azerbaijan:** Thomas de Waal, "Putin's Hidden Game in the South Caucasus," *Foreign Affairs*, June 3, 2024.

92 **the 1921 Treaty of Kars:** For a treatment of Armenian history, see: Thomas de Waal, *The Caucasus: An Introduction* (Oxford University Press, 2010).

92 **Armenia continued to rely on Russia:** For an analysis of Russia's view that it has special rights and obligations in its "near abroad," which imply limitations on the sovereignty of the three states of the region (Armenia, Azerbaijan,

and Georgia), see: S. Neil MacFarlane, "Russia in the Caucasus," in Galina M. Yemelianova and Laurence Broers, eds., *Routledge Handbook of the Caucasus* (Routledge, 2020).

94 **some sort of deal between Baku and Moscow:** "RCDS Insights: Ethnic Cleansing of Nagorno-Karabakh and Russia," Regional Center for Democracy and Security, March 10, 2023.

98 **Olesya Vartanyan, a seasoned South Caucasus analyst:** Olesya Vartanyan, "Armenia Struggles to Cope with Exodus from Nagorno-Karabakh," International Crisis Group, March 4, 2024.

98 **Sociological surveys showed that Karabakh Armenians:** Ivaylo Dinev and Nadja Douglas, "The Political and Cultural Fate of Karabakh Armenians in Armenia," *ZOiS Spotlight*, September 4, 2024.

100 **normalization with Armenia could expand Turkey's influence:** Olesya Vartanyan, "The Window for an Armenia–Azerbaijan Peace Deal Is Closing," *Carnegie Politika*, March 26, 2025.

101 **Armenia's economy has remained deeply dependent on Russia:** Eduard Arakelyan, Karena Avedissian, and Tigran Grigoryan, "Armenia's Structural Dependence on Russia: Trade, Energy, Security," Regional Center for Democracy and Security, October 2024.

CHAPTER 6

108 **Shevardnadze's departure were extremely improvised:** de Waal, *The Caucasus*, 193.

109 **Georgia's population remained overwhelmingly pro-Western:** For polls confirming this, see: "Georgian National Voter Study: August 31–September 10, 2007," International Republican Institute, US Agency for International Development, Baltic Surveys Ltd., The Gallup Organization, IPM; "Public Attitudes Towards Elections in Georgia: Results of a April 2010 Survey Carried Out for NDI by CRRC," National Democratic Institute for International Affairs, April 2010.

111 **Bloomberg published an investigation:** Alberto Nardelli and Ryan Gallagher, "How Russia's Spies Hacked the Entire Nation of Georgia," Bloomberg, October 21, 2024.

113 **Religion occupies a central place:** "Public Opinion Survey: Residents of Georgia," Center for Insights in Survey Research/International Republican Institute, February 2021.

113 **83 percent of the population:** Tsypylma Darieva, "Report 1/2021: Faith, State, and Religious Competition in Georgia," Center for East European and International Studies (ZOiS), January 14, 2021.

115 **GD has been emulating:** Natalie Sabanadze, "Georgia's Imitation Game: Hungary, Russia, and the Rise of the Anti-Liberal International," Heinrich Böll Stiftung Tbilisi—South Caucasus Region, 2024.

CHAPTER 7

119 **caused a devastating famine:** For a history of that period, see: Sarah Cameron, *The Hungry Steppe: Famine, Violence, and the Making of Soviet Kazakhstan* (Cornell University Press, 2018).

120 **she wrote in early 2024:** Zarina Akhmatova, "Deportatsiya chechentsev i ingushey—rana, nezazhivayushhaya 80 let" ["Deportation of Chechens and Ingush—A Wound That Has Not Healed for 80 Years"], Ratel Media, February 24, 2024.

121 **According to the 2021 census:** "National Composition, Religion and Language Proficiency in the Republic of Kazakhstan: Results of the National Population Census of 2021 in the Republic of Kazakhstan," Agency of the Republic of Kazakhstan for Strategic Planning and Reforms, National Bureau of Statistics, Astana, 2023.

124 **attitudes toward Russia overall deteriorated:** Abylay Muzaffar, Medi Edison, Sayat Gani, Serik Beissembayev, and Eric McGlinchey, "Echoes of War: Public Perception of the Russian-Ukrainian War in Central Asia," PaperLab, 2024.

125 **wrote in a damning editorial:** Svetlana Romashkina, "Impressions of the Qantar Memorial," *Vlast*, December 28, 2022.

127 **unofficial third wife of former president:** Reporters with the Organized Crime and Corruption Reporting Project reached out to Nazarbayev and his unofficial third wife, Kurmanbayeva, for comment but did not receive a response.

129 **The radioactive fallout from the tests:** For a full account of Kazakhstan's nuclear history from the Soviet period to the present, see: Togzhan Kassenova, *Atomic Steppe: How Kazakhstan Gave Up the Bomb* (Stanford University Press, 2022).

130 **gave Kazakhstan's "multi-vector foreign policy" a new meaning:** Marie Dumoulin, "Steppe Change: How Russia's War on Ukraine Is Reshaping Kazakhstan," European Council on Foreign Relations, April 13, 2023.

CHAPTER 8

137 **to compare the wars in Ukraine and Gaza:** "Nebenzya ukazal SB OON na raznitsu mezhdu obstanovkoi na Ukraine i v sektore Gaza" ["Nebenzia Pointed Out to the UN Security Council the Difference Between the Situation in Ukraine and the Gaza Strip"], TASS, October 31, 2023.

129 **During the Cold War, the Soviet Union:** For accounts of Soviet foreign policy toward the Middle East, see, for instance: Robert O. Freedman, *Moscow and the Middle East—Soviet Foreign Policy Since the Invasion of Afghanistan* (Cambridge University Press, 1991); Galia Golan, *Soviet Policies in the Middle East—From World War II to Gorbachev* (Cambridge University Press, 1990); Fred Halliday, *Cold War, Third World—An Essay on Soviet-American Relations* (Hutchinson Radius, 1989); Alexei M. Vassiliev, *Russian Policy in the Middle East: From Messianism to Pragmatism* (Ithaca Press, 1993).

139 **Sharansky . . . spent nine years in Soviet prisons:** For Sharansky's account of that experience, see: Natan Sharansky, *Fear No Evil: The Classic Memoir of One Man's Triumph over a Police State* (Public Affairs, 1988).

140 **he and . . . Sharon shared a common enemy:** For Russian foreign policy in the Middle East during the 2000s, see: Rolan Dannreuther, "Russia and the Middle East: A Cold War Paradigm?" *Europe-Asia Studies* 64, no. 3 (May 2012): 543–60; Mark Katz, "Putin's Foreign Policy Towards Syria," *Middle East Review of International Affairs* 10, no. 1 (March 2006): 55–59; Hanna Notte, "Russia in Chechnya and Syria: Pursuit of Strategic Goals," *Middle East Policy Council* 23, no. 1 (Spring 2016): 59–74.

146 **cartoon that displayed BRICS countries:** Sergey Naryshkin, "2024—god geopoliticheskogo probuzhdeniya" ["2024—The Year of Geopolitical Awakening"], *Razvedchik*, no. 4 (December 2023).

147 **Russia launched a military intervention:** For an account of Russia's 2015 intervention, see: Anna Borshchevskaya, *Putin's War in Syria* (I. B. Tauris, 2021).

147 **while maintaining deconfliction channels:** For an account of the Russian–US deconfliction channel in Syria, see: Aaron Stein, "An Unfinished War: Simmering Conflict in a Destroyed State," chap. 6 in *The US War Against ISIS: How America and Its Allies Defeated the Caliphate* (I. B. Tauris, 2022).

148 **destruction of its chemical weapons:** For an account of the Russian role in this effort, see: Hanna Notte, "The United States, Russia, and Syria's Chemical Weapons: A Tale of Cooperation and Its Unravelling," *Nonproliferation Review* 27, nos. 1–3 (2020): 201–24. See also: Matthew Moran, Wyn Q. Bowen, and Jeffrey W. Knopf, *Coercing Syria on Chemical Weapons: A Case Study of Deterrence and Coercive Diplomacy* (Oxford University Press, 2025).

151 **Putin decided it was time:** Syria's new foreign minister, Asaad al-Shaibani, later claimed in an interview with *Al Majalla* magazine that HTS told the Russians days before the November 2024 offensive that the fall of the Assad regime did not need to usher in Russia's departure from Syria. Al-Shaibani claimed that these assurances led Russia to stand aside. Ibrahim Hamidi, "Asaad Shaibani on How Syria Untangled Its Russian Knot," *Al Majalla*, November 18, 2025.

151 **Russian military expert Ruslan Pukhov:** "Uroki Sirii" ["The Lessons of Syria"], *Kommersant*, December 8, 2024.

CHAPTER 9

158 **Russia had a long mercenary tradition:** Anna Borshchevskaya, "Russian Private Military Companies: Continuity and Evolution of the Model," Foreign Policy Research Institute, 2019.

159 **Anna Arutunyan and Mark Galeotti:** Anna Arutunyan and Mark Galeotti, *Downfall: Prigozhin, Putin and the New Fight for the Future of Russia* (Ebury Press, 2024), 45.

159 **new entity called the Wagner Group:** For histories of the Wagner Group's ori-

gins and its evolution over time, see: Jack Margolin, *The Wagner Group: Inside Russia's Mercenary Army* (Reaktion Books, 2024); John Lechner, *Death Is Our Business: Russian Mercenaries and the New Era of Private Warfare* (Bloomsbury, 2025).

159 **Russian operations in Ukraine in 2014:** For a fuller account of Russia's use of mercenaries, volunteers, political technologists, and others as it waged its covert invasion of Ukraine in 2014, see: Anna Arutunyan, *Hybrid Warriors: Proxies, Freelancers and Moscow's Struggle for Ukraine* (Hurst & Co., 2022).

160 **Mohammed Enbis suffered his ordeal:** Account based on interviews conducted in 2022 by the Libyan American Alliance's paralegals with Mohammed Enbis, provided to the author by the Libyan American Alliance, as well as Enbis's complaint filed with the US District Court for the District of Columbia.

161 **bringing the government and armed groups:** Lechner, *Death Is Our Business.*

161 **intelligence agency Molfar has claimed:** "Catalog of Russian PMCs: 37 Private Military Companies of the Russian Federation," Molfar Intelligence Institute, April 24, 2023.

164 **Africa . . . had become Putin's new frontier:** For background on Russia's broader history and interests in Africa, see: Samuel Ramani, *Russia in Africa: Resurgent Great Power or Bellicose Pretender?* (Hurst & Co., 2023).

165 **new mini-Prigozhins might appear:** John Lechner and Sergey Eledinov, "Wagner Mercenaries Declare 'Mission Accomplished' in Mali," *Responsible Statecraft*, June 16, 2025.

CHAPTER 10

171 **Washington and Moscow led an effort:** For a history of US–Russia cooperation within the NPT, see: William C. Potter and Sarah Bidgood, eds., *Once and Future Partners: The US, Russia, and Nuclear Non-Proliferation* (Routledge, 2018) and Sarah Bidgood and William C. Potter, eds., *End of an Era: The United States, Russia, and Nuclear Nonproliferation* (James Martin Center for Nonproliferation Studies, 2021). For a treatment of the role of the US in sustaining the NPT, see: Rebecca Gibson, *The Hegemon's Toolkit: US Leadership and the Politics of the Nuclear Nonproliferation Regime* (Cornell University Press, 2022).

178 **Tensions ran particularly high:** See: Notte, "The United States, Russia, and Syria's Chemical Weapons."

179 **In legacy multilateral institutions:** For a fuller account, see: Hanna Notte, "Russia, the Global South and the Mechanics of the Nuclear Order," *Survival* 66, no. 3 (2024): 49–57.

183 **as a space for residual cooperation:** Richard Gowan, "How the World Lost Faith in the UN," *Foreign Affairs*, November 9, 2023.

186 **had ignored Russia's repeated requests:** United Nations General Assembly, Seventy-Ninth Session, 3rd Plenary Meeting, Official Records (A/79/PV.3*), New York, September 22, 2024.

186 **Russia would seek to move an amendment:** United Nations General Assembly, Seventy-Ninth Session, Agenda Item 123, "Strengthening of the United Nations System," (A/79/L.3), New York, September 20, 2024.

CHAPTER 11

189 **The origins of BRICS:** For a history of BRICS, see: Rachel S. Salzman, *Russia, BRICS, and the Disruption of Global Order* (Georgetown University Press, 2019); Oliver Stuenkel, *The BRICS and the Future of Global Order* (Lexington Books, 2015).

189 **"an international bête noire or pariah":** Viktoria Panova, "BRICS Security Agenda and Prospects for the BRICS Ufa Summit," *International Organisations Research Journal* 10, no. 2 (2015): 119–39.

190 **she also issued a plea and a warning:** Viktoria Panova, "COVID19 Pandemic Has Had Many Impacts," Observer Research Foundation, August 25, 2020.

193 **wanted by the ICC:** The ICC issued arrest warrants for al-Bashir in March 2009 and July 2010 on charges of crimes against humanity, but the suspect is still at large and hence has been neither tried nor convicted.

194 **treatise about Russia's foreign policy:** Sergey A. Karaganov, Alexander M. Kramarenko, and Dmitry V. Trenin, "Russia's Policy Towards World Majority," Higher School of Economics, Council on Foreign and Defense Policy, 2023.

195 **Russian synchronized swimmer Alexandr Maltsev:** Anastasia Stognei, "Fake Games, Cyber Threats and Disinformation: Russia Reacts to Sporting Isolation," *Financial Times*, July 24, 2024.

197 **Reporting from Kazan, the newspaper *Kommersant* cheered:** "BRIKS sblizhaet Indiyu i Kitai" ["BRICS Brings India and China Closer"], *Kommersant*, October 22, 2024.

CHAPTER 12

206 **Soviets also carried out hundreds of tests:** For a history of Soviet nuclear tests, see: "Nuclear Tests," chap. 8 in *Russian Strategic Nuclear Forces*, ed. Pavel Podvig (MIT Press, 2001), 439–566.

208 **deterrence "à la russe":** Dmitry (Dima) Adamsky, *The Russian Way of Deterrence: Strategic Culture, Coercion, and War* (Stanford University Press, 2023). For additional academic work on Russian deterrence, see: Kristin Ven Bruusgaard, "Russian Strategic Deterrence," *Survival* 58, no. 4 (2016): 7–26; Samuel Charap, "Strategic Sderzhivanie: Understanding Contemporary Russian Approaches to 'Deterrence,'" George. C. Marshall European Center for Security Studies, September 2020; Dmitry (Dima) Adamsky, "Quo Vadis, Russian Deterrence? Strategic Culture and Coercion Innovations," *International Security* 49, no. 3 (2025): 50–83.

208 **to help mediate the dispute:** Hanna Notte, "UN Security Council Resolution 1929 on Iran: US-Russian Cooperation and the Quest for Diffuse Reciprocity," in Bidgood and Potter, eds., *End of an Era*.

208 **signed the New START:** For an in-depth perspective on the negotiations of New START, see the account by US lead negotiator Rose Gottemoeller: Rose Gottemoeller, *Negotiating the New START Treaty* (Cambria Press, 2019).

213 **by creating problems for Washington:** See, for instance: Karaganov, Kramarenko, and Trenin, "Russia's Policy Towards World Majority."

213 **Sergey Semenov of the PIR Center:** Sergey D. Semenov, "Scenes from Nonproliferation: Disengagement and Signaling in Russian Policy," chap. 3 in *Security Index Yearbook 2024–2025, Part 1: Global Security in the Times of Transition to a Multipolar World* (PIR Center, 2024).

218 **create and constitute knowledge regimes:** Caner Bakir, "The Vicious Circle of Policy Advisory Systems and Knowledge Regimes in Consolidated Authoritarian Regimes," *Policy and Society* 42, no. 3 (September 2023): 419–39. For scholarship on how Russians navigate unwritten rules and informal practices, see: Alena Ledeneva, "Open Secrets and Knowing Smiles," *East European Politics and Societies* 25, no. 4 (2011): 720–36.

218 **Trenin had published an essay:** Dmitry Trenin, "How Russia Could Recalibrate Its Relationship with Ukraine," Carnegie Russia Eurasia Center, September 10, 2021.

218 **the majority of voices within Russia's strategic community:** Lydia Wachs, "Russian Nuclear Roulette? Elites and Public Debates on Nuclear Weapons in Moscow After Ukraine," *Nonproliferation Review* 30, nos. 4–6 (2023): 173–96.

219 **Trenin and Arbatov engaged in another repartee:** "Akademik Aleksei Arbatov: nuzhno govorit' ne o razoruzhenii, a o vosstanovlenii kontrolya" ["Academician Alexey Arbatov: We Need to Talk Not About Disarmament, but About Restoring Control"], *Interfax*, June 1, 2024; "Professor NIU VShe Dmitrii Trenin: chtoby ne doshlo do mirovoi voiny, nuzhen strakh pered yadernym oruzhiem" ["HSE Professor Dmitry Trenin: To Prevent a World War, We Need Fear of Nuclear Weapons"], *Interfax*, June 2, 2024.

219 **Russian strategic deterrence has long foreseen:** Michael Kofman and Anya Loukianova Fink, "Escalation Management and Nuclear Employment in Russian Military Strategy," *War on the Rocks*, June 23, 2020.

222 ***From Deterrence to Intimidation*:** Dmitry Trenin, Sergei Karaganov, and Sergei Avakiants, *Ot Sderzhivaniia k Ustrasheniiu [From Deterrence to Intimidation]* (Molodaia Gvardiia, 2024).

CHAPTER 13

227 **Kurmasheva and her coeditors:** Alsu Kurmasheva and Regina Khisamova, eds., *Saying No to War: 40 Stories of Russians Who Oppose the Russian Invasion of Ukraine* (Idel Realii, 2022).

228 **Russia has evolved into an abductor state:** Mark Kramer, "From Cold War-Era Spy Swaps to Kidnapping and Criminality in the Putin Era," Davis Center for Russian and Eurasian Studies, August 6, 2024.

231 **assassins hired by the Kremlin:** For a comprehensive history of the Kremlin's

use of spies, see: Shaun Walker, *The Illegals: Russia's Most Audacious Spies and Their Century-Long Mission to Infiltrate the West* (Knopf, 2025).

231 **Investigative journalists followed their trails:** "Diversii s bezopasnogo rasstoyaniya: Kto stoit za novoi taktikoi GRU v Evrope" ["Sabotage from a Safe Distance: Who Is Behind the New GRU Tactics in Europe"], Dossier Center, July 24, 2024; Bojan Pancevski, "A New Spy Unit Is Leading Russia's Shadow War Against the West," *Wall Street Journal*, February 15, 2025.

233 ***The Washington Post* revealed a secret addendum:** "Postanovlenie Zasedaniya Kollegii MID Rossii: Ob utochnenii prioritetnykh napravlenii raboty central'nogo apparata, zagranuchrezhdenii i podvedomstvennykh organizatsii MID Rossii v svete utverzhdeniya novoi Kontseptsii vneshnei politiki Rossiiskoi Federatsii" ["Suspension of the Meeting of the Board of the Ministry of Foreign Affairs of the Russian Federation: On Clarification of Priority Areas of Work of the Central Apparatus, Foreign Institutions and Subordinate Organizations of the Ministry of Foreign Affairs of the Russian Federation in Light of the Approval of the New Concept of Foreign Policy of the Russian Federation"], April 11, 2023.

233 **new foreign policy nihilism in Russia:** "Vladimir Putin's Spies Are Plotting Global Chaos," *Economist*, October 13, 2024.

233 **research team at Leiden University:** Benedicte Dobbinga, "Research: Europe Increasingly Targeted by Russian Sabotage," Universiteit Leiden, January 20, 2025.

233 **A separate dataset . . . based on slightly different metrics:** Seth G. Jones, "Russia's Shadow War Against the West," Center for Strategic & International Studies, March 18, 2025. For another quantitative study, see: Charlie Edwards and Nate Seidenstein, "The Scale of Russian Sabotage Operations Against Europe's Critical Infrastructure," International Institute for Strategic Studies, August 19, 2025.

235 ***Fontanka* revealed that migrants were taken:** " 'Eto vy Baydena sprosite, otkuda oni vzyalis'.' Kak vyglyadit nashestvie smuglykh velosipedistov v Brusnichnom" [" 'You Should Ask Biden Where They Came From.' What the Invasion of Dark-Skinned Cyclists Looks Like in Brusnichny"], Fontanka.ru, November 16, 2023.

240 **harder to attribute any malign activity:** Sidharth Kaushal, "Stalking the Seabed: How Russia Targets Critical Undersea Infrastructure," Royal United Services Institute, May 25, 2023.

243 **investigation into the Christmas Day incident:** Later, a Finnish court would dismiss the criminal case against the crew of the *Eagle S*, referring the incident under the jurisdiction of the UN Convention on the Law of the Sea.

CHAPTER 14

247 **joint press conference in Helsinki:** In his memoir, Trump's former national security adviser John Bolton claims that, before that meeting in Helsinki, Trump asked him whether Finland was "kind of a satellite of Russia."—John

Bolton, *The Room Where It Happened* (Simon & Schuster, 2020). For an account of US foreign policy during Trump's first term, including vis-à-vis Russia, see: Peter Baker and Susan Glasser, *The Divider: Trump in the White House, 2017–2021* (Doubleday, 2022).

249 **Trump's advisers surmised:** Adam Entous, "The Separation: Inside the Unraveling of the U.S.-Ukraine Partnership," *New York Times*, December 30, 2025.

250 **essayist Joshua Craze warned:** Joshua Craze, "USAID: Goodbye to All That?" *New York Review of Books*, March 12, 2025.

251 **the State Department disseminated calls:** Samuel Samson, "The Need for Civilizational Allies in Europe," US Department of State (Substack account), May 27, 2025.

252 **reversed by a new administration:** Ivan Timofeev, "Privedet li poteplenie dialoga Rossii i SShA k otmene sanktsii?" ["Will the Warming of Dialogue Between Russia and the US Lead to the Lifting of Sanctions?"], Russian International Affairs Council, March 7, 2025.

254 **Dimash Alzhanov . . . said in an interview:** Vladimir Radionov, "Budet li konets? Politolog Dimash Al'zhanov pro obeshhanie Trampa zakonchit' voinu v Ukraine" ["Will There Be an End? Political Scientist Dimash Alzhanov on Trump's Promise to End the War in Ukraine"], Respublika.kz, March 11, 2025.

256 **the US was a potential adversary:** Richard Gowan, "U. S. Volte-Face on Ukraine Exposes Depths of Divide in the UN," International Crisis Group, February 26, 2025.

257 **an FSB-affiliated think tank produced a document:** Catherine Belton and Robyn Dixon, "Document Prepared for Kremlin Outlines Hard-Line Negotiating Stance," *Washington Post*, March 12, 2025.

257 **issued a press release warning:** "Imagined Common Enemies: Russia's Foreign Intelligence Service Dreams of an Alliance with Washington Against 'Eurofascism,'" *Meduza*, April 19, 2025.

257 **Others in Moscow argued it was unwise:** The issue was controversially discussed, for instance, at the 33rd Assembly of the Council for Foreign and Defense Policy in Moscow in May 2025.

INDEX

Abil, Yerkin, 124
Abkhazia, 70, 95, 108, 111
Abu Saleh, Dolan, 152–53
Adamsky, Dmitry, 208
Adamyan, Anna, 89, 90
Adamyan, Azat, 89–91, 93, 97, 102, 254
adoptions, 4
Aeroflot, 229–30
Afghanistan, 7, 8, 150, 183, 209
Africa and Africans, 8, 21, 43, 46, 52, 53, 65, 66, 76–79, 82, 84, 85, 158, 160–67, 188, 250, 265, 266, 271; *See also* Sahel, the; *individual countries*
Africa Corps, 162–67, 250, 266, 271
African Initiative (media agency), 78
African National Congress (ANC), 53–60, 62–64, 66, 68, 122, 193
African Peace Initiative, 197
African Union, 186
"African village" (Tver region, Russia), 62
Afrikaners, 62, 251
Agency for the Prohibition of Nuclear Weapons in Latin America and the Caribbean, 180
AI, *See* artificial intelligence
Akhmatova, Zarina, 118–20, 122, 125–27, 129, 130
Akimat, 124, 125
Al Jazeera, 73, 150
Alabuga Polytech, 42–44, 44
Alabuga Special Economic Zone, 42–43, 47, 197
Alabuga Start, 43–44
Alaska summit (2025), 268–69
al-Assad, Bashar, 4, 11, 75, 144, 147–54, 163, 165, 183, 255, 262, 265, 269, 270
al-Assad, Hafez, 147
Alawites, 154
Albatross M5 drone, 42
alcohol consumption, 32
Aleppo, Syria, 149
Alexandra township, South Africa, 58
Al-Farabi Kazakh National University, 123
Algeria, 79, 199
aliyah, 142–43, 145
Aliyev, Ilham, 93, 100
Alliance of Sahel States, 164
Allied Maritime Command (NATO), 240
Almaty, Kazakhstan, 120, 123–26
Alpha Line, 136
al-Sharaa, Ahmed, 154, 269
Alternative für Deutschland, 246
Alt-Info activists, 114
alt-right, 251
Alzhanov, Dimash, 118, 125–27, 254
ANC, *See* African National Congress
ANC Youth Movement, 58
Angel Cakes (coffee shop chain), 24
Angola, 21, 54
Ankara, Turkey, 230
anti-apartheid movement, 55–57, 264
anti-colonialism, 52–53, 60–61, 64, 73, 78, 85, 163, 181, 189
anti-imperialism, 52–55, 57–58, 60, 62, 64, 250
anti-Semitism, 51–52, 140, 141, 145, 146
anti-Westernism, 78, 113, 136, 145–46, 148, 167, 178, 187, 195, 256, 266, 270, 271
anti-woke sentiments, 62, 113, 251
Apartheid, 54–58, 62–64, 68, 264
Arabic language, 73

Ararat (Armenian cognac), 97
Arbatov, Alexey, 216
Argentina, 191, 193
Armenia and Armenians, 35, 38, 89–102, 109, 110, 116, 124, 128, 130, 132, 156, 198, 237, 254, 263–64, 267, 272; *See also* Karabakh Armenians; Nagorno-Karabakh
Armenian Genocide, 92, 99
Arms Control Association, 211; *See also* nuclear arms control
arms trade, 41, 44–46, 225
arsons, 231, 232
artificial intelligence (AI), 194, 200, 222
Artsakh, 89, 98; *See also* Nagorno-Karabakh
Arutunyan, Anna, 159, 162
Asia, 38, 188; *See also* Central Asia
assassinations (incl. assassination attempts), 136, 178, 247, 248
Associated Press, 43
Astana, Kazakhstan, 121, 123, 128, 149, 156
Astana Group, 178
Astana process, 147
asylum seekers, 62, 234–36
ATACMS missiles, 221
Atlantic Ocean, 164
Atlanticism, 264
attestation fraud, 22
Auschwitz concentration camp, 142
Australia, 258
Austria, 182
authoritarianism, 4, 103, 110, 116, 124, 127, 132, 140, 254
autocracy, 111, 217
Avakyants, Sergey, 222
"axis of resistance," 136, 138, 153
"axis of upheaval," 48, 266
Azerbaijan, 20, 35, 89–91, 93–97, 99–102, 254, 267
Azerbaijan Airlines, 100
Azerbaijan Soviet Socialist Republic, 95

Badoo (dating app), 43
Baharoon, Mohammed, 25–26
Baku, Azerbaijan, 100, 263
Baltic Sea, 30, 239
Baltic states, 181, 216, 221, 231–32, 263; *See also* Estonia; Latvia; Lithuania
Balticconnector gas pipeline, 239, 242
Bangalore, India, 22
Bangladeshis, 46
Bangui, Central African Republic, 76–77, 79, 81–83, 162, 165, 250
Bardak, Nagorno-Karabakh, 89, 93, 97, 102
barter, 38, 40
Bashir, Omar al-, 193
"Basic Principles of State Policy of the Russian Federation on Nuclear Deterrence," 220
Bassiani (Tbilisi nightclub), 109, 112
Bavaria, 231
Bayerischer Hof hotel (Munich), 246
BBC, 29, 68
Bedouins, 154
Beissembayev, Serik, 124
Belarus, 38, 132, 157, 158, 186, 206, 219, 220, 230, 254, 256
Belushya Guba, Russia, 205
Ben Gurion Airport (Tel Aviv), 143
Benin, 164
Bennett, Naftali, 143
Berlin, Germany, 230, 232
Beslan school hostage crisis (2004), 69
Biden, Joe, and administration, 18, 22–23, 28, 30, 37, 74, 208–11, 214, 221, 222, 230, 244, 245, 249, 266–67
bioweapons, 75, 85
Birmingham, England, 232
Bisaria, Ajay, 27–28
Black Fortress (Sev Berd), 92
Black Sea, 33, 92
Black Sea fleet, 217
bloggers, 77–78, 151
Bloody January (2022), 125, 127, 128, 130–31
Bloomberg, 111
"Board of Peace," 270
Boisbouvier, Christophe, 79
Bonner, Yelena, 223–24
Border Security Act (Finland), 236
Borrell, Josep, 28, 187

Bossangoa, Central African Republic, 79
Botswana, 44, 55, 161
Bouar, Central African Republic, 82–83
Bout, Viktor, 225
Boxing Day, 238
Bozizé, François, 76, 79
Bratbak, Pål, 240–42
Braw, Elisabeth, 240
Braže, Baiba, 263
Brazil, 10, 21, 22, 195, 197, 199–201, 200, 262
Breakfast Club (South African morning show), 68
Bremmer, Ian, 156
Brest, Belarus, 67
Brexit, 258
BRICS alliance, 10, 10–11, 19, 43, 130, 146, 188–201, 209, 256, 262, 271
BRICS Civil Forum, 190
BRICS Expert Council, 194
BRICS+ Fashion Summit, 188–89, 195
BRICS Games for the Future, 195
BRICS Global Television Network, 194
BRICS International Film Festival, 195
BRICS summit (Kazan, 2024), 198–200
BRICS Theater Schools Festival, 195
BRICS Urban Future Forum, 195
"Bring Back the Fear!" (Trenin), 214
British pound, 192
Buamim, Hamad, 26
Bucha massacre, 143
Bucharest, Romania, 108
Bulgaria, 243
Burevestnik cruise missiles, 270
Burkina Faso, 163, 164, 264
Burundi, 161
Bush, George W., and administration, 248
Bushehr, Iran, 44
Butler, Pennsylvania, 248
Butorin, Pavel, 250
"buzzers," 78

Café Central (Vienna), 172
Cairo, Egypt, 179, 210
Cambridge University, 3
Camp de Roux, 80–81
Canada, 19, 73, 250, 252, 258, 267
cancel culture, 6, 61
capitalism, 55
CAR, *See* Central African Republic
Caravella LLCFZ, 17, 25, 31
Caribbean, 180
Carlson, Tucker, 85–86, 248
Carnegie Moscow Center, 4, 214
Carnegie Russia Eurasia Center, 19
Caspian Pipeline Consortium (CPC), 128
Caspian Sea, 33, 45
Caucasus Barometer survey, 113
Caucasus region, 35; *See also* North Caucasus; South Caucasus
Center for Strategic and International Studies (CSIS), 233
Central African Republic (CAR), 76–77, 79–85, 151, 158–62, 165, 256
Central Asia, 10, 35–37, 51, 91, 123, 130, 196, 254
Central Election Commission (Georgia), 106
Central Intelligence Agency (CIA), 74
Central Training Ground, 206
Centre for Research on Energy and Clean Air (CREA), 24–25, 29, 30
chak-chak, 196
Chanakyapuri, India, 27
Charlie Hebdo, 80
Chatham House, 115
Chechens and Chechnya, 108, 118–20, 140, 230
chelnoki, 33
Chelyabinsk, Russia, 196
chemical weapons, 4, 73, 75, 148
China, 10, 17, 19, 21, 22, 28, 30, 40, 41, 45, 47, 48, 60, 91, 130, 146, 157, 167, 171, 175, 176, 183, 190–91, 196–98, 206, 208, 220, 222, 239, 250, 253, 255, 256, 263–67, 270–71, 273
China Media Group, 263
China National Petroleum Corporation, 21
Christianity (Christian values), 62, 113, 137, 154, 251
Classical Realism, 60
climate, 194, 200
Clinton, Bill, and administration, 248

Clinton, Hillary, 73
CNN, 68
coal, 18
Coalition for Change, 106
Coalition of Patriots for Change (CPC), 76
"Coalition of the Willing," 258
Cold War, 9, 54, 55, 59, 99, 129, 139, 194, 206–8, 214, 228, 233, 272
Collective Security Treaty Organization (CSTO), 92, 93, 101, 125, 128, 131
"collective West," 11, 146, 181, 198, 222, 251
collectivization, forced, 119
colonialism and colonization, 10, 52–53, 58, 77, 78, 107, 121, 123, 164, 181, 186, 189; *See also* anti-colonialism; decolonization; neocolonialism
"color revolutions," 189; *See also specific revolutions, e.g.:* Orange Revolution
Commonwealth of Independent States, 43
communalism, 59
communications cables, undersea, 239–40
communism, 9, 54, 56
Comprehensive Nuclear-Test-Ban Treaty (CTBT), 220
Concert of Europe, 8
Concord (catering company), 159
Congress of South African Trade Unions, 58
conspiracy theories, 73, 85, 104, 156–57
Constitutional Court (South Africa), 63
Cook Islands, 17
corruption, 63
Cossacks, 158
Council of the European Union, 145
Counter Foreign Information Manipulation and Interference Hub (US State Department), 250
counterterrorism efforts, 7, 163
Countryman, Tom, 173
COVID pandemic, 5, 23, 39, 113, 172, 190, 209
CPC (Caspian Pipeline Consortium), 128
CPC (Coalition of Patriots for Change), 76
Craze, Joshua, 250
CREA, *See* Centre for Research on Energy and Clean Air
Crimea, annexation of, 4, 8, 18, 21, 23, 33, 39, 71–72, 118, 143, 178, 189, 208, 209
"CRINK," 48
critical undersea infrastructure (CUI), 239–43
Cross-Border Interbank Payment System, 40
cruise missiles, 36, 141, 208, 247, 270
CSIS (Center for Strategic and International Studies), 233
CSTO, *See* Collective Security Treaty Organization
CTBT (Comprehensive Nuclear-Test-Ban Treaty), 220
Cuba, 21, 263
Cuban Missile Crisis, 207
culture wars, 10, 246, 251
cybersecurity, 237

Dagestan, 146
Damascus, Syria, 149–51, 153, 165
Darassa, Ali, 81
dating apps, 43
decolonization, 120–23, 130, 132
de-dollarization, 40–41, 47, 193, 198, 199, 253, 256
"deep state," 249
"de-escalation zones," 147
Defender of the Fatherland Day, 6–7
democracy, 7, 66, 103, 110, 246
Democratic Republic of the Congo, 83, 161
Deng Xiaoping, 197
Denmark, 238
Deraa, Syria, 150
DHL, 232
"dictatorship of law," 127
diesel, 27
"Difficult but Necessary Decision, A" (Karaganov), 216
DIRCO (South African foreign ministry), 58
DirecTV, 73
disinformation, 70, 73, 86, 231, 232, 250

DOGE (Department of Government Efficiency), 256
Doha, Qatar, 150
Donbas region, 6, 62, 64, 71–72, 162, 182
Donetsk, Ukraine, 139
Dossier Center, 78
drones, 11, 38, 41–44, 47, 82, 138, 144, 145, 163–64, 212, 261–63, 265, 266, 268–70
Druze, 135, 152, 154
"dual containment," 263
dual-use goods, 10, 34–36, 41, 45
Dubai, UAE, 17, 23–26, 29
Dubai Multi Commodities Centre, 26
Dubai Public Policy Research Center, 25–26
Dugin, Alexander, 86
Dultsev, Artem, 230
Dultseva, Anna, 230
Duma, *See* Russian State Duma
Durban, South Africa, 54, 55

Eagle S (oil tanker), 17–18, 20, 25, 30–31, 238–40, 243
East Germany, 54, 214
Eastern Europe, 51, 221, 259
echo chambers, 85–86
Economic Freedom Fighters (EEF), 58
Economist, The, 37, 233
Edelstein, Yuli, 144–45
EEU (Eurasian Economic Union), 38
Egypt, 30, 184, 191, 193, 196, 264
Eilat, Israel, 141
electricity cables, 239
electronics trade, 41
Elkin, Ze'ev, 142, 144–45
Elmendorf Air Force Base, 268
Enbis, Mohammed, 160, 166
Eni, 21
Equatorial Guinea, 164
Equinor, 21
Erdogan, Recep Tayyip, 156
escalation ladders, 206–7, 220–21, 249
Estlink 2 underwater cable, 238
Estonia, 238, 239, 263
Ethiopia, 193, 196
EU, *See* European Union
EU-India summit (2023), 28
Eurasia, 132, 272, 273
Eurasian Economic Union (EEU), 38
Eurasian roundabout, 35–39, 47, 91, 111, 129, 192, 252
euro, the, 40, 192, 198
Europe and Europeans, 8, 73, 148, 185, 217, 219, 231, 235, 246, 251, 257–59, 268, 270
European Bank for Reconstruction and Development, 35
European Union (EU), 18–19, 28, 30, 33–37, 40, 47, 95, 99, 100, 102, 109, 110, 114–16, 140, 145, 163, 181, 187, 239, 246, 252, 258, 262–63, 269
export licensing controls, 36
ExxonMobil, 21

Facebook, 71, 73
facts, truth vs., 75
"fake" Western news, 85
"fakes," law against, 227
family (family values), 61, 62
Fatih district (Istanbul), 33–34
February Revolution (1917), 215
Federal Security Service (FSB), 46, 225, 257
fertilizers, 29
Fico, Robert, 263
Filatova, Irina, 56
financial crisis (1998), 33
Financial Times, 26
Fink, Anya, 219
Finland, 30–31, 233–39, 243, 257–58, 272
Finnish Defense Forces, 236
fishing rights, 240–41
flour exports, 128
Fogel, Marc, 225
Foka, Alain, 79
Fontaine, Richard, 48
Fontanka, 235
Forbidden Stories, 83–84
Force Protection Condition "Charlie," 232
forced collectivization, 119
Foreign Affairs, 48
"foreign influence law" (Georgia), 104–5

Foreign Intelligence Service (SVR), 111, 146, 257
Foreign Press Association, 68
fossil fuels, 18–19, 27, 29, 265; *See also* natural gas; oil production and trade
Fox News, 85
France, 19, 71, 77, 84, 92, 95, 161, 171, 183, 206, 232, 257, 258
Francophone Africa, 79
free speech, 80, 246, 250
Freud, Sigmund, 59
From Deterrence to Intimidation (Trenin et al.), 222
FSB, *See* Federal Security Service
Fula people, 82–83

G7, 19, 190, 195, 252
G8, 38, 190
Gakharia for Georgia, 106
Galeotti, Mark, 159, 162
Galstanyan, Bagrat, 96
gas oil, 27
Gavrilov, Sergey, 112
Gavrilov's Night, 112–13
"gay propaganda," prohibition of, 115
gay rights, *See* LGBTQ rights
Gaza (Gaza war), 62–63, 136–38, 141, 145–47, 153, 184, 198, 250, 269
Gazprom, 1
Gazprom Neft, 19
Gbaya people, 79
GD, *See* Georgian Dream
gender-related language, 173, 180
Geneva, Switzerland, 178, 183, 208, 214, 256
genocide, 63, 74, 181; *See also* Armenian Genocide
Georgia and Georgians, 7, 8, 35, 70, 92, 95, 103–16, 121, 124, 127, 132, 189, 253–54, 264, 272
Georgian Charter, 106
Georgian Dream (GD), 103–16, 127, 132, 253, 254, 264
Georgian National Academy of Sciences, 105
Georgian Orthodox Church, 112, 113
Gerasimov, Valery, 155
Germany, 3, 19, 51, 71, 85, 184–86, 221, 230–32, 239, 246, 258, 261; *See also* East Germany
Gershkovich, Evan, 225, 228–30
glasnost, 32
Glazyev, Sergey, 192
global financial crisis (2008), 189
global information war, 10, 51, 75
Global South, 10, 11, 52, 62, 137, 138, 187, 188
Goethe Institutes, 85
Golan Heights, 135–36, 153
gold, 40, 43, 77, 129, 165, 192
Gomuri, Mako, 112
Google Translate, 80
Gostiny Dvor (Moscow), 1
Gouandjika, Fidèle, 158–59
Gowan, Richard, 184
GPS jamming, 232
grain exports, 73
Grand Café, Le (Bangui, Central African Republic), 80
Greenland, 250, 267, 270
Griner, Brittney, 225
Group of 77 (G77), 180, 184, 185
GRU (Russia's military intelligence service), 159, 231, 243
GUGI (Main Directorate of Deep-Sea Research), 240
Gujarat, India, 17, 25
Gulag literature, 227–28
Gulf countries, 130, 138, 148, 154, 179, 201, 255
Gulf of Guinea, 164, 167
Gulf of Kutch, 18, 26
Gumede, William, 64
Gupta brothers, 63
Guterres, António, 196
Gyumri, Armenia, 92

Hague, The, 178
Haiti, 183
Hakaniemi civil defense shelter, 237
Halperin, Simona, 147
Hama, Syria, 150

Hamas, 62, 135, 136, 141, 146; *See also* October 7, 2023 Hamas attack on Israel
Haniyeh, Ismail, 136
Hanover, Germany, 111
HARDTalk, 29
Haroom Nights, 112
Harris, Kamala, 230
Hayat Tahrir al-Sham (HTS), 149–51
hegemony, 2, 7, 52, 54, 62, 129, 137, 191, 267, 271
Helanterä, Antti, 233–35
Helsinki, Finland, 235, 237, 247
Helsinki Security Forum, 236
Hezbollah, 136, 138
High-Level Dialogue on Global Development, 191
"High-Level Summit on Peace for Ukraine" (Switzerland, 2024), 63
Hill, Fiona, 11
Himmler, Heinrich, 84
Hindus, 59
Hiroshima atomic bombing, 219
Hitler, Adolf, 51, 52
Hola News, 126–27
Holocaust, 3, 84
Holocaust Remembrance Day, 142
Homs, Syria, 150
Hong Kong, 159
Hopkins, Valerie, 228
Houthis, 136, 138
HTS (Hayat Tahrir al-Sham), 149–51
human trafficking, 44
Hungarian Uprising (1956), 72
Hungary, 107, 115–16, 127, 167, 269
Hussein, Saddam, 172
hybrid warfare, 231–34
hydrocarbons, *See* fossil fuels
"hygge," 238
hyperinflation, 32

IAEA, *See* International Atomic Energy Agency
ICC, *See* International Criminal Court
ICJ (International Court of Justice), 63
Idlib, Syria, 149, 184
Ikea, 232
immigration, 142, 144, 244
imperialism, 52, 52–55, 55, 57–58, 58, 60, 62, 64, 65, 79, 137, 139, 250, 251
India, 10, 17–19, 22, 26–31, 59–60, 63, 91, 95, 122, 146, 156, 195–97, 199, 262, 267, 269, 270
India Energy Week, 22, 28
Indian Ocean, 38
Indian Oil Corporation, 28
Indonesia, 191
INF Treaty, *See* Intermediate-Range Nuclear Forces Treaty
inflation, 19, 29, 32, 41, 128
information security, 194
Ingush, 119
Instagram, 121
Institute for Science and International Security (ISIS), 43, 44
Institute of Oriental Studies of the Russian Academy of Sciences, 4
Institute of World Economy and International Relations, 216
insurance providers, 19
intelligence agencies, 74, 77–78, 111, 146, 231, 247, 257
interest rates, 41
Intermediate-Range Nuclear Forces (INF) Treaty, 4, 208, 247
International Affairs, 53
International Atomic Energy Agency (IAEA), 172, 179, 181, 208
International Cable Protection Committee, 241
International Court of Justice (ICJ), 63
International Criminal Court (ICC), 101, 102, 192–93, 201
International Crisis Group, 184
International Day Against Colonialism, 53
International Monetary Fund, 190
International Municipal BRICS Forum, 191
International North-South Transport Corridor, 38
international reserve currency, creation of an, 192

International Society for Fair Elections and Democracy (ISFED), 105–7
International Women's Day, 126
Internet cables, 239
Interpol, 44
Ioffe, Julia, 70
Iran, 10, 11, 20, 38, 41–45, 47, 48, 99, 130, 136, 138–41, 144, 145, 147–49, 151, 153, 154, 156–57, 167, 172, 178, 186, 193, 196, 201, 208, 211–13, 255, 265–67, 270
Iran nuclear deal, *See* Joint Comprehensive Plan of Act (JCPOA)
Iraq, 27, 68, 136, 172, 214, 234
Ireland, 239
ISFED (International Society for Fair Elections and Democracy), 105–7
ISIS, *See* Institute for Science and International Security
Islamic State, 154, 159–60
"Islamist terrorism," 140
Israel, 62–63, 68, 69, 99, 135–48, 153, 154, 184, 255, 266
Israeli Air Force, 144, 147
Israel-Russia Parliamentary Friendship League, 142
Istanbul, Turkey, 33–34, 156, 249
Istanbul University, 34
Italy, 19, 21
Ivanishvili, Bidzina, 104–5, 109–10, 114–16
Ivanov, Igor, 108
Izhevsk, Russia, 44

Jaishankar, Subrahmanyam, 28
Jakeli, Tamar "Tata," 104–7, 109–16, 253–54
James Martin Center for Nonproliferation Studies, 5
Jamnagar District, India, 26
Jamnagar refinery, 269
Japan, 19
Javakheti region (Georgia), 95
Javelin missiles, 247
JCPOA, *See* Joint Comprehensive Plan of Action
Je suis Charlie campaign, 80
Jerusalem, 139
Jewish Agency, 139, 145
Jewish Board of Deputies of South Africa, 84–85
Jews and Judaism, 51–52, 67, 84, 139–44; *See also* anti-Semitism
Joan of Arc, 112
Johannesburg, South Africa, 56, 58, 64, 67, 68, 74, 79, 192–93, 198
Johnson, Boris, 248
Joint Base Andrews, 230
Joint Comprehensive Plan of Action (JCPOA), 208, 211–12, 247
journalists and journalism, 29, 68, 69, 74–75, 81, 85, 86, 125, 126, 195, 225–28, 231, 239; *See also individual journalists*

Kahn, Herman, 207
Kalfon, Yomtov, 142
Kallas, Kaja, 246, 263
kalsarikännit, 238
kamikaze drones, 42–43
Kandla, India, 17, 25, 26
Karabakh Armenians, 90, 91, 94–95, 97–98, 101, 102, 111, 132, 152, 265
Karaganov, Sergey, 194, 213, 216–20, 222
Kara-Murza, Vladimir, 230
Kasrils, Ronnie, 56
Kavelashvili, Mikheil, 116
Kazakh Bubble (Instagram channel), 121
Kazakh language, 121, 122, 130
Kazakh Soviet Socialist Republic, 119
Kazakh Telegraph Agency, 131
Kazakhstan, 35, 37, 38, 117–32, 198, 199, 206, 254, 263, 272
Kazan, Russia, 130, 195–200, 224, 226, 228, 229
Kazan Federal University, 196
Kedmi, Yakov, 145
Kendall-Taylor, Andrea, 48
kerosene, 27
KGB, 46, 140
Kharkiv, Ukraine, 56–57
Kharkiv offensive, 213–15, 221
Khmeymim base (Syria), 144, 147–49, 151

Khrushchev, Nikita, 9
Kim Jong Un, 45–46
kipyatilnik, 227
Kiryat Moriah, 139
Klimkin, Pavlo, 46–47
Klimov, Andrey, 111
Knesset (Israel), 142
Kofman, Michael, 219
Komi Republic, 196
Kommersant, 197, 216, 220
Komsomolsk-on-Amur, Russia, 45–46
Korean War, 54
Kramer, Mark, 228
Krasnaya Zvezda, 258
Krasnodar, Russia, 69
Krieger, Rico, 230
Kuleba, Dmytro, 65, 265
Kundera, Milan, 229
Kurds, 154
Kurmasheva, Alsu, 223–31, 242, 250
Kursk region (Russia), 46
Kyiv, Ukraine, 59, 71–72, 144, 157
Kyrgyz Soviet Socialist Republic, 119
Kyrgyzstan, 35, 38

Lachin Corridor, 94
Laleli Industrialists and Businessmen's Association, 35
Laleli market (Istanbul), 33–35, 38
Langa, Bheki, 56–58, 64–65, 77, 122
Lapid, Yair, 143
Lapland, 235
Latin America, 73, 95, 180, 181
Latvia, 242–43, 263
Lavrentiev, Alexander, 149, 178
Lavrov, Sergey, 51, 85, 101, 123, 150, 211, 251, 258
"law against LGBT propaganda" (Georgia), 105
Law of Return (Israel), 143
"law on parallel exports" (Russia), 34
leaks (leaked documents), 21, 43, 127, 140
Lebanon, 135, 136, 138
Lefortovo prison (Moscow), 225, 229
Leiden University, 233
Leipzig, Germany, 232
Leningrad, siege of, 142
Leningrad University, 21
Leopard tanks, 221
Lesotho, 161
"LGBT propaganda," 104, 105, 113, 114
LGBTQ rights, 104–6, 110, 112–15, 250, 253–54
liberalism (liberal values), 6, 8, 48, 60, 61, 113, 115, 116, 132, 180, 249–51, 253–54, 258, 272
"Liberation Day," 252
Libya, 158, 160, 163, 165, 167
Libyan American Alliance, 166
Libyan Civil War, 71, 147, 151
Libyan National Army (LNA), 160, 163
Lieberman, Avigdor, 144
Life Is an Unpaired Boot (Petkevich), 227–28
Lik, Kevin, 230
"like-minded group," 184–85
Likhachev, Alexey, 205–6
liquefied natural gas (LNG), 18, 29
Lisi Wonderland (Tbilisi), 113–14, 254
Lithuania, 232, 239, 263
"little green men," 71–72
LNA, *See* Libyan National Army
LNG, *See* liquefied natural gas
Lomonosov Moscow State University, 39
London, England, 24
Los Angeles, Calif., 97
Lukashenko, Alexander, 157
Lukoil, 269
Lukyanov, Fyodor, 5, 178, 184, 214, 247, 258–59, 269
Lula da Silva, Luis Inácio, 262, 264
Lynd, Hillary, 65

Madagascar, 161
Maduro, Nicolás, 196, 262
MAGA, 251, 258
Magnitsky Act, 4
Main Directorate of Deep-Sea Research (GUGI), 240
Majdal Shams (Golan Heights), 135–36, 152–54
Majdal Shams attack, 147
Makhachkala, Dagestan, 146

Malema, Julius, 58
Mali, 161, 163, 164, 166, 183–84
Maltsev, Alexandr, 195
Manama, Bahrain, 150
Manchuria, 53
Mannerheim, Gustaf, 234
Mapaila, Solly, 58
Mariupol, Ukraine, 104, 161
Markarova, Oksana, 246
marriage rights, 105, 113
Marx, Karl, 3
Marxism-Leninism, 58
Mashal, Khaled, 141
Masis, Armenia, 97–98
Matochkin Strait, 205
May 9 Victory Day parade (Moscow), 156, 254, 261–66
McBride, Derrick, 54–55
McBride, Robert, 54–56, 58, 59, 64–65, 68, 77, 122
McCain, John, 18
McGlynn, Jade, 85
media law (Kazakhstan), 126–27
Mediterranean Sea, 164
Medvedev, Dmitry, 2, 208, 215, 240, 245, 252
Mekdad, Faisal, 6
Melnichenko, Andrey, 23
"memory diplomacy," 85
mercenaries, 158; *See also* Wagner Group
Mexico, 73, 186, 231
Middle Corridor, 91
Middle East, 27, 71, 73, 74, 91, 95, 135–41, 150, 154, 158, 201, 247, 255, 266, 267, 272; *See also individual countries*
Middle East Quartet, 140
migrants, 231, 234–35, 242
Mikkeli, Finland, 238
Milan, Italy, 189
Milei, Javier, 193
military training, 56, 161, 236
militias, 81, 136, 138, 147, 154
Miller, Alexey, 1
Minnikhanov, Rustam, 196
missiles, 44, 45, 138, 140, 209, 217, 221, 247, 269; *See also* cruise missiles; drones
MK, *See* uMkhonto we Sizwe ("Spear of the Nation")
Modi, Narendra, 28, 156, 196, 262
Moldova, 132
Molfar, 161
Molotov cocktails, 234
Moran Security Group, 159
Moscow, Russia, 1–2, 6–7, 33, 56–57, 59, 69, 97, 155, 156, 158, 188, 254, 261–65
Moscow Institute of National Economy, 56
Moscow State Institute of International Relations, 123
Moscow State University, 39
Moscow Treaty (Strategic Offensive Reductions Treaty), 208
Moskva (battleship), 217
Mothers and Daughters (Bonner), 223–24
Mozambique, 21
Mufamadi, Sydney, 58–59, 63, 68
multiculturalism, 248
multilateralism, 180
multipolarity (multipolar world), 53, 61, 180, 195, 213
Mumbai, India, 17
Munich Security Conference, 246, 256
"Munich speech" (Putin), 7
Muratov, Dmitry, 216
Muslims, 42, 59, 140, 146, 224
"mutually assured destruction," 207

Nabiullina, Elvira, 1, 38–42, 47, 162, 192, 198–200, 252
NAFO (North Atlantic Fella Organization), 182
Nagasaki atomic bombing, 219
Nagorno-Karabakh, 89–95, 99–102, 254; *See also* Karabakh Armenians
Nakheel Mall (Dubai), 23
Namibia, 184, 186
Naryshkin, Sergey, 146
Nasrallah, Hassan, 136
National Committee on BRICS Research, 189
National Defense Training Association (MPK), 236–37

national liberation, struggles for, 55–56, 78
National Party (South Africa), 54, 62
Nativ agency, 143
NATO, *See* North Atlantic Treaty Organization
NATO Defense College, 214
NATO Maritime Centre for the Security of Critical Undersea Infrastructure, 240–42
natural gas, 18, 29, 101, 160
Navalny, Alexey, 178
Nazarbayev, Nursultan, 127
Nazis and Nazism, 51, 84, 142, 157, 261, 264
neocolonialism, 10, 52–53, 58, 107, 181, 186
neoliberalism, 64
Nepalis, 46
Netanyahu, Benjamin, 136–37, 141, 142, 144, 153, 262
Netherlands, 233
New Delhi, India, 27–28, 199–201
New Development Bank, 190
New Island (St. Petersburg restaurant), 159
New START agreement, 2, 207–10, 267
New York City, 183, 184, 189, 209, 256
New York Review of Books, The, 250
New York Times, The, 228, 240
NGOs, *See* non-governmental organizations
Nicaragua, 186, 256
Nicholas II, Czar, 53, 215
Niger, 163–64
Nigeria, 161, 199
Niinistö, Sauli, 235
9/11 attacks, 7
"no-action motions," 186
Non-Aligned Movement, 194
nondollar currencies, 40
non-governmental organizations (NGOs), 104, 105, 108
nonproliferation treaty (NPT), 171–80, 186, 207, 209
Nord Stream gas pipelines, 239–40
North Atlantic Fella Organization (NAFO), 182
North Atlantic Treaty Organization (NATO), 52, 53, 57, 59, 71, 99, 108, 116, 148, 167, 199, 206, 209, 211, 217, 218, 220, 232, 234, 238–42, 257, 258, 269, 272
North Caucasus, 146, 147
North Karelia, 235
North Korea, 10, 41, 45–47, 48, 172, 186, 213, 252, 255, 256, 264, 265, 271
Northwood, England, 240, 241
Norway, 21, 234, 238–41
Novaya Zemlya, Russia, 205–6, 220
Novorossiysk, Russia, 128
NPT, *See* nonproliferation treaty
nuclear arms control, 2, 5, 10, 48, 177, 179, 185, 206–13, 216, 222, 267
nuclear deterrence, 207–8, 215–20
nuclear doctrine, Russian, 221–22
nuclear energy, 29, 44, 129, 130, 171, 173–74, 205, 255
nuclear escalation ladder, 206–7, 216, 249
nuclear "multipolarity," 213
nuclear war, 207, 214–16, 219, 222, 231
nuclear weapons, 2, 6, 10–11, 47, 73–74, 129, 171–74, 177, 206–8, 211, 214–22, 237, 242, 257, 262, 265, 266, 270, 271; *See also* nuclear arms control

Obama, Barack, and administration, 3–4, 208, 209, 245, 248
Ochberg, Isaac, 67, 84
October 7, 2023 Hamas attack on Israel, 62, 136–39, 146, 147, 153, 154, 184
Odesa, Ukraine, 56
"offensive information campaign," 233
Office of Foreign Assets Control (US Treasury), 25
oil price caps (price cap coalition), 10, 19–23, 25, 26, 28–31, 34, 190, 269
oil production and trade, 10, 17–20, 22, 26–30, 30, 128, 159, 160, 252, 269, 270
oil tankers, 10, 11, 17–18, 20–26, 30–31, 36–40, 238–40, 243, 252, 269
oligarchs, Russian, 1, 41, 104, 110, 116
Olmert, Ehud, 140–42
Olympic games (Paris), 195, 232

Olympic Park (Sochi, Russia), 61
OPEC+, 22
Open Skies Treaty, 208
Operation Chechevitsa, 119
Operation Rising Lion, 266
Orange Revolution (Ukraine), 7, 71–72, 189
Orbán, Viktor, 107, 115, 127
Oreshnik missiles, 221
Organization for Security and Co-operation in Europe (OSCE), 92, 108
Organization for the Prohibition of Chemical Weapons (OPCW), 178
Organization of the Petroleum Exporting Countries (OPEC), 22
Organized Crime and Corruption Reporting Project, 38
OSCE Minsk Group, 92
Ottoman Empire, 92
Overchuk, Alexey, 101
Oxford University, 3

Pact for the Future, 184–87
pager attacks, Israeli, 136
Pakistan, 184
Palestinians and Palestine, 62, 137, 139, 146
Palm Jumeirah (Dubai), 23
Palmyra, Syria, 159–60
Panama Canal, 250, 267
Pandora Papers, 127
Pankisi Gorge (Georgia), 108
Panova, Viktoria, 189–90, 194, 199–201
PaperLab, 124, 131
Paris, France, 189, 195, 232
Pashinyan, Nikol, 93–96, 100, 101, 156, 198, 254, 263–64
Patriot Media Group, 77, 78
Patriot missiles, 138
Pazylbekova, Aigerim, 121–23
Peninsular Maritime India Private Limited, 17
People's Soviet of Workers of Petropavlovsk, 117–18, 130, 131
perestroika, 27, 32
Persian Gulf, 138, 270; *See also* Gulf countries
Peskov, Dmitry, 1, 211, 228, 233, 250, 262
Petkevich, Tamara, 227–28
Petropavlovsk, Kazakhstan, 117–18, 121, 130, 224
Peulh people, 82–83
Pew Research Center, 113
P5 states, 206
Pietiläinen, Kari, 236
pikkujoulu, 238
pipelines, 128, 239–42
PIR Center, 213
Platform to Protect Whistleblowers in Africa, 83
Pokrovsk, Ukraine, 270
Poland, 67, 181, 216, 232, 257, 263
Politico, 102
Politkovskaya, Anna, 136
Polyana 1389 Hotel (Sochi, Russia), 5
Polyansky, Dmitry, 187
Polymetal, 129
Popasna, Ukraine, 161
Pope, Edmund, 225
populism, 63, 64, 193
pornography, 46
Porvoo, Finland, 31
Poseidon underwater drones, 270
post-Western order, 8, 53, 190, 201
Potentiel Centrafricain, Le, 79–80
Prague, Czech Republic, 224–26
Pravda network, 78
preemptive nuclear use, 216, 218
Pretoria, South Africa, 59
price cap coalition, *See* oil price caps
Prigozhin, Pavel, 166
Prigozhin, Yevgeny, 77, 78, 155–59, 161–63, 165, 166, 271
Primakov, Yevgeny, 140
Primakov Readings (2024), 101
prisoner exchanges, 179, 225, 230–31
propaganda, 10, 51, 61, 72–74, 77, 78, 84, 86, 104, 105, 113, 114, 145, 222, 250, 263, 270
"proxy rebellion," 11
Pukhov, Ruslan, 151
Puri, Hardeep Singh, 29
Pushkin, Alexander, 123
Putin, Viktor, 142

Putin, Vladimir
at Alaska Summit, 268–69
anti-Semitism of, 145, 146
as anti-woke leader, 61–62
and Armenia, 92, 93
attack on Western liberalism, 6
and Azerbaijan, 100
and BRICS, 19, 189–97, 199, 201
and China, 41, 191, 197, 255, 263
on collapse of Soviet Union, 68
and COVID pandemic, 5
and Crimea annexation, 18
and "decade of humiliation," 32
and decline of the West, 259
on de-dollarization, 40–41
early career of, 32–33
and Georgian Dream, 110, 116
Gostiny Dvor speech (2023) of, 1–2
ICC arrest warrant for, 101, 192–93
and India, 270
and Israel, 136–37, 140–44, 153
and Kazakhstan, 122, 127, 128, 130
on mission of Russia, 264
and multipolarity, 53
Munich speech (2007) of, 7
and Elvira Nabiullina, 38–39, 42
non-Western countries' support for, 11, 58, 62–64
and North Korea, 45, 47
and nuclear arms, 206–8, 210–11, 218–21
political violence of, 136
and post-Soviet Eurasia, 132
and Yevgeny Prigozhin, 155–59, 162
and prisoner exchanges, 225, 228, 230–31
and Igor Sechin, 20, 21
and Margarita Simonyan, 73
and Paula Slier, 75
and Syria, 147–49, 151–52
Trump and MAGA's affinity for, 247, 249, 251
and Ukraine (Ukraine War), 2, 8–9, 11–12, 91, 145, 244–45, 249, 254, 261, 262, 271–73
and US-Russia "reset," 3–4
Valdai speeches of, 5–6, 10, 61
at Victory Parade (2025), 262–66
and Western sanctions, 34, 232–33

Qaddafi, Muammar al-, 147
Questions I Never Asked, The (documentary), 84–85

racism, 57, 66, 78
Radchenko, Sergey, 233
Radio France Internationale (RFI), 79
Radio Free Europe/Radio Liberty (RFE/RL), 224–25, 227, 250
Radio Ndeke Luka, 81
Raisina Dialogue, 199
Ramaphosa, Cyril, 58, 193, 196
rare-earth elements, 192
Ras Al Khaimah, UAE, 29
Real America's Voice, 245
Red Army, 56, 142, 264
Red Sea, 138, 163
Red Square, 261, 264–65
Reliance Industries, 26, 29, 269
renminbi, 40
Republican Party, 247–48
reserve currency, creation of an international, 192
"reset," US-Russia, 3–4, 7, 71, 208
Respublika, 254
RFE/RL, *See* Radio Free Europe/Radio Liberty
RFI (Radio France Internationale), 79
RIA Novosti, 69
Rio de Janeiro, Brazil, 201
Riyadh, Saudi Arabia, 249, 256
Rogachev, Ilya, 84–85
Rosatom, 129, 205, 206
Rose Revolution (Georgia), 7, 108, 189
Rosneft, 1, 20, 21, 28, 29, 31, 269, 270
Rossiya (Russian state television network), 69
Rossotrudnichestvo, 194
Rostov-on-Don, Russia, 155–57
roundabout trade, *See* Eurasian roundabout
RT (formerly Russia Today), 68–79, 86, 108, 127, 263

RT America, 72, 73
RT Arabic, 73
RT Balkan, 73
RT Hindi, 73
RT India, 270
Rubio, Marco, 250, 262
Russia in Global Affairs (journal), 5
Russia-Africa Summit (St. Petersburg, 2023), 53
Russian Academy of Sciences, 191
Russian Army, 132, 157, 227, 229
Russian Central Bank, 1, 38–41, 269
Russian elites, 9, 23, 63, 192, 215, 248, 249
Russian Empire, 92, 118–19, 124
Russian Federal Assembly, 194, 206, 210
Russian films, 70
Russian Houses, 85, 123, 164, 194, 250
Russian language, 3, 62, 95, 109, 120–23, 130
Russian music, 3
Russian Navy, 217, 240
Russian "shadow fleet," 10, 11, 20–26, 30–31, 36–40, 240, 252, 269
Russian State Duma, 4, 39, 41, 192
Russian state TV, 151
Russo-Georgian War (2008), 8, 70, 189
Rwanda, 76
Ryabkov, Sergey, 188–89, 200, 209–10

Saakashvili, Mikheil, 108–9
Sabanadze, Natalie, 115, 116
sabotage, 231–33, 238–43
SACP (South African Communist Party), 54
"Sacred War" (song), 263
Sahel, the, 10, 151, 163–65, 167, 256, 266
St. Petersburg (formerly Leningrad), Russia, 21, 40, 53, 78, 142, 158, 159, 191, 234
St. Petersburg International Economic Forum, 73, 211, 220
Sakharov, Andrey, 224
sanctions, 2, 4, 9–10, 18, 20, 22–26, 28, 30, 33, 34, 36–41, 48, 60, 72–74, 91, 109, 110, 137, 143, 145–47, 149, 178, 183, 190, 191, 208, 211, 213, 232–33, 247, 249, 252, 254, 255, 269, 270
Saudi Arabia, 22–23, 27, 193, 198
Saydnaya prison (Damascus), 151
Saying No to War (Kurmasheva), 227
Schengen visas, 235
Scholz, Olaf, 221, 246
Sciutto, Jim, 221
Sechin, Igor, 1, 20–23, 28, 29, 31, 41, 162, 196, 269, 270
Second Chechen War, 108
Second Palestinian Intifada, 140
Second Sino-Japanese War, 264
secondary sanctions, 37, 38
secularism, 248
Security Council (Russia), 215; *See also* UN Security Council
Seitak, Bibarys, 121
"self-deterrence," 221
Semenov, Sergey, 213
Semipalatinsk, Kazakhstan, 119, 129
Serbia, 263
Sergei's Courtyard (Jerusalem), 141
Sev Berd (Black Fortress), 92
Sevastopol, Crimea, 2
Shahed drones, 42–45, 82, 144, 212, 265, 266, 268
Shanghai Cooperation Organization, 192
Sharansky, Avital, 139
Sharansky, Natan, 139–40, 142, 144
Sharon, Ariel, 140, 141
Shen Haixiong, 263
Shevardnadze, Eduard, 108
Shoigu, Sergey, 1, 155–56, 205–6, 220
Short, Philip, 21
"Shouting Hill" (Golan Heights), 135
Siberia, 74
Sikka, India, 29
Silicon Valley, 215
siloviki, 21
Simonyan, Margarita, 6, 69, 70, 73–74, 100, 107, 131, 146, 157, 197–98, 245–46, 263, 270
Singapore, 181
Sisi, Abdel Fattah el-, 264
Sisulu, Lindiwe, 64
Sisulu, Walter, 64
Six Day War (1967), 135, 139
SIZOs, 226, 227

Skripal family, 178, 247
Slavonic Corps, 159, 160
Slier, Paula, 67–72, 74–79, 84–86, 108, 127, 165, 193–94
Slovakia, 263
Slovenia, 230
Sloviansk, Ukraine, 72
Snowden, Edward, 3
Sobchak, Anatoly, 32
Sobyanin, Sergey, 155, 261
Sochi, Russia, 4–5, 61, 97, 143, 148, 226
socialism, 9, 56, 57
Society for Worldwide Interbank Financial Telecommunications (SWIFT), 40
South Africa, 10, 53–60, 62–65, 67, 72, 74, 78, 84–85, 122, 189, 191–94, 196–98, 251, 262, 264
South African Broadcasting Corporation, 68
South African Communist Party (SACP), 54, 58
South African foreign ministry (DIRCO), 58
South Caucasus, 10, 35–37, 91, 92, 99, 100–102, 111, 254, 267, 272
South Ossetia, 70, 95, 107–8, 111
Sovcomflot, 20, 25
Soviet Union (USSR), 3, 11, 21, 27, 32, 54–56, 65–66, 68, 72, 78, 92, 95, 99, 119–20, 122–24, 129, 137, 139, 140, 142, 158, 182, 206, 207, 214, 227–28, 233, 234, 262, 264
Soweto uprising, 55
space exploration, 209
Spanish language, 73
"speed dating" negotiations, 174
Sputnik (Russian news agency), 100
SSD (unit at GRU headquarters), 243
Stalin, Joseph, 51, 119, 182, 224
Stamba Hotel (Tbilisi), 104, 109
Statoil, 21
Stepanakert, Nagorno-Karabakh, 89, 94, 97
S-300 air defenses, 141
stoykost, 9, 47, 249, 271
Strategic Offensive Reductions Treaty (Moscow Treaty), 208
"strategic parasitism," 219
Strategic Stability Dialogue, 208, 209
Strong Georgia, 106
Stubb, Alexander, 236
Sudan, 161, 186, 193
sugar exports, 128
suicide drones, 42–43
"suitcase trade," 33, 40
Sullivan, Jake, 210–11
Sun Ship Management, 25
Sunni Muslims, 154
sustainable development, 194
Svalbard archipelago, 241
SVR, *See* Foreign Intelligence Service
Sweden, 239, 243, 257–58, 272
SWIFT banking system, 40
Switzerland, 63, 178
Syria, 4, 6, 11, 73, 75, 135–36, 138, 141, 144, 147–54, 159–60, 162, 163, 165–66, 178, 183–84, 186, 213, 234, 247, 255, 265, 269–71
Syrian Constitutional Committee, 178
Syrian Democratic Forces, 154
System for Transfer of Financial Messages, 40
Syunik province (Armenia), 101

Tabuni, Omar, 166
tactical nuclear weapons, 221, 237
Tagzym memorial (Almaty, Kazakhstan), 125, 131
Taiwan, 198
Tajikistan, 35
Taksim Square (Istanbul), 34
Taliban, 150, 183
tariffs, 252, 256, 267
Tartus base (Syria), 148, 149, 151
Tatar language, 224
Tatars and Tatarstan, 42, 82, 196, 224, 225
Taurus missiles, 221
Tavush province (Armenia), 95–96, 101
Tbilisi, Georgia, 70, 103–7, 109, 110, 112–14, 253
Tbilisi First Public School, 105
Tbilisi Pride, 104–5, 112–13, 253, 254
Tekhnoexport, 21
Telegram, 80, 130, 215

Tengiz oil field (Kazakhstan), 128
Thucydides, 267
Time magazine, 245
Timofeev, Ivan, 252
Tinder, 43
Tinzaouten, Mali, 163
Togo, 164
Tokayev, Kassym-Jomart Kemeluly, 118, 122, 125, 127–30, 198, 263
Tomahawk missiles, 269
Torture Victim Protection Act (1991), 166
totalitarianism, 217
Touadéra, Faustin-Archange, 77, 159, 162
traditional values, 6, 10, 61–62, 264
transgenderism, 6
Traoré, Ibrahim, 264
Treaty of Brest-Litovsk, 67
Treaty of Kars, 92
Trenin, Dmitry, 156, 194, 200–201, 213–15, 217–22
Trier, Germany, 3
Tripoli, Libya, 71, 160
"troll factories," 77–78
Trump, Donald, and administrations, 11, 73, 153, 201, 208, 211, 222, 244–59, 264, 266–70
"Trump Heights," 153
truth, facts vs., 75
Truth and Reconciliation Commission (South Africa), 55
Tsar Bomba, 206
Tskhinvali, Georgia, 70
Turkey, 10, 22, 33–38, 35, 91, 92, 99–100, 102, 130, 147–49, 153, 154, 156, 167, 178, 179, 183, 196, 199, 250
Turunen, Marko, 235–36
Tutkov, Dima, 24
TV Dozhd, 265
TV Imedi, 106
Tver region (Russia), 62
Twelve-Day War, 266, 268, 270
Twitter, 71, 181–82
"tyranny of minor differences," 59

UAE, *See* United Arab Emirates
Ubangi River, 83
Ufa, Russia, 38–39
UK, *See* United Kingdom
Ukraine; *See also* Donbas region
- and BRICS alliance, 196–97
- indictment of Margarita Simonyan by, 74
- Orange Revolution in, 7, 71–72, 189
- during Soviet period, 57, 264
- Wagner Group in, 159

Ukraine invasion and war
- as anti-colonialist war, 52–55, 60–61, 84, 85
- attack on *Moskva,* 217
- and Azerbaijan, 91, 93, 99
- and bioweapon rumors, 75
- BRICS countries and, 190–92, 196–97
- and China, 41, 47
- as civil war, 59–60
- comparisons with violence in Holy Land, 62–63
- domestic Russian opposition to, 227
- drone attacks on Russia, 261–63
- drones and other weapons in, 42–45, 265, 270
- and Eurasian roundabout, 35, 46
- and Finland, 236–38
- and Gaza war, 137–39
- and Georgia, 103, 104, 109, 110, 113, 116
- and Israel, 142–45
- and Kazakhstan, 120–22, 124, 126–32
- Kharkiv offensive, 213–15, 221
- and multipolarity, 61
- and North Korea, 45–47
- and nuclear arms control, 172–79, 206, 210, 231
- and oil exports, 18, 26–29
- and overall Russian foreign policy, 11–12, 181–84, 267, 271–72
- Yevgeny Prigozhin and, 78
- as "proxy war," 52, 57–58, 250
- Putin's actions immediately preceding, 6–7
- reaction of non-Western countries to, 11, 59–61, 64–65
- and Russian elites, 23–24
- Russia's aims and justification for, 1–2, 8–10, 118

and sanctions, 37, 211
as "special military operation," 51, 181
suffering wrought by, 12, 273
and Syria, 148, 151
Dmitry Trenin's skepticism about, 218
Donald Trump and, 244–52, 254, 256–58, 268–69
Wagner Group's role in, 161–62
Ulken, Kazakhstan, 129
Ulyanov, Mikhail Ivanovich, 180–82, 211–13
uMkhonto we Sizwe ("Spear of the Nation," MK), 55–57, 62, 63, 64
UN, *See* United Nations
UN General Assembly, 130, 176, 184–87, 189, 256
UN High Commissioner for Refugees, 256
UN Panel of Experts for North Korea, 213
UN Security Council, 137, 147, 148, 154, 183, 185, 206, 208, 256, 267, 270
UN Special Commission for the Disarmament of Iraq, 172
UN Summit of the Future, 184–87
Unbearable Lightness of Being, The (Kundera), 229
undersea communications cables, 239–40
Union Buildings (Pretoria, South Africa), 59
Union of Writers (Soviet Union), 182
Unité pour la paix en Centrafrique, 81
United Arab Emirates (UAE), 20, 23–26, 29, 30, 43, 193; *See also* Dubai
United Kingdom (UK), 19, 171, 178, 183, 206, 232, 240, 248, 257, 258
United National Movement (UNM) (Georgia), 106, 108–9
United Nations (UN), 10, 71, 108, 137, 140, 143–44, 172–80, 183–87, 196, 206, 210, 271; *See also specific headings*
United States (US); *See also specific topics*
and arms control, 2, 171, 206–11, 216, 219, 220, 222, 267
in battle of resources, 47
and BRICS, 146, 189, 198, 256
"dual containment" policy of, 263
echo chambers in, 85
European military bases of, 232
hegemony of, 7, 54, 62, 137, 191, 271
intelligence agencies of, 74, 77–78, 231, 247
and Nagorno-Karabakh, 92
NGOs financed by, 108
and Niger, 163–64
"reset" in relations with Russia, 3–4, 7, 71, 208
RT in, 70–71
Russia's "compartmentalization" of relations with, 266–67
and Syria, 147, 148
tariffs imposed by, 252, 256, 267
and United Nations, 183
University of Bangui, 79
Ural Mountains, 44
US Agency for International Development (USAID), 4, 18, 250
US Air Force, 266, 268
US Congress, 4, 253
US Department of Government Efficiency (DOGE), 256
US dollar, 2, 10, 27, 37, 38, 40, 190, 192, 193, 198, 199, 252–53, 256; *See also* de-dollarization
US presidential election (2016), 4, 8, 73, 77–78, 247
US presidential election (2024), 74, 244, 264
US State Department, 250, 251
US Treasury, 19, 25, 40
Ushakov, Yuri, 197, 198
USSR, *See* Soviet Union
Ust-Luga, Russia, 30
Utkin, Dmitry, 165
Uzbekistan, 35

Vakulenko, Sergey, 19, 22
Valdai Discussion Club, 4–6, 10, 61, 220, 269
Vance, JD, 244–46, 251, 256–57
Varma, Venkatesh, 59–60
Varshavka Sky shopping center (Moscow), 2